The
Electric Pressure
Cooker COOKBOOK

The Electric Pressure Cooker Cookbook

200 FAST AND FOOLPROOF RECIPES FOR EVERY KIND OF MACHINE

BARBARA SCHIEVING

Creator of the popular blog *Pressure Cooking Today*

HARVARD COMMON PRESS

Brimming with creative inspiration, how-to projects, and useful
information to enrich your everyday life, Quarto Knows is a favorite
destination for those pursuing their interests and passions. Visit our
site and dig deeper with our books into your area of interest:
Quarto Creates, Quarto Cooks, Quarto Homes, Quarto Lives,
Quarto Drives, Quarto Explores, Quarto Gifts, or Quarto Kids.

© 2017 Quarto Publishing Group USA Inc.
Text © 2017 Barbara Schieving

First Published in 2017 by The Harvard Common Press, an imprint of The Quarto Group,
100 Cummings Center, Suite 265-D, Beverly, MA 01915, USA.
T (978) 282-9590 F (978) 283-2742 QuartoKnows.com

The Harvard Common Press titles are also available at discount for retail, wholesale, promotional, and bulk purchase.
For details, contact the Special Sales Manager by email at specialsales@quarto.com or by mail at The Quarto Group,
Attn: Special Sales Manager, 401 Second Avenue North, Suite 310, Minneapolis, MN 55401, USA.

21 20 19 18 17   2 3 4 5

ISBN: 978-1-55832-896-9

Library of Congress Cataloging-in-Publication Data

Names: Schieving, Barbara, author.
Title: The electric pressure cooker cookbook : 200 fast and foolproof recipes
    for every kind of machine / Barbara Schieving.
Description: Beverly, MA, USA : Harvard Common Press, an imprint of The
    Quarto Group, [2017] | Includes index.
Identifiers: LCCN 2017027609 | ISBN 9781558328969 (pbk.)
Subjects: LCSH: Pressure cooking. | Electric cooking. | LCGFT: Cookbooks.
Classification: LCC TX840.P7 S39 2017 | DDC 641.5/87--dc23 LC record available at https://lccn.loc.gov/2017027609

Design and Layout: Rita Sowins / Sowins Design
Photography: Barbara Schieving

Printed in Canada

To my husband and my kids—the joy in my life
and the reason I pressure cook.

And to my *Pressure Cooking Today* blog readers—
those who have been there from
the beginning and those just joining me on this
pressure cooking journey.

Contents

Preface:
Under Pressure

Like many of you, I'm a busy mom and under pressure to get delicious, healthy meals on the table fast. Now, thanks to my electric pressure cooker, mealtime has never been quicker or easier.

Growing up, my mom used an old-fashioned stovetop pressure cooker to cook a pot roast on Sundays. The regulator on top wiggled and jiggled and made scary noises. It always made me a little nervous—although I was too little to remember, my older siblings loved to tell the story of when my stepmother's old stovetop pressure cooker exploded, blasting food everywhere—even the ceiling! Still, despite that mishap, I grew up knowing meals made in a pressure cooker were fast and delicious.

Pressure cookers fell out of favor at my house when my mom got her first microwave. While there's no denying a microwave's convenience, it's simply not possible to get the rich flavor of a long-simmered meal from a microwave.

Many years later, after becoming a mom myself, I began hearing about electric pressure cookers. I was impressed when I read how much pressure cooker technology had improved and saw all the safety features on the new pressure cookers. I was also intrigued by how easy electric pressure cookers were to use—set-it-and-forget-it easy. I also remembered the home-cooked dinners of my childhood and knew I had to try one.

I really did fall in love with my electric pressure cooker after making my first recipe. I appreciated how quick and easy it was to make meals in the pressure cooker, and I loved having only one pot to wash. And the food tasted great— tender, fall-apart meats; soups that tasted as though they'd simmered for hours; and pasta and rice dishes cooked to perfection.

All 200 recipes in this cookbook are recipes I enjoy with my family. I've included 50 of the most popular recipes from my website, *Pressure Cooking Today* (www.pressurecookingtoday.com), and created 150 all-new electric pressure cooker recipes that I'm sure will become new favorites. The recipes in this cookbook are a good mix of old-fashioned American favorites, international cuisines with an American flair, and healthy meals with trendy ingredients. Of course, I had to include some decadently delicious pressure cooker desserts as well. I'm so excited to share these new recipes with you!

Thanks for joining me on my journey to make quicker and better-tasting meals using today's modern, easy-to-use electric pressure cookers.

Barbara Schieving

Introduction:
Getting the Most from Your Electric Pressure Cooker

There is a pressure cooking renaissance going on right now. You can make better tasting meals in a fraction of the time using today's modern, easy-to-use electric pressure cookers. As with any new tool, there are a few things you'll need to know before you get cooking— let's get started.

ADVANTAGES OF USING AN ELECTRIC PRESSURE COOKER

Pressure cooking, in general, offers certain advantages over the oven, stove, or slow cooker.

- **FASTER COOK TIME.** Electric pressure cookers let you cook meats, stews, soups, beans, stocks, and broths in a fraction of the time they take to cook on the stove, in the oven, or with the slow cooker—and foods still taste like they've been cooking for hours!

- **BETTER FLAVOR.** The pressure inside the pot raises the boiling point, which forces liquid into tough foods, making them tender, and the high heat promotes caramelization, adding depth of flavor.

- **BETTER NUTRIENT RETENTION.** The longer you cook fruits and vegetables in water, the more nutrients they lose. When you pressure cook your vegetables, you use a shorter cook time—keeping nutrients in your food and making your meals healthier.

- **COOK FROM FROZEN.** Forget to thaw the meat? No problem! No thawing required before pressure cooking. (This works best for smaller cuts of meat.)

- **COST SAVINGS.** Ovens and stoves use a lot of energy as they cook. Pressure cookers require less energy, have shorter cook times, and don't heat up your house.

- **EASY CLEANUP.** One-pot cooking means only one pot to clean.

In addition, there are some unique advantages to electric pressure cookers instead of stovetop pressure cookers:

- **SAFETY.** Electric pressure cookers have several built-in safety features to prevent mishaps, including automatic pressure control, heating and pressure sensors, lid detection, and heating plates that distribute heat evenly.

- **CONVENIENCE.** You don't have to stand at the stove to adjust the heat so that whatever you're cooking doesn't boil over—the electric pressure cooker automatically regulates the heat and pressure. Go play with your kids, pay bills, or clean the kitchen and set the table while the electric pressure cooker does all the work.

- **CONSISTENT RESULTS.** Once you figure out the right cook time for your pressure cooker you'll come back to a perfectly cooked dish—every time.

- **KEEP WARM SETTING.** Unlike a stovetop pressure cooker, you don't need to worry about being home to turn off the pot; most electric pressure cookers automatically switch to the Keep Warm setting when the pressure cook time ends.

GETTING TO KNOW YOUR ELECTRIC PRESSURE COOKER

The earliest pressure cookers were created on a simple concept: Food cooks hotter and faster inside a pressure-sealed pot. (The scientific explanation involves raising the boiling point of water, which allows pressure cookers to cook food about 40°F (4.5°C) hotter than it could cook on the stovetop.) Electric pressure cookers use technology to enhance this process—for instance, by using sensors to regulate the temperature and pressure automatically inside the pot during cooking.

Electric pressure cookers place the cooking pot inside a housing unit that includes a heating element and sensors as well as the operating controls. The lid contains a gasket to ensure it fits snugly against the housing and a pressure release valve and small float valve that allow pressure to release safely, if needed.

There are many brands of electric pressure cookers currently on the market. (Some brands prefer the term "multi-cookers" because they offer slow cooking features; however, they all operate similarly, and, for simplicity, I refer to them all as *pressure cookers* throughout the book.) I own several brands and often use two at the same time. Some brands in my kitchen include:

INSTANT POT. The Instant Pot pressure cooker is the one I use most in my kitchen. I really like the stainless steel pot for browning and that the cooker tells me when it's preheated and ready to sauté ingredients. It's quiet, comes in a variety of models, and sizes range from 3 quart to 8 quart (2.8 to 7.5 L). The Instant Pot is a multi-cooker, and some models offer high- and low-pressure settings and also function as slow cookers, rice cookers, and yogurt makers. The Instant Pot has limited availability in stores but is available at Amazon and other online retailers.

FAGOR. Fagor has been selling stovetop pressure cookers worldwide for decades, and they've recently entered the electric pressure cooker market with two quality products: the LUX multi-cooker and the more affordable Premium Pressure Cooker. The LUX was recently chosen as the top-rated multi-cooker in *Good Housekeeping*'s "Multi-Settings Cooker Reviews." I really like the buttons on the Fagor pressure cookers. Fagor pressure cookers come with a nonstick pot, though they recently began offering the LUX LCD with a stainless steel pot. You'll find Fagor pressure cookers at specialty kitchen stores as well as online.

POWER PRESSURE COOKER. The Power Pressure Cooker is one of the best-selling electric pressure cookers on the market. It comes in three sizes—6 quart, 8 quart, and 10 quart (5.7, 7.5, and 9.5 L)—and it's an affordable option for a larger pressure cooker. Currently it offers only a nonstick pot, which makes for easy cleanup but doesn't brown quite as well as a stainless steel pot. A favorite on QVC, the Power Pressure Cooker XL is now available in many retail stores, including Costco and Sam's Club.

CUISINART. My first electric pressure cooker was a 6-quart (5.7 L) Cuisinart, so I have a fondness for it. It doesn't tout itself as a multi-cooker, and I like the straightforward buttons. Select High or Low Pressure, set the cook time, and press start—no wondering whether to use the chicken button or the stew button. It comes with a nonstick pot that can get scratched if you're not careful. The Cuisinart is available at specialty kitchen stores as well as online.

As the popularity of electric pressure cookers has exploded, many manufacturers have added electric pressure cookers or multi-cookers to their offerings. Breville, Farberware, Black & Decker, and T-fal now offer 6-quart (5.7 L) electric pressure cookers, which operate similarly to the models I've discussed.

Electric Pressure Cooker Parts

The various electric pressure cooker brands use slightly different terms to refer to the cooker's parts; however, these parts are similar among all brands. For your convenience, I've included a quick explanation of the terms I use throughout the book.

COOKING POT. Made of stainless steel, ceramic, or nonstick aluminum, this removable pot is where the magic happens. (Do not confuse this with the *housing*, also called the *exterior* or *stationary pot*—you can seriously damage your electric pressure cooker if you try to cook without the cooking pot inside the housing.)

PRESSURE RELEASE VALVE. Also called a *pressure limit valve*, *pressure regulator knob*, *steam release handle*, *steam release reset button*, and *rapid release button*, this plastic piece is located on the lid's exterior and controls whether the pressure inside the pot is allowed to escape. While the different brands have different names for this knob, it's the same basic principal: Use it to either seal the pressure cooker or to allow the steam to escape and let the pressure release quickly.

SEALING RING. Made of tough, food-grade silicone, this removable ring attaches to the underside of the lid. When locked in place, this ring creates the airtight seal that lets the pressure cooker come to pressure. This is also called a *silicone gasket*, *rubber grommet*, or *rubber gasket*, depending on the brand.

FLOAT VALVE. Also called a *floating valve* or *pressure limit valve*, this small valve is one of the safety features of electric pressure cookers. As your pressure cooker comes to pressure, the float valve is pushed up until the mini gasket seals the cooker. When the float valve rises, the lid locks to prevent it from being opened while the contents are at pressure. When this valve drops, you can carefully remove the lid and continue with your recipe.

Selecting a Button

As with the pressure cooker components, even though different pressure cooker brands use different names for the buttons, all pressure cookers operate similarly. The recipes in this cookbook are designed to work in *any* electric pressure cooker—regardless of what the control panel looks like or how many buttons it has.

If you have a multi-cooker with additional buttons, your user manual should have an in-depth explanation of the different buttons and how they work. I recommend familiarizing yourself with them. However, these manuals don't always clarify that the buttons are simply convenience settings with preprogrammed cook times. Pressure cookers currently on the market cannot sense what you are actually cooking in the pot.

So, don't worry—you're not going to "mess up" by using the Meat button when you cook chicken soup. Nearly all the buttons on electric pressure cookers cook at High Pressure, so it really doesn't matter if you choose the Meat, Stew, or Poultry button. You can even cook desserts using the Meat button with no problem, as long as you adjust the cook time accordingly.

Initial Walk-Through

An easy way to familiarize yourself with your electric pressure cooker is to test it using only water. The steps in this process are repeated every time you cook at pressure, though they won't always be written in this much detail in the recipe.

1. Place the pressure cooking pot inside the housing. *Get in the habit of checking that the inner pot is there before you start pouring in ingredients!*

2. Add 1 cup (235 ml) water to the pressure cooking pot.

3. Check that the lid is properly assembled with the sealing ring in position and the float valve in place. Close and lock the lid. Verify that your pressure cooker is positioned so that steam vents away from cabinets.

4. Make sure the pressure release valve is in the Sealed position. The term for this position varies by brand (*Sealing* for Instant Pot; *Pressure* for Fagor and Cuisinart). Read your user manual for the exact term on your electric pressure cooker.

5. Select the Manual/High Pressure setting and set 5 minutes for the cook time. (Or, to test a multi-cooker setting, select one of the preprogrammed pressure cooking buttons and set a 5-minute cook time.)

6. Watch while the pressure cooker does all the work. It takes about 5 minutes for the water to heat up and build pressure; some steam will release from the float valve while pressure is building. The steam causes the float valve to rise and seal, but the timer won't start until the pot reaches pressure—only then does the timer start counting down.

7. When the cook time ends, carefully turn the pressure release valve to the Venting position so that steam can escape and the pressure can release. Again, the exact term varies by brand (*Venting* for Instant Pot, *Steam* for Fagor). Avoid placing your hands, face, or arms directly over the valve—the steam is very hot and can burn. (When my daughter first started using her electric pressure cooker, the steam and the noise made her a little nervous, so she used a wooden spoon to turn the valve.)

8. Once the steam disperses completely, you should hear the float valve drop. When this happens, the lid unlocks. Carefully remove the lid, tilting it so that steam vents away from you. The pressure cooking pot is hot—use hot pads or silicone mitts to remove it.

9. Don't forget to turn off the pressure cooker! (Sometimes I unplug my pressure cooker to make sure it isn't still cooking on the Keep Warm setting without my noticing.)

That's it! Now that you're familiar with your pressure cooker, let's get started with some easy pressure cooking recipes, such as Cilantro-Lime Rice (page 255) or Strawberry Applesauce (page 274). Before you know it, you'll be making fabulous pressure cooker meals and wondering how you ever cooked without it!

PRESSURE COOKING TERMINOLOGY

When my daughter first began using a pressure cooker, she was a little intimidated by the unfamiliar terms she encountered in my recipes. Many cooks who are new to pressure cooking feel this way; however, once you learn the terminology, you'll be confident and ready to get cooking.

Releasing Pressure

One of the first things to learn about pressure cooking is when and how to release the pressure. When the cook time ends, the cooker beeps. At this point, the recipe directs you how to release the pressure in the pressure cooking pot, using one of the following methods:

NATURAL PRESSURE RELEASE. A *natural pressure release* is when you leave the pressure release valve in the Sealed position when the cook time ends; this lets the pressure release slowly, without you doing anything. After the cook time expires, most electric pressure cookers automatically switch to the Keep Warm setting and the pressure inside the cooking pot begins to drop slowly. Food inside the cooking pot continues to cook as the pressure decreases. A natural pressure release can take from 5 to 30 minutes—the time varies depending on the ingredients and amount of liquid in the cooking pot.

The pressure cooker will not open until all pressure is released. When the pressure is fully released, the float valve drops and the lid unlocks and opens easily. There is no beep or signal when the pressure is released, though sometimes you can hear the float valve drop if you're close by.

Use a natural pressure release any time you need to release the pressure gradually—particularly for soups and grains, which are known to foam inside the pressure cooking pot, and for large cuts of meat, which need to rest after cooking to tenderize the meat.

QUICK PRESSURE RELEASE. A *quick pressure release* (or *rapid release*) is when you turn the pressure release valve to the Venting position and let the steam release quickly after the cook time ends. (Remember, the exact term for the valve varies by brand.) Unlike a natural pressure release, a quick pressure release results in a strong jet of steam coming from the pressure release valve. This is normal. If drops of liquid or foam start to emerge from the pressure release valve, simply switch the valve back to the Sealed position and use an intermittent pressure release (see following).

When you use a quick pressure release, you know the pressure is fully released when the steam fully dissipates and the float valve drops. You cannot unlock the lid until all the pressure is released.

A quick pressure release stops the cooking quickly to avoid overcooking; it is well suited for ingredients such as potatoes and vegetables that need to stop cooking while they're tender but still hold their shape.

INTERMITTENT PRESSURE RELEASE. An *intermittent pressure release* is the best way to release pressure for foods such as pastas, soups, and certain grains, which are prone to foaming or spitting if you try to release pressure with a quick release. With this method, you open and close the pressure release valve in intervals. This allows the pressure to escape more quickly than a natural pressure release and also prevents foam from coming out of the pressure release valve. With some foods, one or two closed intervals is all I need before I can leave the valve in the Venting position; with other foods, if the foaming is particularly bad, I will close the valve and wait a minute or two, then slide the valve to Venting again and continue opening and closing the valve as needed.

ABBREVIATED NATURAL RELEASE. The different types of pressure releases can also be combined; for example, in many recipes in this cookbook, I let the pressure release naturally for a number of minutes, then use a quick pressure release to release any remaining pressure. Combining the two release options reduces waiting time yet gives you many of the benefits of a natural pressure release, such as reducing foam and tenderizing meats.

KEEP WARM SETTING. When the pressure cook time ends, most models will automatically switch to the Keep Warm setting. This setting continues to heat food at a low temperature. Check your manual for details on how the Keep Warm setting works in your brand.

HELPFUL TIP: I prefer to turn off the pressure cooker after pressure cooking and set a kitchen timer to beep and remind me when to release the pressure. If you prefer to leave the pressure cooker on once the pressure cook time ends and let the Keep Warm setting keep track of the elapsed time, that's a great option too. The pressure begins to release naturally either way, so choose what works best for you.

Sautéing, Simmering, and Browning

Sautéing ingredients before cooking results in richer, more complex flavors; it is a cornerstone of cooking meats and soups and is necessary for flavorful gravies and sauces.

One big advantage of using a pressure cooker is sautéing foods directly in the pressure cooking pot before pressure cooking. The buttons on pressure cookers vary from brand to brand, though, most include a button for sautéing ingredients, and many also have buttons for browning and simmering. Often, the trick is simply finding the right button! (For example, some models of the Instant Pot use Sauté adjusted to More for browning and Sauté adjusted to Less for simmering. Some electric pressure cookers simply use a pressure setting without the lid in place; for instance, the Power Pressure Cooker XL sautés using the Chicken setting without the lid.) Consult your pressure cooker's user manual to identify the capabilities of your machine.

Since there is so much variety between machines, the recipes in this book use two terms for cooking techniques: *Simmer/Sauté* and *Browning/Sauté*. Use what works best according to your cooking preferences and your machine's capabilities. As you would sauté on a stovetop, use these buttons only when the lid is off.

SIMMER/SAUTÉ. When you see this term in a recipe, select either the Simmer or Sauté button. The Simmer feature uses a lower heat than the Sauté feature and is best for thickening sauces and soups.

BROWNING/SAUTÉ. Likewise, when you see this term, use either the Browning or Sauté button to cook. The Browning feature uses a higher heat than the Sauté feature, so your meats and vegetables (such as onions, carrots, and celery) cook more quickly on Browning than on Sauté.

Here are some tips to get the best results from the Browning/Sauté settings:

• Select the Browning/Sauté button to preheat the pot. Do not add any oil or ingredients to the cooking pot before it has finished preheating.

• Electric pressure cooking pots are slightly raised in the middle, so the oil will run to the sides, which may make foods stick when placed in the middle of the pot. To prevent sticking, you can use a pastry brush to spread the oil around the pot, but I prefer to pick up the pressure cooker and swirl the oil around.

• Don't crowd the pot by adding too much food at the same time. This is especially important with meats—if they are packed tightly in the pot, they will steam, not brown.

• When cooking vegetables, stir frequently to promote even cooking. In contrast, when cooking meats, place the meat in the pot and do not stir. Periodically test with a fork by gently lifting part of the meat; do not turn it until the meat releases easily from the pot.

- If foods cook too quickly (for example, a sauce boiling too rapidly), use a hot pad to lift the inner pot a few inches (about 7.5 cm) away from the heating element on the bottom of the pot or remove the pot from the pressure cooker briefly. If your machine has the capability, switch to a lower heat setting.

- After you finish browning, many recipes have you deglaze, or add liquids to, the hot pan. When you brown vegetables or meats, they release juices that caramelize on the bottom of the pot, called *fond*, which adds delicious flavor to sauces and gravies. Adding a liquid—such as broth, juice, wine, or even plain water (don't use dairy, which could curdle)—loosens the fond from the bottom of the pot. Immediately after adding the liquid, stir, scraping up any browned bits from the bottom of the pot to flavor the sauce. The fond should be golden-brown to dark brown; if it turns black, your food will taste burnt.

- When I'm cooking recipes that use a lot of liquids, I'll often sauté the meat and vegetables, add the liquids to deglaze, and leave the Browning/Sauté setting on while I add the rest of the ingredients. This starts heating the liquids and cuts down on the time it takes to come to pressure.

PRESSURE COOKING EQUIPMENT

There are some pressure cooking accessories I use often enough that I consider them truly essential to pressure cooking. Luckily, they are also affordably priced, making it easier to add them to your kitchen arsenal. Other accessories simply make life easier or are needed for certain recipes only —they're nice to have, but not absolutely necessary.

All items listed below are used in the recipes in this cookbook. You may already have some of these items. If you don't, you may have dishes and pans in your kitchen that will make good substitutes—if a dish is ovenproof and fits easily in the cooking pot, it should be safe to use in the electric pressure cooker.

Essentials

TRIVET. A trivet or a rack with feet keeps ingredients or other bowls off the bottom of the pressure cooking pot. While many pressure cookers include a trivet, consider purchasing a second—a few of my recipes use an additional trivet for stacking items.

STEAMER BASKET. Like a trivet, a steamer basket keeps foods out of the water; however, the steamer basket is more substantial and has small holes like a colander. This gadget really helps those foods that break down easily in water retain their shape—I consider it essential for cooking potatoes—and it also makes vegetables easy to remove from the pressure cooking pot.

EXTRA SILICONE RING. I keep an extra silicone ring on hand in case the original gets damaged, but I consider it a must-have when cooking mild-flavored breakfasts or desserts to avoid a transfer of smell and flavor—the last thing you want is to have tonight's cheesecake tasting slightly like yesterday's barbecue.

SLING. A sling makes it much easier to remove pots from the pressure cooker. You can make your own sling by folding a long strip of aluminum foil in thirds lengthwise. However, if you'd like a longer-lasting sling, cut a large silicone pastry mat lengthwise into strips—mine are about 4 inches (10 cm) wide and 26 inches (66 cm) long. The silicone makes a great nonslip surface that helps the pan stay in place on the sling as you lower it into the cooking pot. Carefully tuck the ends of the sling away from the contents of the pan before you lock the lid in place.

INSTANT-READ THERMOMETER. I consider this essential for verifying that larger cuts of meat are cooked to a safe internal temperature. The thermometer also helps you check that cheesecakes and other desserts are set.

Specialty Items

SMALL CAKE PAN. I use my 7 × 3-inch (18 × 7.5 cm) round cake pan for cakes, lasagnas, pot-in-pot rice, and so much more. You can use almost any ovenproof, flat-bottomed pan or glass dish that fits in your pressure cooking pot.

IMMERSION BLENDER. While you can use any blender for these recipes, an immersion blender lets you blend creamy soups directly in the pressure cooking pot without having to worry about spilling hot liquid when you transfer it to a blender. (If you have a nonstick cooking pot, be careful not to scratch your pot with an immersion blender.)

SPRINGFORM PAN. A 6- or 7-inch (15 or 18 cm) springform pan is the perfect size for making cheesecake in a 6-quart (5.7 L) pressure cooker. It also works well for cooking cakes and quiches.

GLASS CUSTARD CUPS. These small 6-ounce (170 g) glass custard cups are perfect for cooking single-serve items such as mini desserts and egg muffins.

CANNING JAR LIFTER TONGS. I like to use these to remove glass custard cups or Mason jars from my pressure cooker. They're also handy for removing fresh corn on the cob from the pressure cooking pot.

PRESSURE COOKING POINTERS

READ THE ENTIRE RECIPE BEFORE COOKING. Few things in the kitchen are more frustrating than getting halfway through a recipe and realizing you don't have an ingredient or that the food needs to chill for hours before you can continue. Plus, having foods measured and chopped before you start cooking can help cut your stress level as you cook. In addition, many recipes have serving suggestions at the end, so reading to the end helps you plan ahead so that you have these items ready when you need them.

UNDERSTAND RECIPE TIMING. While pressure cooking is fast, it doesn't happen in an instant. When you start the pressure cooker, the heating element turns on and starts to heat your food, building the steam that puts the "pressure" in pressure cooking. The time spent coming to pressure is similar to time spent preheating an oven or waiting for water to boil—it isn't counted in the cook time. *The recipe cook time does not start until the pressure cooker reaches pressure.* The time it takes for your pressure cooker to reach pressure could be as quick as 5 minutes when cooking with small amounts of liquid or as long as 30 minutes if your ingredients are cold or your pot is filled with lots of liquid.

TRUST YOUR SENSES. You'll be more successful and avoid mistakes in the kitchen if you learn to trust your instincts and your senses. Remove the cooking pot from the pressure cooker housing immediately if you smell burning while sautéing. Use a quick pressure release and open the lid if you see steam escaping from around the sides of the lid—you don't have a proper seal. Don't be afraid to take action if something doesn't seem right!

RECOGNIZE THERE'S MORE THAN ONE RIGHT WAY TO PRESSURE COOK. One of the best features of pressure cooking is its flexibility; often, there are many ways to approach cooking certain items. For example, I prefer to cook beans using a quick soak method (1 minute at pressure with 1 hour soak time), but you can also soak your beans overnight or even increase the pressure cook time in the recipe to accommodate the unsoaked beans. While none of these methods is "right" or "wrong," you will find you prefer some methods over others. Use what works best for you!

USE THESE RECIPES WITH A STOVETOP PRESSURE COOKER. All recipes in this cookbook can also be cooked in a stovetop pressure cooker. Simply bring your stovetop pressure cooker to pressure using a medium-high heat and then reduce the heat to the lowest setting necessary to maintain pressure. Start timing the cook time once your stovetop pressure cooker reaches pressure.

USE THE MINIMUM LIQUID REQUIRED. The minimum amount of liquid required varies among the different brands of pressure cookers; consult your user manual to find your brand's minimum amount. However, many brands do not acknowledge that the minimum amount of liquid required can also depend on what you're cooking. Many ingredients release liquid as they cook, so you can use less liquid to begin with; for example, many of my chicken recipes use less than the minimum amount of water because the chicken releases liquid as it cooks.

REDUCE OR DOUBLE RECIPES. When reducing a recipe, do not reduce the liquids below ½ to 1 cup (120 to 235 ml) cooking liquid. For example, when reducing my Cheesy Potatoes au Gratin (page XX), I halve all ingredients except the broth and spices added below the steamer basket. After steaming the potatoes, I simply discard half the remaining cooking liquid and continue with the recipe.

You can generally use the same cook time specified in the original recipe, as the timing is based more on the thickness of the food than on the amount. Therefore, when you reduce a recipe, don't cut the cook time if the thickness of the food remains the same—especially when cooking meat. For example, whether you cook 2 pork chops or 6 pork chops, the cook time stays the same if all the pork chops are the same thickness.

When doubling a recipe, never fill the pot above the maximum fill line, typically two-thirds full or half full for foods that foam. (For this reason, I don't recommend doubling most pasta recipes in this book.) However, the same principles for cook time apply to doubling a recipe—as long as the thickness of the food is the same, you can generally use the recipe's original cook time. Be aware that a fuller pot takes longer to come to and release pressure, which increases the overall time, and you may need to reduce the recipe cook time to compensate.

HIGH-ALTITUDE COOKING. I live about 4,000 feet (1.2 km) above sea level, which is considered high altitude, and I occasionally need to change a recipe to adjust for that. Water boils at a lower temperature at high altitudes, so foods may need a slightly longer cook time. The technical rule is to add 5 percent more cook time at 3,000 feet (0.9 km) above sea level, 10 percent for 4,000 feet (1.2 km) above sea level, and so on, increasing by 5 percent every additional 1,000 feet (0.3 km). For example, at my altitude, if a recipe has a cook time of 30 minutes at sea level, technically I should add an extra 3 minutes to account for my altitude (0.10×30 minutes = 3 minutes extra).

That said, I rarely adjust for altitude, especially for foods with short cook times.

Occasionally, I need to increase my cook times by a few minutes, especially with beans and grains. The recipes in this cookbook were tested at various altitudes and should not need any adjustment below 5,000 feet (1.5 km).

CHECK THE TEMPERATURE. As discussed in the Selecting a Button section (see page 14), your pressure cooker does not have a sensor that monitors what's cooking in the pot; each button only starts a preprogrammed cook time. The only way to know that your foods have reached the desired internal temperature is to use an instant-read thermometer.

I highly recommend getting in the habit of checking the temperature of pressure cooked foods. Common safe internal temperatures are as follows:

Breads and cakes	210°F	(100°C)
Baked potatoes	205°F	(96°C)
Chicken thighs and wings	180°F	(82°C)
Beef (well-done)	165°F	(74°C)
Chicken breasts	165°F	(74°C)
Turkey breasts	165°F	(74°C)
Ground beef (e.g., meatloaf)	155°F	(68°C)
Cheesecake	150°F	(65.5°C)
Beef (medium)	145°F	(63°C)
Fish	145°F	(63°C)
Pork	145°F	(63°C)
Beef (rare)	125°F	(51.5°C)

THICKEN SAUCES AND GRAVIES AFTER PRESSURE COOKING. Since pressure cooking requires liquid to achieve pressure, you'll generally thicken the flavorful pressure cooking liquids *after* pressure cooking. Using flour or cornstarch before pressure cooking can interfere with the pressure cooking process. Skip flouring your meat before browning it and use the flour in a slurry at the end to thicken the gravy.

I intentionally use many methods for thickening sauces and gravies in my recipes. A cornstarch slurry (whisking cornstarch and cold water) is probably the easiest method, but I also use a flour slurry, a roux, and blended vegetables, or I simmer sauces until they're reduced. As long as you add it after pressure cooking, there's no right or wrong thickener—switch them up as desired!

COOKING FOODS THAT FOAM OR FROTH. Pressure cooking manuals often have warnings about cooking foods that foam in your pressure cooker, and for good reason—

if cooked improperly, these foods can interfere with maintaining and releasing pressure. Common foods that froth and foam include pastas, soups, applesauce, beans and split peas, grains such as barley and oatmeal, and high-starch items like potatoes.

When cooking these foods, never fill the pot more than halfway. When the cook time ends, turn off the pressure cooker. Use a natural pressure release or an intermittent release, if necessary. If foam starts to come out of the pressure release valve, close it and wait a few minutes. If it works with your recipe, you may also add 1 or 2 tablespoons (15 to 30 ml) oil to the liquids in the cooking pot to reduce the foaming.

COOKING FROZEN MEATS. You get better results if you don't cook large cuts of frozen meat. A frozen roast doesn't brown well, cook as evenly, or absorb marinades—and it's hard to judge how much time it will take. However, if you want to cook from frozen, lots of people do. A good rule is to add 5 minutes of cook time per inch (2.5 cm) of thickness.

If your recipe calls for diced meat, but you forgot to defrost it the night before, use your pressure cooker to defrost and partially cook smaller cuts of frozen meats, such as chicken breasts. Simply pour 1 cup (235 ml) water into your pressure cooking pot, place a trivet in the bottom, and arrange the frozen chicken breasts on the trivet. Lock the lid in place. Select High Pressure and 1 minute cook time. When the cook time ends, turn off the pressure cooker. Use a quick pressure release. Remove the chicken from the pot and dice it into small pieces and continue with the recipe as directed.

PLAN AHEAD. Making a meal plan that covers several days can save you even more time in the kitchen. Here are some tricks I use in my own cooking:

• Plan your meals to double up on common items. For example, make a double batch of white rice to eat with a meal like Beef and Broccoli (page 174), and save half the rice for Ham Fried Rice (page 256) the next day.

• When you bring meat home from the grocery store that you don't plan to use right away, cut it into bite-size pieces and freeze them flat. Bite-size pieces of meat thaw quickly, and you can use them frozen, without thawing or changing the recipe timing.

• Chop all the vegetables you'll use throughout the week at the same time so that they're ready to go on busy nights. Try to plan multiple meals that use the same vegetables, for instance, Creamy Chicken and Wild Rice Soup (page 80) and Pasta Fagioli (page 92). Store the different amounts in separate containers.

• Chopped onion freezes well, so if a recipe uses only half an onion, dice the entire onion and freeze half for another recipe.

• Freeze leftovers in single-serve portions. Many soups freeze well, but soups with noodles, potatoes, or rice freeze better if you freeze the noodles, potatoes, or rice in separate single-serving bags and reheat the two separately.

REHEAT FOODS. Reheating in the pressure cooker helps keep foods moist and avoids the changes in flavor and texture that you get from reheating in the microwave. To reheat leftovers, pour 1 cup (235 ml) water into the pressure cooking pot and place a trivet in the bottom. Put the food in an ovenproof dish and place the dish on the trivet. Cook on High Pressure for about 5 minutes, depending on the amount of the food, and use a quick pressure release.

CONVERTING A REGULAR RECIPE FOR A PRESSURE COOKER

Before you try to convert your favorite recipes for the electric pressure cooker, I recommend cooking several recipes from this cookbook to become familiar with the process. Once you have some experience and feel ready to start converting recipes to pressure cooker recipes, remember that even the most experienced cooks do not always get perfect results on the first try—look at recipe conversion as a process.

Keep a notebook and write down the changes you make to the original recipe and tweaks you'd like to try the next time you make it—if it's not written down, it's unlikely you'll get the same results! Once you adapt a couple of recipes, it gets easier. You'll learn to trust your instincts.

When I find a recipe I'm interested in converting to a pressure cooker recipe, I answer the following questions:

1. Is the recipe a good choice for the pressure cooker?

Because the pressure cooker requires liquid to achieve pressure, an ideal pressure cooker recipe calls for some liquid. Recipes originally written for slow cookers with marinades—as well as stovetop recipes for most soups, meats with gravy, and legumes and grains—are generally easily adapted to the pressure cooker.

If you want a crispy fried coating on your meat or veggies, or if you're cooking meat that's very lean or expensive and already tender, the pressure cooker is probably not the best method.

The pressure cooker excels at turning tough, fatty meats into tender, succulent meals. It also makes quick soups that taste like they've simmered all day long, and it's perfect for cooking vegetables—I love it for potatoes and spaghetti squash. The pressure cooker is the only way I cook rice now, and it makes cooking dried beans a breeze.

Not every recipe is faster to cook in the pressure cooker, but even if it's not faster, it's often easier and tastier cooked this way. You get long-simmered, marinated flavors in a fraction of the time.

2. How do I know what cook time to use?

I find it's much easier to modify an existing pressure cooker recipe than to start from scratch by using a chart to figure out cook times and amounts of liquid needed—especially when cooking multiple ingredients at the same time. I've intentionally developed recipes for this book that use a variety of meats, so you can use this cookbook as a resource in adapting your own recipes.

For example, we eat a lot of chicken at my house, so I've created recipes using whole chicken, bone-in and boneless breasts (both diced and whole), thighs, wings, and legs. If you want to adapt your favorite chicken recipe to the pressure cooker, just match the major ingredients (meats and vegetables) in your recipe with a similar recipe in this cookbook and use that as a guide for cook time and amount of liquid.

If you can't find a similar recipe here or online, use a reliable chart to determine the cook time for the main ingredient in your recipe. (Cooking charts appear in your pressure cooker's user manual and are widely posted on a number of pressure cooking websites.)

When converting a pasta recipe, whether you use regular, gluten-free, or whole wheat pasta, you generally divide the cook time listed on the package by 2, then subtract 1 minute. After cooking at High Pressure, if the pasta is not cooked through, select Simmer/Sauté and simmer until the pasta is cooked as desired

To find the proper cook time for meat, I generally reduce the cook time for meat recipes cooked in the oven or on the stove by 50 to 75 percent. For example, if you're cooking a roast that requires 3 hours in the oven, start with 1 hour cook time in the pressure cooker. Test for doneness with an instant-read thermometer. If the roast needs more time, add up to 30 minutes more of cook time, depending on the internal temperature.

3. What if ingredients have different cook times?

If you're cooking a dish with meat, the size and shape of the meat matters more than the amount. A large 3-pound (1.36 kg) whole roast needs to cook much longer at High Pressure than 3 pounds (1.36 kg) of the same roast cut into bite-size pieces. Consider whether you can cut your meat so that its cook time matches the cook time for the other ingredients. For example, small bite-size pieces of chicken breast have the same cook time as white rice, so cutting the chicken into bite-size pieces lets you cook the chicken and rice at the same time.

Another option for quick-cooking items is to wrap them in aluminum foil or put them on a trivet on top of the longer-cooking item to slow their cook time.

If you can't change the size or shape of your ingredients to have similar cook times, consider cooking the ingredient with the longest cook time first and adding the other ingredients and cooking for a few minutes longer. For example, if you think your meat will take 50 minutes to pressure cook and your vegetables will take 5 minutes, cook the meat for 45 minutes and release the pressure. Add the veggies, return the lid, bring the pot back to pressure, and cook for 5 minutes more.

4. How much liquid should I use?

Generally you need at least 1 cup (235 ml) liquid; however, there are instances where you can use less liquid, like when you use ingredients that contain lots of water, such as chicken, fruit, or vegetables. For specific ingredients, consult a recipe in this cookbook or your pressure cooker's user manual.

Since there's very little liquid lost when you pressure cook with an electric pressure cooker, you generally have to reduce the liquid in recipes such as soups and braises so that you don't water down the flavor. A good starting point is reducing the liquid by 25 percent.

5. Do I need to adjust when I add my ingredients to the pressure cooker?

While many recipes can keep the same order as the original recipe, there will be times you need to make modifications. For example, if your recipe starts with a roux or flouring your meat before browning, you need to change the recipe. Flour can create a layer on the bottom of the pressure cooking pot that prevents it from coming to pressure. To prevent issues created by flour or other thickeners, add these ingredients after you release the pressure. Combine the thickener with a little water to make a slurry before adding it to the pot (see Beef and Broccoli, page 174).

Jarred syrups and sauces may have thickeners that settle to the bottom of the pressure cooking pot, and dairy products such as heavy cream, yogurt, and cheese can settle or curdle. Add these ingredients after pressure cooking as well.

6. Should I use a natural or quick pressure release?

As discussed in the Releasing Pressure section (see page 15), meats generally benefit from a natural pressure release; if you're cooking meats with pasta or vegetables that you're worried about overcooking, use a quick pressure release.

TROUBLESHOOTING GUIDE

Once in a while, something goes wrong in the pressure cooking process—it happens to even the best cooks! While many pressure cooker user manuals include brand-specific troubleshooting tips, here is a list of common problems I'm asked about by readers of my blog, *Pressure Cooking Today*, and my family and friends. In many cases, you can save the meal and get things back on track!

MY LID WON'T LOCK INTO PLACE. Sometimes if the liquid in the pot is hot, the steam pushes the float valve up and the safety mechanism won't let you lock the lid in place again. Make sure the pressure release valve is in the Venting position so that steam can release, and push the float valve down with the end of a wooden spoon.

STEAM IS COMING FROM MY LID. First, determine where the steam is coming from. If steam is coming from the pressure release valve, double-check that the valve is actually on the lid and is in the Sealing position. If steam is coming from the sides of the lid, it means the lid isn't sealing properly. There are a few reasons for this. To check, turn off the pressure cooker and use a quick pressure release. When the lid unlocks, remove the lid and check to see that the sealing ring and float valve are properly in place and free of any food particles. If either the float valve or sealing ring needs to be adjusted, wait until the lid is cool enough to handle to avoid the risk of burns.

In rare cases, steam escapes from the sides of the lid because the sealing ring is brittle or broken. If you notice issues with your sealing ring, unfortunately, the only solution is to replace it.

If you notice the steam early in the cooking process, adjust the pressure release valve or the lid and restart the High Pressure cook time. If you suspect a number of minutes went by before you noticed the problem, you may need to add more liquid to your pressure cooking pot or reduce the cook time—there's no hard rule for how much, so make your best guess.

IT'S TAKING FOREVER FOR MY INGREDIENTS TO COME TO PRESSURE. Remember, if you're cooking a dish like soup with a lot of liquid or if the ingredients are cold, it can take as many as 30 minutes for the pressure cooker to come to pressure.

If that's not the problem, you should double-check that the pressure cooker hasn't been unplugged by mistake. Also, check that you added enough liquid to the pressure cooking pot—pots cannot reach High Pressure without sufficient liquid, and bigger 8- and 10-quart (7.5 and 9.5 L) cookers may need more liquid than their smaller 5- and 6-quart (4.7 and 5.7 L) counterparts.

MY MEAT SCORCHES DURING THE BROWNING PROCESS. In these situations, there are a number of options. If possible, lower the heat setting and add more oil to the pot. If your recipe calls for them, be sure to have liquids measured and ready to add as soon as you're done browning. You can also lift the cooking pot away from the heating element to slow the cooking process briefly.

THE COOK TIME HAS ENDED, BUT MY FOOD ISN'T COOKED. If your pasta or meat is nearly done, it's best not to return the pot to High Pressure. Rather, select Simmer/ Sauté and finish cooking the dish on that setting. Food can also finish cooking on the Keep Warm setting—simply lock the lid in place and wait a few minutes more.

However, if your meat isn't close to the proper temperature or isn't as fall-apart tender as you'd like, lock the lid in place and pressure cook it again for additional time.

Also, if quicker-cooking foods such as vegetables are done, but your meat is not, remove these ingredients from the cooking pot and place them in a bowl covered with aluminum foil. Once your meat is cooked, return the vegetables to the cooking pot and heat through.

MY SAUCE OR GRAVY IS TOO THIN. Different ingredients release different amounts of liquid as they cook, so it's hard to judge the exact amount of thickeners you need before pressure cooking. For example, chicken injected with water before freezing releases more liquid than a fresh chicken breast. If your original recipe calls for a thickener, remember that thickeners need to reach a temperature near the boiling point before they activate (the exact temperature depends on your altitude), so continue to Simmer/Sauté to heat your dish. If your sauce is still is too thin, mix an equal ratio of thickener and water and add it to your sauce, or simply let the sauce simmer a little longer until the liquid reduces.

If the original recipe doesn't call for a thickener and your sauce is too thin, make a slurry by whisking 2 tablespoons cornstarch (16 g) with 2 tablespoons (30 ml) cold water until smooth and add it to your sauce.

MY SAUCE OR GRAVY IS TOO THICK. Don't be afraid to add a little extra liquid and stir until it reaches the consistency you like. The liquid doesn't have to be water—choose something that matches the ingredients in your meal.

MY SAUCE OR GRAVY IS LUMPY. Don't panic! Whisk the sauce vigorously, pour it through a fine-mesh sieve or strainer, or use an immersion blender to purée it smooth. Lumpy sauce often results from adding dry thickeners to a hot pot or from not stirring to incorporate them completely with the water, so double-check this step in the future.

MY SILICONE RING SMELLS LIKE YESTERDAY'S DINNER. Unfortunately, the silicone sealing ring and the mini gasket on the float valve have a tendency to take on strong smells, particularly after cooking flavorful, savory meats and soups. I've tried many remedies—lemon juice, vinegar, baking soda, and other food-safe cleaners—but haven't yet found anything that will completely get rid of the smell.

I like to use one ring for savory foods and an extra sealing ring only for mild foods, such as oatmeal and cheesecake. My daughter prefers to use three rings: one for savory dishes, one for breakfasts, and one saved just for cheesecake. She keeps her savory sealing ring inside a sealed zipper bag to keep the smell from transferring to her cupboards. In contrast, I like to store my lids upside down on the pressure cooking pot in my pantry so that the sealing ring has a chance to air out. Again, there's not a right or wrong way to do it.

{ Chapter 1 }

Breakfasts

Breakfast is the most important meal of the day, and it's also my favorite meal. Here's a great selection of quick, get-you-out-the-door-fast recipes mixed with a handful of slow-morning indulgent recipes.

Very Berry Steel Cut Oats

YIELD:
8 SERVINGS

TIP: Chia seeds have a mild nutty flavor and are a good source of protein. If you don't have them on hand, omit them and reduce the water.

My daughter and her family are crazy about pressure cooker steel cut oats, and she makes a big batch that lasts for a couple of days. She likes the oatmeal thick and loaded with fresh berries. The heat from the oats warms the berries so they melt in your mouth, and the thick oats cool quickly with a splash of cold milk so her family doesn't have to wait as long to eat. I'm sure you'll enjoy it as much as they do!

2 tablespoons (28 g) unsalted butter
2 cups (352 g) steel cut oats
6½ cups (1.5 L) water
½ cup (120 ml) heavy cream
¼ cup (60 g) packed light brown sugar
¼ cup (21.25 g) dried cranberries
¼ teaspoon salt
¼ cup (44 g) chia seeds
1 teaspoon vanilla extract
1½ cups (255 g) fresh berries (raspberries,
**   blackberries, blueberries, or sliced strawberries)**
Sliced almonds, for garnish
Milk, for serving

Select Simmer/Sauté and melt the butter in the pressure cooking pot. Add the oats. Toast for about 3 minutes, stirring constantly, until they smell nutty. Stir in the water, heavy cream, brown sugar, cranberries, and salt. Lock the lid in place. Select High Pressure and 10 minutes cook time.

When the cook time ends, turn off the pressure cooker. Let the pressure release naturally for 10 minutes and finish with a quick pressure release. When the valve drops, carefully remove the lid. Stir in the chia seeds and vanilla. Cover and let sit for 5 minutes until the oats reach your desired thickness. Top with the berries, and finish with a sprinkle of sliced almonds and a splash of milk.

Carrot Cake Steel Cut Oats

YIELD:
6 SERVINGS

....

TIP: If you don't have pumpkin pie spice, make your own: Combine ½ teaspoon ground cinnamon, ¼ teaspoon ground ginger, ¼ teaspoon ground nutmeg, and ⅛ teaspoon ground cloves.

The flavors of the classic dessert in a hearty, heart-healthy breakfast.

1 tablespoon (14 g) unsalted butter
1 cup (176 g) steel cut oats
1 quart (946 ml) water
1 cup (110 g) grated carrots
3 tablespoons (60 g) pure maple syrup, plus more for serving
2 teaspoons ground cinnamon
1 teaspoon pumpkin pie spice
¼ teaspoon salt
¾ cup (110 g) raisins, plus more for serving
¼ cup (44 g) chia seeds
Chopped nuts, for serving
Milk, for serving

Select Simmer/Sauté and add the butter to the pressure cooking pot to melt. Add the oats. Toast for about 3 minutes, stirring constantly, until they smell nutty. Stir in the water, carrots, maple syrup, cinnamon, pumpkin pie spice, and salt. Lock the lid in place. Select High Pressure and 10 minutes cook time.

When the cook time ends, turn off the pressure cooker. Let the pressure release naturally for 10 minutes and finish with a quick pressure release. When the valve drops, carefully remove the lid. Stir in the raisins and chia seeds. Cover and let sit for 5 to 10 minutes until the oats reach your desired thickness. Serve topped with more raisins, maple syrup, chopped nuts, and milk.

Apple-Cinnamon Oatmeal

YIELD:
2 TO 3 SERVINGS

....

TIP: I top my oatmeal with sliced almonds, extra brown sugar, and a splash of milk around the edges to cool it down. Oatmeal really is a blank slate—change up the toppings to fit what you have on hand.

Old-fashioned oatmeal made in the pressure cooker is perfect for busy mornings. This dish is ready in no time, giving you the chance to enjoy your coffee before your day starts!

1 tablespoon (14 g) unsalted butter
2 cups (470 ml) water
1 cup (156 g) old-fashioned oats
1 cup (150 g) diced apple
2 tablespoons (30 g) packed light brown sugar
¼ teaspoon ground cinnamon
¼ teaspoon salt

Select Simmer/Sauté and melt the butter in the pressure cooking pot. Add the water, oats, apple, brown sugar, cinnamon, and salt. Lock the lid in place. Select High Pressure and 1 minute cook time.

When the cook time ends, turn off the pressure cooker. Let the pressure release naturally for 10 minutes and finish with a quick pressure release. When the valve drops, carefully remove the lid. Stir the oatmeal and serve hot with your choice of toppings.

Oatmeal for One

YIELD:
I SERVING

....

TIP: This oatmeal has no added sugar, allowing you to control just how much sweetness you need to start your day.

On weekdays in our busy home, everyone fixes their own breakfast. On cold, snowy days, I crave a hearty, warm breakfast that will keep me going until lunch. Making a single batch of oatmeal in the pressure cooker doesn't save a lot of time, but you can cook the oatmeal in the same bowl you'll eat it in, and you can leave the kitchen while it cooks without worrying that your oatmeal will boil over.

½ cup (78 g) old-fashioned oats
1 cup (235 ml) water
Pinch salt

In a small, deep, ovenproof bowl with at least a 2-cup (470 ml) capacity, stir together the oats, water, and salt. Put a trivet in the pressure cooking pot and add 1 cup (235 ml) water. Place the bowl on the trivet. Lock the lid in place. Select High Pressure and 2 minutes cook time.

When the cook time ends, turn off the pressure cooker. Let the pressure release naturally for 5 minutes and finish with a quick pressure release. When the valve drops, carefully remove the lid. Stir the oatmeal and serve hot with your choice of toppings.

Cherry-Orange Breakfast Quinoa

This light, fluffy quinoa combines a rise-and-shine orange flavor with tart cherries in a quick fiber- and protein-packed breakfast that will keep you full all morning.

2¼ cups (540 ml) water
1½ cups (276 g) uncooked quinoa, well rinsed
2 tablespoons (24 g) sugar
Juice of 1 orange
Zest of 1 orange
¼ teaspoon salt
½ cup (80 g) dried cherries, chopped
Milk, sliced almonds, and sugar, for topping

In the pressure cooking pot, combine the water, quinoa, sugar, orange juice, orange zest, and salt. Lock the lid in place. Select High Pressure and 1 minute cook time.

When the cook time ends, turn off the pressure cooker. Let the pressure release naturally for 10 minutes and finish with a quick pressure release. When the valve drops, carefully remove the lid. Fluff the quinoa with a fork and stir in the cherries. Serve hot topped with milk, sliced almonds, and more sugar, if desired.

Crustless Ham and Cheese Quiche

YIELD:
4 TO 6 SERVINGS

....

TIP: This recipe is easy to customize to your taste. Load this quiche with sausage, bacon, and ham for a hearty meat lover's special or substitute roasted vegetables for the ham for a healthy start to your day.

No crust plus your pressure cooker equals no fuss. This crustless quiche is loaded with ham, cheese, and scallions and cooks up light and fluffy.

6 large eggs, well beaten
$\frac{1}{2}$ cup (120 ml) milk
$\frac{1}{8}$ teaspoon salt
$\frac{1}{8}$ teaspoon freshly ground black pepper
1 cup (150 g) diced ham
2 large scallions, white and green parts, chopped
1 cup (115 g) shredded Cheddar cheese
$\frac{1}{4}$ cup (20 g) shredded Parmesan cheese

Put a metal trivet in the bottom of the pressure cooking pot and add 1$\frac{1}{2}$ cups (360 ml) water.

In a large bowl, whisk the eggs, milk, salt, and pepper. Set aside.

Spray a 7-inch (18 cm) round cake pan or 1$\frac{1}{2}$-quart (1.4 L) ovenproof dish with nonstick cooking spray. Add the ham, scallions, and Cheddar and mix well. Pour the eggs over the ham mixture and stir to combine. Sprinkle the top with Parmesan. Use a sling to place the dish on the trivet. Lock the lid in place. Select High Pressure and 20 minutes cook time.

When the cook time ends, turn off the pressure cooker. Let the pressure release naturally for 10 minutes and finish with a quick pressure release. When the valve drops, carefully remove the lid. Lift out the dish. You can serve this immediately or pop the dish in a preheated broiler and broil until the top is lightly browned.

Hash Brown Breakfast Casserole

YIELD:
6 SERVINGS

TIP: My family prefers crisp bacon. If the bacon doesn't brown evenly in the pressure cooking pot, after I transfer it to a plate, I put it in the microwave for 30 seconds to crisp up.

When you crave something a little more substantial to start the day, this easy one-pot hash brown breakfast casserole is sure to become a favorite.

3 slices bacon, coarsely chopped
½ cup (80 g) chopped onion
2 cups (420 g) frozen hash brown potatoes
8 large eggs
¼ cup (60 ml) milk

¼ teaspoon salt
¼ teaspoon freshly ground black pepper
¾ cup (90 g) shredded Cheddar cheese, divided

Spray a 7-inch (18 cm) round cake pan or a 1½-quart (1.4 L) baking dish with nonstick cooking spray.

Select Browning/Sauté and add the bacon to the pressure cooking pot. Fry for about 5 minutes until crisp, stirring occasionally. Transfer the bacon to a paper towel–lined plate, leaving the bacon fat in the pot. Add the onion. Sauté for 3 minutes, stirring frequently. Transfer the onion to the prepared pan and add the cooked bacon and hash browns. Set aside.

In a large bowl, whisk the eggs, milk, salt, and pepper. Mix in ½ cup (60 g) Cheddar. Pour the egg mixture over the hash browns and bacon and stir to combine. Sprinkle the remaining ¼ cup (30 g) Cheddar on top—do not stir.

Put a trivet in the bottom of the pressure cooking pot and add 1 cup (235 ml) water. (You don't need to clean the pot after cooking the onion. The water will help clean it as the casserole cooks.) Center the dish on a sling and carefully lower it onto the trivet. Lock the lid in place. Select High Pressure and 20 minutes cook time.

When the cook time ends, turn off the pressure cooker. Let the pressure release naturally for 10 minutes and finish with a quick pressure release. When the valve drops, carefully remove the lid and use a paper towel to blot up any water that collected on the casserole. If desired, brown the cheese under a preheated broiler for a few minutes before serving.

Mexican Breakfast Casserole

YIELD:
6 SERVINGS

TIP: Queso fresco is a fresh-tasting, mild Mexican cheese that's easily crumbled. If it's not available in your area, substitute a shredded Mexican cheese blend.

Spice up your morning with this easy, meaty, cheesy, Mexican-inspired casserole. The tortillas dissolve into the eggs, giving the casserole body and a great corn flavor.

4 (5 inches, or 13 cm) corn tortillas, torn into bite-size pieces
1 tablespoon (15 ml) vegetable oil
1 pound (454 g) ground chorizo or Italian sausage
8 large eggs
1/3 cup (78 ml) milk
1/2 teaspoon salt
1/4 teaspoon freshly ground black pepper

1 can (4 oz, or 113 g) diced mild green chilies
1/2 cup (59 g) crumbled queso fresco
3 scallions, white and green parts, chopped
1/2 cup (58 g) shredded Cheddar cheese

Spray a 7-inch (18 cm) round cake pan with a generous amount of nonstick cooking spray. Place the tortilla pieces in the prepared pan.

Select Browning/Sauté to preheat the pressure cooking pot. When hot, add the vegetable oil and chorizo. Cook for about 5 minutes, stirring frequently, until brown and crumbled. Use a slotted spoon to transfer to a paper towel–lined plate. Set aside. Drain any excess fat from the pot.

In a large bowl, whisk the eggs, milk, salt, and pepper. Stir in the green chilies, queso fresco, scallions, and browned chorizo. Pour the egg mixture into the prepared pan and stir to combine. Sprinkle the top with Cheddar.

Put a trivet in the bottom of the pressure cooking pot and add 1 cup (235 ml) water. Center the pan on a sling and carefully lower it onto the trivet. Lock the lid in place. Select High Pressure and 25 minutes cook time.

When the cook time ends, turn off the pressure cooker. Let the pressure release naturally for 10 minutes and finish with a quick pressure release. When the valve drops, carefully remove the lid. Lift out the dish. If desired, broil until the cheese is lightly browned.

Maple-Almond-Raisin Breakfast Risotto

....

TIP: This dish tastes great the next day as well. Add more almond milk before you rewarm it to get that creamy consistency back.

This breakfast risotto is similar to rice pudding but has less fat and sugar. You may find yourself eating it for dessert as well.

2 tablespoons (28 g) unsalted butter

1½ cups (288 g) arborio rice

1 quart (946 ml) unsweetened almond milk, plus more as needed

½ cup (75 g) raisins

¼ cup (80 g) pure maple syrup, plus more for serving

¼ cup (60 g) packed light brown sugar

1 teaspoon vanilla extract

½ teaspoon ground cinnamon

¼ teaspoon salt

Sliced almonds, for serving

Select Browning/Sauté and melt the butter in the pressure cooking pot. Stir in the rice. Cook for about 3 minutes, stirring frequently, until fragrant. Stir in the almond milk, raisins, maple syrup, brown sugar, vanilla, cinnamon, and salt. Lock the lid in place. Select High Pressure and 6 minutes cook time.

When the cook time ends, turn off the pressure cooker. Let the pressure release naturally for 5 minutes and finish with a quick pressure release. When the valve drops, carefully remove the lid. Stir the mixture. Add more almond milk, if needed, to achieve a creamy consistency. Serve topped with maple syrup, sliced almonds, and a splash of almond milk.

Parmesan, Spinach, and Tomato Egg Muffins

YIELD:
6 SERVINGS

....

TIP: These keep for 1 week in the refrigerator, and they also freeze well. To reheat, microwave on high power for about 30 seconds.

These egg muffins are like crustless mini quiches. This colorful spinach-tomato version is loaded with healthy veggies and makes a great meal on the run.

8 large eggs
¼ cup (60 ml) milk
¼ teaspoon salt
⅛ teaspoon freshly ground black pepper
1 cup (30 g) fresh baby spinach, chopped
½ cup (90 g) diced seeded tomato
2 scallions, white and green parts, sliced
⅓ cup (26.6 g) shredded Parmesan cheese

Spray 6 (6-ounce, or 170 g) ovenproof custard cups with nonstick cooking spray.

In a large bowl, whisk the eggs, milk, salt, and pepper until just blended. Evenly divide the spinach, tomato, and scallions among the custard cups. Pour the egg mixture over the veggies. Sprinkle the Parmesan over each.

Pour 1 cup (235 ml) water into the pressure cooking pot and place a trivet in the bottom. Place 3 custard cups on the trivet and place a second trivet on top. Place the remaining 3 cups on it. Lock the lid in place. Select High Pressure and 6 minutes cook time.

When the cook time ends, turn off the pressure cooker. Let the pressure release naturally for 5 minutes and finish with a quick pressure release. When the valve drops, carefully open the lid and remove the cups.

{ Chapter 2 }

Sandwiches, Wraps, Tacos, and More

Sandwiches (and all their variations) aren't just for lunch—on a busy day, a sandwich is the perfect quick-to-make, quick-to-eat dinner. With your electric pressure cooker, you can make the sandwich fillings ahead of time and freeze them in single-serve or family-size portions.

Asian Chicken Lettuce Wraps

YIELD:
6 SERVINGS

TIP: If you're unable to find butter lettuce, Boston and Bibb lettuce are close substitutes. In a pinch, iceberg or romaine lettuce can also work, or substitute corn or flour tortillas and make Asian chicken tacos.

Meet my easy pressure cooker version of the popular restaurant lettuce wraps. The crunchy vegetables and pop of color from the scallions and carrots will have your family asking for this again and again.

1 tablespoon (15 ml) vegetable oil

1½ pounds (680 g) ground chicken

3 cloves garlic, minced

1 cup (235 ml) reduced-sodium chicken broth

½ cup (120 ml) hoisin sauce

¼ cup (60 ml) low-sodium soy sauce

1 teaspoon chili-garlic sauce, plus more for serving

½ cup (98 g) white rice

1 can (8 oz, or 227 g) sliced water chestnuts, drained and diced

1 tablespoon (8 g) cornstarch

1 tablespoon (15 ml) cold water

1 cup (130 g) frozen diced carrots, thawed

3 scallions, white and green parts, sliced

2 heads butter lettuce, for serving

Select Browning/Sauté to preheat the pressure cooking pot. When hot, add the vegetable oil and chicken. Cook for about 5 minutes, crumbling with a spoon, until browned. Add the garlic and cook for 1 minute more, stirring frequently. Stir in the chicken broth, hoisin sauce, soy sauce, and chili-garlic sauce. Stir in the rice and water chestnuts. Lock the lid in place. Select High Pressure and 4 minutes cook time.

When the cook time ends, turn off the pressure cooker. Let the pressure release naturally for 10 minutes and finish with a quick pressure release. When the valve drops, carefully remove the lid.

In a small bowl, whisk the cornstarch and cold water until smooth. Add the slurry to the pot. Select Simmer/Sauté and cook, stirring constantly, until the sauce reaches your desired thickness. Stir in the carrots and scallions. Serve wrapped in lettuce leaves topped with more chili-garlic sauce or Sriracha, if desired.

Sweet Pork Tostadas

YIELD:
8 SERVINGS

TIP: Cutting the pork into bite-size pieces before cooking reduces the cook time dramatically and makes this a quick and tasty weeknight meal.

Think traditional tostada—a crispy corn shell topped with refried beans, lettuce, tomatoes, cheese, and guacamole—but with the addition of restaurant-style sweet pork. It's anything but ordinary.

1 can (7 ounces, or 200 g) diced green chilies
2 cups (470 ml) cola, divided
½ cup (130 g) chunky salsa
⅓ cup (75 g) packed light brown sugar
2 tablespoons (32 g) tomato paste
2 teaspoons chili powder
¼ teaspoon ground cumin
4 pounds (1.8 kg) boneless pork shoulder, trimmed and cut into 1-inch (2.5 cm) cubes

1 cup (235 ml) red enchilada sauce
8 (5 inches, or 13 cm) white corn tortillas
Refried beans, for serving
Shredded lettuce, for serving
Shredded Mexican cheese, for serving
Guacamole, for serving
Fresh salsa, for serving

In the pressure cooking pot, combine the green chilies, 1 cup (235 ml) cola, the chunky salsa, brown sugar, tomato paste, chili powder, and cumin. Stir to combine. Add the pork. Lock the lid in place. Select High Pressure and 25 minutes cook time.

When the cook time ends, turn off the pressure cooker. Let the pressure release naturally for 10 minutes and finish with a quick pressure release. When the valve drops, carefully remove the lid.

Pour the pot's contents into a colander to drain the juices; discard them. Shred the pork and put it back into the cooking pot. Stir in the remaining 1 cup (235 ml) cola and enchilada sauce. Select Browning/Sauté and cook until the sauce heats through.

Preheat the oven to 350°F (180°C, or gas mark 4). Lightly spray the tortillas with cooking spray. Place them on a baking sheet and bake for about 5 minutes until crisp and starting to brown. Spread the tortillas with refried beans and top with the pork, lettuce, cheese, guacamole, and salsa.

Shredded Chicken Taco Filling

YIELD:
12 SERVINGS

....

TIP: If you have a stand mixer, put your cooked chicken in the bowl and use the paddle attachment to shred it. The chicken is shredded in just a few minutes.

This chicken taco filling is so versatile. It's great for taco salads, enchiladas, burritos, and more, and it's very convenient—you don't even have to thaw the frozen chicken. My neighbor likes this recipe so much, she makes it every week.

2 tablespoons (30 ml) olive oil
1 large onion, diced
6 large boneless skinless chicken breasts, frozen
1 can (10 ounces, or 284 g) diced tomatoes and
   green chilies (Ro-Tel Original)
1 tablespoon (8 g) chili powder
1 teaspoon salt
½ teaspoon freshly ground black pepper

Select Browning/Sauté to preheat the pressure cooking pot. Add the oil and onion. Sauté for about 3 minutes until tender. Add the chicken, tomatoes and green chilies, chili powder, salt, and pepper. Lock the lid in place. Select High Pressure and 12 to 15 minutes cook time, depending on how large your chicken, breasts are. (If using thawed chicken, reduce the cook time by a couple of minutes.)

When the cook time ends, turn off the pressure cooker. Use a quick pressure release. When the valve drops, carefully remove the lid. Remove the chicken from the pressure cooker, but do not discard the juices in the pot. Shred the chicken and return it to the cooking pot, stirring to combine it with the tomatoes and juices. Select Simmer/Sauté. Cook for about 5 minutes, uncovered, stirring occasionally, until all the liquid is absorbed. Serve immediately or divide into 1-cup (about 200 g) portions and freeze for later.

Carnitas Street Tacos

TIP: Make life easier before a big get-together. Prepare the taco meat early in the morning or even a day ahead and reheat it in the pressure cooker with a little reserved cooking liquid.

I have a favorite taqueria that serves upscale little street tacos with pretty pink pickled onions on top. The pickled onions add color, a burst of flavor, and a nice crunch to the taco—and they're easy to make.

FOR PICKLED ONIONS:

1 small red onion, thinly sliced and quartered

1 cup (235 ml) hot water

½ cup (120 ml) apple cider vinegar

1 tablespoon (12 g) sugar

1 teaspoon salt

⅛ teaspoon red pepper flakes

FOR TACOS:

1 tablespoon (3 g) dried oregano

2 teaspoons ground cumin

2 teaspoons salt

1 teaspoon freshly ground black pepper

2 tablespoons (30 ml) olive oil

6 pounds (2.7 kg) boneless pork shoulder, trimmed and cut into 4 equal pieces

1 cup (235 ml) fresh orange juice (from about 2 large oranges)

2 onions, quartered

8 cloves garlic, smashed

2 jalapeño peppers, seeded, ribbed, and chopped

Small corn tortillas, queso fresco, fresh cilantro, lime juice, and sour cream, for serving

TO MAKE THE PICKLED ONIONS: In a small bowl, combine the red onion and hot water. Let soak for 1 minute. Drain. In a pint-size (470 ml) Mason jar, whisk the cider vinegar, sugar, and salt until dissolved. Add the red pepper flakes and red onion to the jar. Let sit at room temperature for 1 hour. Drain before using.

TO MAKE THE TACOS: In a small bowl, stir together the oregano, cumin, salt, pepper, and olive oil. Rub this paste over the pork pieces. In the pressure cooking pot, stir together the orange juice, onions, garlic, and jalapeños. Add the pork to the pot. Lock the lid in place. Select High Pressure and 50 minutes cook time.

When the cook time ends, turn off the pressure cooker. Let the pressure release naturally for 10 minutes and finish with a quick pressure release. When the valve drops, carefully remove the lid. Using a large fork or slotted spoon, carefully transfer the meat to a large platter and shred it with 2 forks. Discard any excess fat as you shred. Strain the juices in the cooking pot and set aside.

Serve immediately or crisp the pork before serving. To crisp, preheat the broiler. Line a rimmed baking sheet with aluminum foil and spread the pork in a single layer. Broil for 3 to 5 minutes, or until the edges of the pork start to brown and crisp.

Place the shredded pork in a serving bowl and ladle ½ cup (120 ml) reserved cooking liquid over the pork. Serve in warmed tortillas topped with the pickled red onions. Finish with queso fresco, chopped fresh cilantro leaves, a squeeze of lime juice, and sour cream, if desired.

Carne Asada Tacos

YIELD:
6 SERVINGS

TIP: If you fancy fajitas, sauté sliced onions and bell peppers in a little vegetable oil in a skillet over medium-high heat while the beef cooks. Add these to the warmed tortillas just before serving.

Cooking flank steak in the pressure cooker tenderizes the meat, leaving it melt-in-your-mouth delicious.

1 tablespoon (8 g) chili powder
1 teaspoon ground cumin
1 teaspoon garlic powder
1 teaspoon onion powder
½ teaspoon salt
½ teaspoon freshly ground black pepper
2 pounds (907 g) flank steak, cut into
  ¼-inch -thick (0.6 cm) strips
¼ cup (60 ml) water
¼ cup (60 ml) fresh lime juice
¼ teaspoon liquid smoke (optional)
Warmed tortillas, queso fresco, and pico de gallo, for serving

In a large bowl, stir together the chili powder, cumin, garlic powder, onion powder, salt, and pepper. Use clean hands to rub the spices into the steak until it is evenly coated.

In the pressure cooking pot, combine the water, lime juice, liquid smoke (if desired), and steak. Lock the lid in place. Select High Pressure and 12 minutes cook time.

When the cook time ends, turn off the pressure cooker. Use a quick pressure release. When the valve drops, carefully remove the lid. Select Simmer/Sauté and cook for about 10 minutes until all the liquid is gone, stirring frequently. Serve in the warmed tortillas topped with queso fresco and pico de gallo.

Greek Tacos

YIELD:
8 SERVINGS

....

TIP: This Greek taco meat freezes very well. Freeze in individual portions for quick, easy meals.

This delightful Greek version of tacos is made with tender chunks of seasoned pork braised in herbs and lemon juice, served on warm pita bread with lettuce, tomatoes, and cool, creamy tzatziki sauce.

FOR PORK:

1 teaspoon dried marjoram

½ teaspoon salt

¼ teaspoon freshly ground black pepper

2 tablespoons (30 ml) olive oil

4 pounds (1.8 kg) boneless pork shoulder, trimmed and cut into 1-inch (2.5 cm) cubes

½ cup (120 ml) fresh lemon juice

¼ cup (60 ml) water

Pita bread, diced tomato, and lettuce, for serving

FOR TZATZIKI SAUCE:

1 small cucumber, peeled, seeded, and shredded

¼ teaspoon salt

1 cup (230 g) plain Greek yogurt

1 tablespoon (15 ml) fresh lemon juice

1 teaspoon dried dill weed

1 clove garlic, minced or pressed

⅛ teaspoon freshly ground black pepper

TO MAKE THE PORK: In a small bowl, stir together the marjoram, salt, pepper, and olive oil. Rub this paste all over the cubed pork. Add the lemon juice and water to the pressure cooking pot. Place the pork in the pot. Lock the lid in place. Select High Pressure and 25 minutes cook time.

TO MAKE THE TZATZIKI SAUCE: While the pork cooks, in a fine-mesh strainer, toss the cucumber with the salt. Let the cucumber drain for 15 minutes over a bowl or the sink to remove excess water. In a medium-size bowl, stir together the drained cucumber, yogurt, lemon juice, dill weed, garlic, and pepper until well combined.

When the cook time ends, turn off the pressure cooker. Let the pressure release naturally for 10 minutes and finish with a quick pressure release. When the valve drops, carefully remove the lid. Using a slotted spoon, transfer the meat to a serving dish. Serve on pita with diced tomatoes, shredded lettuce, and tzatziki sauce.

Ground Beef Tacos

YIELD:

4 TO 6 SERVINGS

TIP: The cook time in this recipe assumes the ground beef is frozen in a flat square. If you're using more than 1 pound (454 g) of meat, or if your meat is frozen in a thick slab or ball, you may need to add more High Pressure or Browning/Sauté cook time.

My mom's favorite taco was a ground beef taco. You're going to love that you can start with frozen ground beef and go from frozen to fiesta in 15 minutes.

1 cup (235 ml) water
2 teaspoons chili powder
½ teaspoon ground cumin
½ teaspoon garlic powder
1 teaspoon onion powder

¼ teaspoon salt
Dash cayenne pepper
1 pound (454 g) frozen lean ground beef

Add the water to the pressure cooking pot and stir in the chili powder, cumin, garlic powder, onion powder, salt, and cayenne. Add the frozen ground beef. Lock the lid in place. Select High Pressure and 5 minutes cook time.

When the cook time ends, turn off the pressure cooker. Use a quick pressure release. Select Browning/Sauté and cook the mixture for about 5 minutes, stirring frequently, until the water evaporates and the beef is browned and crumbled.

Serve as desired, in flour tortillas or crisp taco shells, with cheese, salsa, lettuce, and tomatoes.

Barbecue Beef Brisket Tacos

YIELD:
8 SERVINGS

....

TIP: If you prefer, buy prepared coleslaw at the deli counter instead of making your own.

These tacos are a fusion of Mexican and barbecue flavors. I first tasted this fantastic flavor combination at a neighborhood street fair, where a local barbecue restaurant serves this as their Wednesday special. I couldn't resist re-creating these at home in the pressure cooker, so now I can have them any day of the week.

FOR COLESLAW:
½ cup (115 g) mayonnaise
2 tablespoons (30 ml) apple cider vinegar
2 teaspoons sugar
¼ teaspoon salt
4 cups (280 g) coleslaw mix

FOR FILLING:
½ cup (120 ml) water
2 tablespoons (15 g) chili powder
1 tablespoon (18 g) salt
1 teaspoon freshly ground black pepper
1 teaspoon garlic powder
½ teaspoon cayenne pepper
3 pounds (1.36 kg) flat-cut beef brisket, halved equally
8 (4 inches, or 10 cm) flour tortillas
½ cup (125 g) barbecue sauce, for serving

TO MAKE THE COLESLAW: In a large bowl, stir together the mayonnaise, cider vinegar, sugar, and salt. Add the coleslaw mix and stir until well combined. Refrigerate until serving.

TO MAKE THE FILLING: In the pressure cooking pot, stir together the water, chili powder, salt, pepper, garlic powder, and cayenne. Add the brisket, fat-side up. Lock the lid in place. Select High Pressure and 60 minutes cook time.

When the cook time ends, turn off the pressure cooker. Let the pressure release naturally for 10 minutes and finish with a quick pressure release. When the valve drops, carefully remove the lid. Transfer the brisket to a rimmed baking sheet and shred the meat.

To serve, top the tortillas with 2 tablespoons (28 g) brisket and a drizzle of barbecue sauce, then finish with the coleslaw.

Cheesy Baked Chicken Taquitos

YIELD:
10 SERVINGS

TIP: My family prefers flour tortillas, but corn tortillas work, too.

Taquitos are small, rolled tacos that are often deep-fried. I've created a baked version filled with a chicken and cheese filling that comes together quickly in the pressure cooker.

½ cup (120 ml) water

¼ cup (32 g) green salsa, plus more for serving

1 teaspoon chili powder

½ teaspoon onion powder

½ teaspoon ground cumin

½ teaspoon garlic powder

½ teaspoon salt

¼ teaspoon freshly ground black pepper

2 large chicken breasts, fresh or frozen

1 tablespoon (15 ml) fresh lime juice

1 package (3 ounces, or 85 g) cream cheese, cubed

10 (6 inches, or 15 cm) flour tortillas

1½ cups (173 g) shredded Colby Jack cheese

3 tablespoons (3 g) fresh chopped cilantro leaves

2 scallions, white and green parts, chopped

Guacamole and sour cream, for serving

Preheat the oven to 400°F (200°C, or gas mark 6). Line a baking sheet with aluminum foil and lightly coat it with nonstick cooking spray.

In the pressure cooking pot, stir together the water, green salsa, chili powder, onion powder, cumin, garlic powder, salt, and pepper. Add the chicken. Lock the lid in place. Select High Pressure and 10 minutes cook time.

When the cook time ends, turn off the pressure cooker. Use a quick pressure release. When the valve drops, carefully remove the lid. Remove the chicken, shred it, and return it to the pot. Select Simmer/Sauté and cook uncovered for about 5 minutes, stirring occasionally, until all the liquid is absorbed. Stir in the lime juice. A little at a time, stir in the cream cheese until melted.

Divide the chicken mixture among the tortillas, placing it near the bottom. Top with the Colby Jack, cilantro, and scallions. Tightly roll the tortilla around the filling. Place each taquito, seam-side down, on the prepared baking sheet. Spray the tops with cooking spray. Bake for 10 to 15 minutes until crisp and golden-brown on the ends, turning seam-side up halfway through the baking time. Serve with guacamole, green salsa, and sour cream, if desired.

Chicken Quesadillas with Avocado Salsa

YIELD:
4 SERVINGS

....

TIP: I like to cook my quesadilla in a dry skillet, but my daughter likes to butter her tortillas before she cooks them.

Spicy chicken and creamy avocado salsa blend beautifully inside a crisp, golden-brown tortilla. Cooking the filling in the pressure cooker gets this meal on the table in a snap!

FOR QUESADILLAS:

1 can (14.5 ounces, or 411 g) diced tomatoes, with liquid

1 can (4.5 ounces, or 128 g) diced green chilies, with liquid

1 teaspoon chili powder

½ teaspoon garlic powder

½ teaspoon onion powder

¼ teaspoon ground cumin

¼ teaspoon salt

2 large boneless skinless chicken breasts, fresh or frozen

8 (10 inches, or 25 cm) flour tortillas

2 cups (230 g) shredded Monterey Jack cheese

FOR AVOCADO SALSA:

1 large ripe avocado, peeled, pitted, and diced

½ cup (80 g) diced red onion

2 tablespoons (2 g) chopped fresh cilantro leaves

1 tablespoon (15 ml) fresh lemon juice

TO MAKE THE QUESADILLAS: In the pressure cooking pot, mix together the tomatoes, green chilies, chili powder, garlic powder, onion powder, cumin, and salt. Add the chicken. Lock the lid in place. Select High Pressure and 8 minutes cook time for fresh chicken, and 10 minutes if using frozen chicken.

TO MAKE THE AVOCADO SALSA: While the chicken cooks, in a small bowl, gently mix together the avocado, red onion, cilantro, and lemon juice. Set aside.

When the cook time ends, turn off the pressure cooker. Let the pressure release naturally for 5 minutes and finish with a quick pressure release. When the valve drops, carefully remove the lid. Transfer the chicken to a plate and shred it. Return the shredded chicken to the cooking pot and stir to combine with the tomatoes and juices. Select Browning/Sauté. Cook for about 5 minutes, uncovered and stirring occasionally, until all the liquid is absorbed or evaporates.

Put 1 tortilla in a skillet. Spread $1/4$ cup (28.75 g) Monterey Jack on top. Scatter 2 tablespoons (28 g) avocado salsa over the cheese. Top with $1/3$ cup (67 g) shredded chicken and an additional $1/4$ cup (28.75 g) shredded cheese. Finish with a second tortilla on top. Cover the skillet and cook over medium heat until the tortilla is golden-brown. Flip and cook for a few minutes more, covered, until the tortilla is golden-brown and the cheese melts. Remove from the skillet and use a pizza cutter to slice the quesadilla into 6 wedges. Repeat with the remaining ingredients.

Buffalo Chicken Tender Sandwiches with Blue Cheese Sauce

YIELD:
4 SERVINGS

TIP: I prefer Frank's RedHot sauce, but feel free to substitute your favorite.

The blue cheese sauce cools the heat from the spicy buffalo chicken. If you're a fan of buffalo chicken wings, I know you'll cheer for this easy-to-make sandwich.

FOR BUFFALO CHICKEN:
½ cup (120 ml) water
2 tablespoons (30 ml) hot sauce
12 chicken tenders, frozen or fresh
4 sub rolls, split and toasted
Romaine or iceberg lettuce leaves, for serving
1 small red onion, thinly sliced

FOR BLUE CHEESE SAUCE:
⅓ cup (75 g) mayonnaise
⅓ cup (75 g) sour cream
1 tablespoon (15 ml) lemon juice
Pinch salt and freshly ground black pepper
⅓ cup (40 g) blue cheese, crumbled

TO MAKE THE BUFFALO CHICKEN: Add the water and hot sauce to the pressure cooking pot and stir to combine. Add the chicken tenders. Lock the lid in place. Select High Pressure and 2 minutes cook time.

When the cook time ends, turn off the pressure cooker. Let the pressure release naturally for 5 minutes and finish with a quick pressure release. When the valve drops, carefully remove the lid. Use a slotted spoon to transfer the chicken to a plate. Shred the chicken using 2 forks and return it to the liquid in the cooking pot. Select Simmer/Sauté. Cook for about 5 minutes, uncovered and stirring occasionally, until all the liquid is absorbed or evaporates.

TO MAKE THE BLUE CHEESE SAUCE: In a small bowl, whisk the mayonnaise, sour cream, lemon juice, and salt and pepper, until smooth. Stir in the blue cheese.

TO MAKE THE SANDWICHES: Place a scoop of shredded chicken on the bottom of the sub roll and top with lettuce and red onion. Spread the top roll with blue cheese sauce and place it on top of the sandwich. Serve any remaining blue cheese sauce for dipping, if desired.

Chicken Salad Sandwiches

YIELD:
6 SERVINGS

....

TIP: If your favorite chicken salad is loaded with celery, grapes, scallions, and pecans, double the amounts used in the recipe.

Chicken salad sandwiches are perfect for everyday lunches yet elegant enough to serve at parties on mini croissants. The celery, pecans, and grapes combine to add crispy, crunchy, juicy notes to brighten each bite.

2 large boneless skinless chicken breasts,
   diced into bite-sized pieces
1½ cups (360 ml) water
¼ cup (60 g) mayonnaise
¼ cup (60 g) sour cream
1 teaspoon fresh lemon juice
½ teaspoon salt
¼ teaspoon freshly ground black pepper
½ cup (60 g) diced celery
½ cup (75 g) quartered grapes
1 scallion, white and green parts, chopped
¼ cup (28 g) chopped pecans, toasted
6 sandwich rolls or mini croissants, halved and toasted

In the pressure cooking pot, combine the diced chicken and water. Lock the lid in place. Select High Pressure and 4 minutes cook time.

When the cook time ends, turn off the pressure cooker. Use a quick pressure release. When the valve drops, carefully remove the lid. Transfer the chicken to a plate to cool and discard the cooking water.

In a large bowl, stir together the mayonnaise, sour cream, lemon juice, salt, and pepper. Add the cooled chicken, celery, grapes, and scallion. Gently toss to combine. Cover and chill for at least 1 hour. Stir in the pecans just before serving on the toasted sandwich rolls or mini croissants.

Tropical Teriyaki Chicken Wraps

YIELD:
6 SERVINGS

TIP: If you're trying to reduce carbs, serve this as a lettuce wrap. This chicken also works well served over rice for a Hawaiian-themed rice bowl.

Teriyaki chicken is typically grilled, but this quick-cooking pressure cooker version is so flavorful you won't miss the grill at all. The colorful, fresh pineapple salsa really pulls this dish together.

FOR TERIYAKI CHICKEN:
18 chicken tenders
Salt and freshly ground black pepper, for seasoning
¼ cup (60 ml) low-sodium soy sauce
2 tablespoons (30 g) packed light brown sugar
2 tablespoons (30 ml) rice vinegar
2 tablespoons (30 ml) pineapple juice
¼ teaspoon garlic powder
¼ teaspoon ground ginger
2 tablespoons (16 g) cornstarch
2 tablespoons (30 ml) cold water
6 large tortillas
Chopped romaine lettuce, for serving

FOR FRESH PINEAPPLE SALSA:
2 cups (310 g) fresh pineapple cubes (½ inch, or 1 cm)
⅓ cup (55 g) finely chopped red onion
¼ cup (4 g) chopped fresh cilantro leaves
1 small jalapeño pepper, seeded and finely chopped
2 tablespoons (30 ml) fresh lime juice
1 tablespoon (15 g) packed light brown sugar

TO MAKE THE TERIYAKI CHICKEN: Season the chicken tenders with salt and pepper. Set aside. In the pressure cooking pot, stir together the soy sauce, brown sugar, rice vinegar, pineapple juice, garlic powder, and ginger. Add the chicken. Lock the lid in place. Select High Pressure and 3 minutes cook time.

TO MAKE THE FRESH PINEAPPLE SALSA: While the chicken cooks, in a large bowl, combine the pineapple, red onion, cilantro, and jalapeño. In a small bowl, whisk the lime juice and brown sugar. Add this to the pineapple mixture and toss to combine. Set aside.

When the cook time ends, turn off the pressure cooker. Use a quick pressure release. When the valve drops, carefully remove the lid. Transfer the chicken to a bowl and shred it into large pieces with 2 forks. Leave the juices in the pot.

In a small bowl, whisk the cornstarch and cold water until smooth. Select Simmer/Sauté and add the slurry to the pot, stirring constantly until the sauce thickens. Stir 1 cup (235 ml) thickened sauce into the shredded chicken.

To serve, place a tortilla on a plate. Layer with a spoonful of teriyaki chicken, pineapple salsa, and lettuce. If desired, spoon more teriyaki sauce on top. Fold in the tortilla ends and roll into a wrap.

Shredded Barbecue Chicken Sandwiches

YIELD:
8 SERVINGS

TIP: Toasting the rolls helps keep the sauce from making them soggy—so don't skip that step.

When you're craving pulled pork but need something quicker, these shredded barbecue chicken sandwiches are just the ticket.

2 cups (500 g) barbecue sauce, divided, plus more for serving
1 cup (235 ml) water
1 teaspoon liquid smoke
1 large onion, quartered
3 cloves garlic, smashed
4 large boneless skinless chicken breasts
8 sandwich rolls, toasted

In the pressure cooking pot, stir together 1 cup (250 g) barbecue sauce, the water, and liquid smoke. Add the onion, garlic, and chicken breasts. Lock the lid in place. Select High Pressure and 6 minutes cook time.

When the cook time ends, turn off the pressure cooker. Let the pressure release naturally for 5 minutes and finish with a quick pressure release. When the valve drops, carefully remove the lid. Transfer the chicken to a plate and shred it with 2 forks. Strain the cooking liquid, reserving 1/2 cup (120 ml).

Return the chicken to the cooking pot and add the remaining 1 cup (250 g) barbecue sauce and reserved cooking liquid. Stir to combine. Select Simmer/Sauté and bring the mixture to a simmer, stirring frequently. Serve on toasted rolls topped with barbecue sauce.

Three-Ingredient Pulled Pork

YIELD:
8 SERVINGS

....

TIP: I brown the roast to deepen the flavor a bit, but you can skip that step if you're in a hurry or feeling a bit lazy. Some days are like that.

Pulled pork doesn't have to take all day. This easy pulled pork gives you the flavor of slow-cooked pulled pork in a fraction of the time—and with only three ingredients, you're out of the kitchen in a flash.

2 tablespoons (30 ml) vegetable oil
4 pounds (1.8 kg) boneless pork shoulder,
    trimmed and cut into 4 equal pieces
2 cups (500 g) barbecue sauce, divided, plus more for serving
½ cup (120 ml) water
8 sandwich rolls, toasted

Select Browning/Sauté and add the vegetable oil to the cooking pot. When the oil is hot, add 2 pieces of pork. Brown for about 3 minutes per side. When browned, transfer to a platter and repeat with the remaining 2 pieces.

Add 1 cup (250 g) barbecue sauce and ½ cup (120 ml) water to the cooking pot. Add the browned pork and any accumulated juices. Lock the lid in place. Select High Pressure and 60 minutes cook time.

When the cook time ends, turn off the pressure cooker. Use a natural pressure release. When the valve drops, carefully remove the lid. Carefully transfer the meat to a bowl and shred it with 2 forks, discarding any excess fat.

Strain the cooking liquid into a fat separator and reserve ½ cup (120 ml). Return the shredded pork to the cooking pot. Stir in the remaining 1 cup (250 g) barbecue sauce and reserved cooking liquid. Select Simmer/Sauté and bring to a simmer, stirring frequently. Serve on toasted rolls with more barbecue sauce, if desired.

Easy French Dip Sandwiches

YIELD:
4 SERVINGS

TIP: I generally have the butcher slice meat for me; if you slice it yourself, put the roast in the freezer for about 30 minutes before slicing—meat is easier to slice when it's slightly frozen.

French dip sandwiches don't get much easier than this! The meat cooks in an easy-to-make beef and onion broth that starts with a packet of dried onion soup mix, so there's not even any chopping to do.

$1\frac{1}{2}$ **pounds (680 g) boneless beef top round roast,**
   thinly sliced
1 can (14.5 fluid ounces, or 429 ml)
   reduced-sodium beef broth
1 packet dried onion soup mix
1 teaspoon finely crushed dried rosemary
$\frac{1}{2}$ teaspoon garlic powder
Butter, for the sub rolls
4 sub rolls, sliced lengthwise
8 slices of provolone cheese

In the pressure cooking pot, combine the beef, beef broth, onion soup mix, rosemary, and garlic powder. Lock the lid in place. Select High Pressure and 10 minutes cook time.

When the cook time ends, turn off the pressure cooker. Let the pressure release naturally for 10 minutes and finish with a quick pressure release. When the valve drops, carefully remove the lid.

Remove the meat from the broth. Strain the broth and skim off any fat. Butter and toast the sub rolls under a preheated broiler. Top each roll with meat and 2 slices of cheese. Broil again, just until the cheese melts and starts to bubble. Serve the broth in small cups for dipping.

Egg Salad Sandwiches

YIELD:
4 SERVINGS

TIP: The pressure cooker makes great hard-boiled eggs that are easy to peel—the shells practically fall off. The perfect cook time varies a bit for everyone, so if 6 minutes is a little too long for you, reduce the High Pressure cook time by 1 minute or use a quick pressure release.

I am crazy about making hard-boiled eggs in the pressure cooker. Now we keep hard-boiled eggs in the fridge all the time, and it's easy to make these quick egg salad sandwiches.

8 large eggs
¼ cup (60 g) mayonnaise
¼ cup (60 g) sour cream
1 teaspoon yellow mustard
Salt and freshly ground black pepper, for seasoning
¼ cup (30 g) diced celery
1 scallion, white and green parts, chopped
8 slices white bread
Lettuce leaves, for serving

Put a steamer basket in the pressure cooking pot and add 1 cup (235 ml) water. Carefully place the eggs in the steamer basket. Lock the lid in place. Select High Pressure and 6 minutes cook time.

While the eggs cook, prepare a large bowl of ice water and set aside.

When the cook time ends, turn off the pressure cooker. Let the pressure release naturally for 6 minutes and finish with a quick pressure release. When the valve drops, carefully remove the lid. Immediately transfer the steamer basket with the eggs into the ice water to stop the cooking. When completely cool, peel and dice the eggs. Set aside.

In a large bowl, mix together the mayonnaise, sour cream, and mustard. Season with salt and pepper to taste. Add the diced eggs, celery, and scallion. Gently toss to combine. Spread 4 slices of bread with egg salad, then top with a lettuce leaf and the remaining 4 slices of bread.

Sweet-and-Spicy Sloppy Joes

YIELD:
8 SERVINGS

TIP: If your family likes green bell peppers, dice one and add it with the onion.

There's no need to buy sloppy joe sauce in a can when it's so easy and inexpensive to make your own from ingredients you probably already have in your cupboard.

2 pounds (907 g) lean ground beef
1 tablespoon (15 ml) vegetable oil
1 cup (160 g) diced onion
4 cloves garlic, finely chopped
1 can (28 ounces, or 794 g) crushed tomatoes in purée
1 cup (235 ml) water
1 tablespoon (15 g) packed light brown sugar
2 tablespoons (30 ml) Worcestershire sauce
2 teaspoons chili powder
1 teaspoon dry mustard
½ teaspoon salt
¼ teaspoon freshly ground black pepper
8 sandwich buns, toasted

Select Browning/Sauté. Brown the ground beef for about 5 minutes in the pressure cooking pot, stirring occasionally until the beef crumbles and is no longer pink. Transfer to a paper towel–lined plate. Drain any excess fat from the pot.

Add the vegetable oil and onion to the cooking pot. Sauté for about 3 minutes until tender. Add the garlic and sauté for 1 minute more. Stir in the tomatoes, water, brown sugar, Worcestershire sauce, chili powder, dry mustard, salt, and pepper. Add the browned beef and stir to combine. Lock the lid in place. Select High Pressure and 5 minutes cook time.

When the cook time ends, turn off the pressure cooker. Use a quick pressure release. When the valve drops, carefully remove the lid. Select Browning/Sauté and cook for about 5 minutes, stirring frequently, until the sauce reaches your desired thickness. Serve on toasted buns.

Beef and Bean Burritos

YIELD:
6 SERVINGS

TIP: The spice level in this recipe is mild. If you like things a little hotter, double the chili powder.

My daughter prefers her burritos with rice and beans as well as meat. This recipe lets you cook all three at the same time.

2 tablespoons (30 ml) vegetable oil, divided

1 pound (454 g) lean ground beef

1 cup (160 g) diced onion

3 cloves garlic, minced

2 teaspoons chili powder

1 teaspoon ground cumin

$\frac{1}{4}$ teaspoon salt

1 can (15 ounces, or 425 g) black beans, drained and rinsed

1 cup (235 ml) reduced-sodium beef broth

$\frac{1}{2}$ cup (93 g) long-grain white rice

1 can (4 ounces, or 115 g) diced green chilies

Juice of 1 lime

2 tablespoons (2 g) chopped fresh cilantro leaves (optional)

6 burrito-size tortillas

Shredded Monterey Jack cheese, for serving

Salsa, for serving

Select Browning/Sauté to preheat the cooking pot. When hot, add 1 tablespoon (15 ml) vegetable oil and the ground beef. Cook for about 5 minutes, stirring frequently, until the beef is browned and crumbled. With a slotted spoon, transfer the beef to a paper towel–lined plate.

Add the remaining 1 tablespoon (15 ml) vegetable oil and onion to the cooking pot. Sauté for about 3 minutes, stirring occasionally, until the onion is tender. Add the garlic and cook for 1 minute more. Stir in the browned beef, chili powder, cumin, and salt. Sauté for 2 minutes. Add the black beans, beef broth, rice, and green chilies. Lock the lid in place. Select High Pressure and 3 minutes cook time.

When the cook time ends, turn off the pressure cooker. Let the pressure release naturally for 10 minutes and finish with a quick pressure release. When the valve drops, carefully remove the lid. Stir in the lime juice and cilantro.

Warm the tortillas in the microwave for 1 minute. Spread a small amount of the beef and bean mixture down the center of each tortilla and top with Monterey Jack and salsa. Fold the ends of the tortillas over and roll them up.

Shredded Beef Burritos

YIELD:
8 SERVINGS

....

TIP: If you like a smothered burrito, top these with your favorite enchilada sauce and shredded cheese. Broil for 2 to 4 minutes until the cheese is bubbly. Watch closely because the cheese browns quickly once it starts.

My son adores this classic burrito—tender, juicy, not-too-spicy shredded beef wrapped in a soft flour tortilla and served with his favorite toppings. Customize this for your family with their favorite toppings.

½ cup (120 ml) reduced-sodium beef broth
3 tablespoons (23 g) chili powder
½ teaspoon smoked paprika
½ teaspoon ground cumin
½ teaspoon garlic powder
½ teaspoon dried oregano
½ teaspoon salt
½ teaspoon freshly ground black pepper

1 (3 pounds, or 1.4 kg) chuck roast, cut into 3 equal pieces
Burrito-size flour tortillas
Shredded cheese, Mexican rice, and black beans, for filling (optional)
Sour cream, guacamole, fresh salsa, for serving (optional)

In the pressure cooking pot, stir together the beef broth, chili powder, paprika, cumin, garlic powder, oregano, salt, and pepper. Add the roast pieces. Lock the lid in place. Select High Pressure and 50 minutes cook time.

When the cook time ends, turn off the pressure cooker. Let the pressure release naturally for 10 minutes and finish with a quick pressure release. When the valve drops, carefully remove the lid. Transfer the beef to a work surface and shred it with 2 forks, discarding any fat. Transfer the cooking liquid to a fat separator. Return the shredded beef and 1 cup (235 ml) cooking liquid to the cooking pot and stir to combine. Select Simmer/Sauté and cook, uncovered and stirring occasionally, until most of the liquid is absorbed or evaporates.

Place ½ cup (about 115 g) beef in the center of a tortilla, add cheese and additional fillings of your choice (if desired). Fold in the edges and roll up into a burrito. Repeat with the remaining tortillas. Served topped with sour cream, guacamole, and fresh salsa (if desired).

Bacon-Avocado Sliders

YIELD:
6 SERVINGS

TIP: You get a more flavorful, juicier burger if you don't use lean ground beef.

Sliders are always fun to serve when you have a crowd. These tasty sliders can be browned ahead of time and finished right before serving so that you can enjoy the party, too.

8 slices bacon, halved widthwise
2 pounds (907 g) ground beef (don't use lean ground beef)
Salt and freshly ground black pepper, for seasoning
12 slider buns, toasted
1 avocado, peeled, pitted, and sliced

Select Browning/Sauté and add the bacon to the pressure cooking pot in small batches. Fry for about 3 minutes, until crisp but still soft, stirring frequently. Transfer to a paper towel–lined plate to cool. Turn off the pressure cooker and remove the cooking pot from the pressure cooker. Leave the bacon fat in the pot.

In a large bowl, mix together the ground beef, 1 tablespoon (15 ml) bacon fat, and the cooked bacon, crumbled. Form the mixture into 12 patties, about 3 ounces (85 g) each and slightly wider than the buns. Season generously with salt and pepper.

Return the cooking pot to the pressure cooker. Select Browning/Sauté. Add the sliders, 4 at a time, and cook for about 3 minutes per side to brown. Transfer to a plate when browned.

When all patties are browned, place a trivet in the cooking pot and add 1 cup (235 ml) water. Place the browned patties on the trivet, staggering them as you stack them. Lock the lid in place. Select High Pressure and 3 minutes cook time.

When the cook time ends, turn off the pressure cooker. Use a quick pressure release. When the valve drops, carefully remove the lid. Serve the sliders on toasted buns topped with avocado and your favorite burger toppings.

Cuban Sandwiches

YIELD:
8 SERVINGS

TIP: You can purchase bottled Mojo sauce at the grocery store—add 1 cup (235 ml) sauce to the pressure cooking pot before you add the pork.

My husband and I had our first Cuban sandwich when we were in Miami on vacation. It was love at first bite.

⅓ cup (78 ml) olive oil
10 cloves garlic, minced or pressed
¾ cup (175 ml) fresh orange juice
¾ cup (175 ml) fresh lime juice
1 teaspoon dried oregano
1 teaspoon ground cumin
1 teaspoon salt
1 teaspoon freshly ground black pepper
4 pounds (1.8 kg) boneless pork shoulder, trimmed and cut into 4 equal pieces
Dijon mustard, for serving
8 Cuban bread rolls or sub rolls, sliced lengthwise
8 slices black forest ham
8 slices Swiss cheese
8 sandwich-size dill pickles

Select Browning/Sauté and add the olive oil to the cooking pot. When the oil is hot, add the garlic and sauté for 30 seconds. Stir in the orange juice, lime juice, oregano, cumin, salt, and pepper. Use a ladle to remove 1 cup (235 ml) of this Mojo sauce for dipping the sandwiches. Add the pork to the pot. Lock the lid in place. Select High Pressure and 60 minutes cook time.

When the cook time ends, turn off the pressure cooker. Let the pressure release naturally. When the valve drops, carefully remove the lid. Carefully transfer the meat to a bowl and shred it with 2 forks, discarding any excess fat. Skim the fat off the liquid in the pot. Add ½ cup (120 ml) cooking liquid to the shredded pork.

Spread mustard on the bottom halves of the rolls. Top with cooked pork, ham, cheese, and pickles. Place the top half of the roll on top. Put the sandwiches into a preheated panini press and grill for 5 to 6 minutes until the cheese melts and the bread is toasted. If you don't have a panini press, cook the sandwich in a heavy skillet weighed down with a heavy lid or pan. Serve with the reserved Mojo sauce for dipping.

Steak and Cheddar Sandwiches

YIELD:
4 TO 6 SERVINGS

....

TIP: Lightly butter the hamburger buns and toast in a 350°F (180°C, or gas mark 4) oven for about 5 minutes until golden-brown.

A classic hot beef and Cheddar sandwich gets kicked up a notch with steak. Don't skip the hot sauce in the cheese sauce—it doesn't add much heat, but it does add a ton of flavor.

FOR STEAK:

1 to 3 tablespoons (15 to 45 ml) vegetable oil, divided

2 pounds (907 g) boneless beef sirloin steak, sliced against the grain into ¼-inch-thick (0.6 cm) slices

½ cup (120 ml) reduced-sodium beef broth

½ teaspoon garlic powder

½ teaspoon salt

½ teaspoon freshly ground black pepper

8 onion hamburger buns, toasted

FOR CHEESE SAUCE:

2 tablespoons (28 g) unsalted butter

2 tablespoons (14 g) all-purpose flour

1 cup (235 ml) milk

2 teaspoons hot sauce (I use Frank's RedHot)

¼ teaspoon salt

1½ cups (173 g) shredded Cheddar cheese

TO MAKE THE STEAK: Add 1 tablespoon (15 ml) vegetable oil to the pressure cooking pot and quickly brown the beef strips on one side. Work in batches, adding more vegetable oil as needed, until all the meat is browned on one side. Transfer the meat to a plate when browned.

Add the beef broth, garlic powder, salt, and pepper to the cooking pot and stir to combine. Return the browned beef to the pot. Lock the lid in place. Select High Pressure and 12 minutes cook time.

TO MAKE THE CHEESE SAUCE: While the beef cooks, in a medium-size saucepan over medium heat, melt the butter. Sprinkle in the flour and cook until bubbling. Gradually whisk in the milk a little at a time until the sauce is smooth and thick. Whisk in the hot sauce and salt. Add the Cheddar a handful at a time and stir until melted and smooth. Remove from the heat.

When the cook time ends, turn off the pressure cooker. Use a quick pressure release. When the valve drops, carefully remove the lid. To serve, top each bun with a mound of beef slices and ladle cheese sauce on top.

Easy Moo Shu Pork

YIELD:
6 SERVINGS

TIP: To change things up or to cut some carbs, serve the Moo Shu Pork in lettuce leaves.

A favorite at Chinese restaurants, this easy pressure cooker version uses Mexican tortillas instead of the traditional moo shu pancakes.

1 tablespoon (15 ml) vegetable oil

2 large eggs, beaten

½ cup (120 ml) water

¼ cup (60 ml) low-sodium soy sauce

2 tablespoons (32 g) smooth peanut butter

1 tablespoon (20 g) honey

1 tablespoon (15 ml) white vinegar

½ teaspoon Sriracha

¼ teaspoon garlic powder

¼ teaspoon ground black pepper

1½ pounds (680 g) pork loin or boneless pork chops, sliced into thin strips

1 package (8 ounces, or 227 g) fresh mushrooms, thinly sliced

1 can (8 ounces, or 227 g) bamboo shoots, sliced matchstick style

2 tablespoons (16 g) cornstarch

3 tablespoons (45 ml) cold water

2 teaspoons sesame oil

1 bag (14 ounces, or 397 g) coleslaw

1 scallion, white and green parts, chopped

12 thin flour tortillas

Select Simmer/Sauté to preheat the pressure cooking pot. When hot, add the vegetable oil and coat the bottom of the pot. Add the eggs and cook for about 3 minutes, without stirring, to create an omelet. Turn off the pressure cooker. Transfer the omelet to a cutting board and slice it into small, thin pieces.

Add the water, soy sauce, peanut butter, honey, white vinegar, Sriracha, garlic powder, and pepper to the pressure cooking pot and stir to combine. Stir in the pork, mushrooms, and bamboo shoots. Lock the lid in place. Select High Pressure and 5 minutes cook time.

When the cook time ends, turn off the pressure cooker. Use a quick pressure release. When the valve drops, carefully remove the lid.

In a small bowl, whisk the cornstarch and cold water until smooth. Add the slurry to the pot. Select Simmer/Sauté and simmer for a few minutes, stirring constantly, until the sauce thickens. Stir in the sesame oil, coleslaw, and chopped egg. Transfer to a serving bowl and garnish with scallions. To serve, divide the pork mixture among the tortillas and roll up to enclose.

{ Chapter 3 }

Soup's On

Soups made in the pressure cooker taste exactly like soups that simmer for hours on the stovetop. No need to serve your family soup from a can when you can have many homemade soups from your pressure cooker to the table in under 30 minutes.

Creamy Chicken and Wild Rice Soup

YIELD:
6 SERVINGS

TIP: My *Pressure Cooking Today* blog readers have had success substituting regular wild rice in this recipe instead of the long-grain wild rice blend.

A rich, creamy chicken and wild rice soup loaded with chicken, long-grain and wild rice, carrots, onions, and celery. This warm, hearty soup is perfect for cold snowy days.

2 tablespoons (32 g) unsalted butter

1 cup (160 g) chopped onion

1 cup (130 g) diced carrots

1 cup (120 g) diced celery

2 large boneless skinless chicken breasts, diced into bite-sized pieces

2 cans (14.5 fluid ounces, or 429 ml, each) reduced-sodium chicken broth

1 package (6 ounces, or 170 g) Uncle Ben's Long-Grain and Wild Rice (discard seasoning packet)

1 tablespoon (1 g) dried parsley

1 teaspoon salt

½ teaspoon freshly ground black pepper

Dash red pepper flakes

2 tablespoons (16 g) cornstarch

2 tablespoons (30 ml) cold water

4 ounces (113 g) cream cheese, cubed

1 cup (235 ml) milk

1 cup (235 ml) half-and-half

Select Browning/Sauté and melt the butter in the pressure cooking pot. Add the onion, carrots, and celery. Sauté for about 5 minutes, stirring occasionally, until the vegetables are tender. Stir in the chicken, chicken broth, rice, parsley, salt, pepper, and red pepper flakes. Lock the lid in place. Select High Pressure and 5 minutes cook time.

When the cook time ends, turn off the pressure cooker. Let the pressure release naturally for 5 minutes and finish with a quick pressure release.

In a small bowl, whisk the cornstarch and cold water until smooth. Select Simmer/Sauté and add the slurry to the pot stirring constantly. Stir in the cream cheese until melted. Stir in the milk and half-and-half, heat through—do not bring to a boil—and serve.

Louisiana Gumbo

TIP: Gumbo is traditionally served over steamed or dirty rice.

Gumbo is a Louisiana stew thickened with a flavorful roux and loaded with veggies, chicken, sausage, and seafood.

½ cup (120 ml) vegetable oil, divided

1 pound (454 g) Andouille sausage, halved lengthwise and cut into ¼-inch -thick (0.6 cm) slices

3 large boneless skinless chicken breasts

½ cup (56 g) all-purpose flour

1 large onion, diced

2 ribs celery, sliced

½ green bell pepper, chopped

4 cloves garlic, minced

5 cups (1.2 L) reduced-sodium chicken broth

1 can (14.5 ounces, or 411 g) diced tomatoes

2 cups (about 200 g) frozen sliced okra

1 tablespoon (15 ml) Worcestershire sauce

½ teaspoon cayenne pepper

8 ounces (227 g) small cooked shrimp, peeled and deveined

Salt and freshly ground black pepper, for seasoning

2 scallions, white and green parts, sliced, for garnish

Select Browning/Sauté to preheat the pressure cooking pot. Add ¼ cup (60 ml) vegetable oil and the sausage. Cook for about 3 minutes until browned. Transfer to a plate. Add the chicken. Cook for about 3 minutes per side to brown. Transfer to a cutting board and cut the chicken into bite-size pieces.

Add 2 tablespoons (30 ml) vegetable oil to the cooking pot and sprinkle the flour over the oil. Cook for about 10 minutes, stirring constantly, until the roux is medium to dark brown. Transfer to a bowl to cool.

Add the remaining 2 tablespoons (30 ml) vegetable oil to the cooking pot along with the onion, celery, and green bell pepper. Sauté for about 3 minutes, stirring occasionally, until the onion is tender. Add the garlic and cook for 1 minute more. Stir in the chicken broth, tomatoes, okra, Worcestershire sauce, cayenne, chicken, and sausage. Lock the lid in place. Select High Pressure and 4 minutes cook time.

When the cook time ends, turn off the pressure cooker. Let the pressure release naturally for 5 minutes and finish with a quick release. When the valve drops, carefully remove the lid. Select Simmer/Sauté and add the roux to the pot. Stir until the gumbo thickens. Add the shrimp and stir to combine. Season with salt and pepper to taste.

Chicken and Gnocchi Soup

YIELD:
6 SERVINGS

TIP: Gnocchi are small dumplings made from potato and flour. Look for them in the pasta section at the market.

This soup is a copycat version of a popular restaurant soup, but making it in the pressure cooker is so easy, you may never go out for it again.

1 tablespoon (14 g) unsalted butter

1 cup (160 g) diced onion

½ cup (60 g) diced celery

2 cloves garlic, minced

1½ quarts (1.4 L) reduced-sodium chicken broth

2 large boneless skinless chicken breasts, fresh or frozen

2 tablespoons (3 g) dried parsley

½ teaspoon dried thyme

⅛ teaspoon red pepper flakes (optional)

2 packages (1 pound, or 454 g, each) potato gnocchi

1 cup (110 g) finely shredded carrots

1 cup (30 g) coarsely chopped fresh spinach

3 tablespoons (24 g) cornstarch

3 tablespoons (45 ml) cold water

2 cups (470 ml) half-and-half

Salt and freshly ground black pepper, for seasoning

Select Browning/Sauté and melt the butter in the pressure cooking pot. Add the onion and celery. Sauté for about 3 minutes, stirring occasionally. Add the garlic and sauté for 1 minute more. Stir in the chicken broth, chicken, parsley, thyme, and red pepper flakes (if desired). Lock the lid in place. Select High Pressure and 4 minutes cook time.

When the cook time ends, turn off the pressure cooker. Use a quick pressure release. When the valve drops, carefully remove the lid. Transfer the chicken to a cutting board and cut it into bite-size pieces. Return the chicken to the pot and add the gnocchi and carrots. Lock the lid in place. Select High Pressure and 1 minute cook time.

When the cook time ends, turn off the pressure cooker. Let the pressure release naturally for 15 minutes and finish with a quick pressure release. When the valve drops, carefully remove the lid. Add the spinach and stir until wilted.

In a small bowl, whisk the cornstarch and cold water until smooth. Select Simmer/Sauté and add the slurry to the pot, stirring constantly until the soup thickens. Stir in the half-and-half. Season with salt and pepper to taste and serve.

White Chicken Chili

YIELD:
6 SERVINGS

TIP: You can make this recipe with cooked chicken as well. I often buy a rotisserie chicken to use in quick, easy recipes like this, or I'll use leftover chicken from another meal. The total cook time is the same with cooked or uncooked chicken.

This is my favorite chili! It's quick to make—only 5 minutes in the pressure cooker—but tastes like it's been simmering all day.

1 tablespoon (15 ml) vegetable oil

1 large onion, diced

2 cloves garlic, minced or pressed

3 cups (about 1 pound, or 454 g) diced chicken

2 cans (14.5 fluid ounces, or 429 ml, each) reduced-sodium chicken broth

1 jar (16 ounces, or 454 g) salsa verde

1 can (4 ounces, or 113 g) diced green chilies

1 teaspoon ground cumin

¼ teaspoon red pepper flakes

2 cans (15.5 ounces, or 440 g, each) cannellini beans or other white bean, drained and rinsed

2 tablespoons (16 g) cornstarch

3 tablespoons (45 ml) cold water

Salt and freshly ground black pepper, for seasoning

Sour cream, diced avocado, tortilla chips, and shredded cheese, for serving

Select Browning/Sauté and add the vegetable oil to the pressure cooking pot. When the oil is hot, add the onion. Sauté for about 3 minutes, stirring occasionally, until the onion is tender. Add the garlic and cook for 1 minute more. Stir in the chicken, chicken broth, salsa verde, green chilies, cumin, red pepper flakes, and beans. Lock the lid in place. Select High Pressure and 5 minutes cook time.

When the cook time ends, turn off the pressure cooker. Let the pressure release naturally for 5 minutes and finish with a quick pressure release.

In a small bowl, whisk the cornstarch and cold water until smooth. Select Simmer/Sauté and add the slurry to the pot, stirring constantly until the chili thickens. Season with salt and pepper to taste. Served topped with sour cream, diced avocado, tortilla chips, and shredded cheese, if desired.

Spicy Chicken Soup

TIP: You can use frozen boneless skinless chicken breasts in this recipe. Adjust the cook time to 11 minutes. You can also substitute 2 tablespoons (7 g) dried onion and 1 teaspoon dried minced garlic for the fresh onion and garlic. Add these ingredients to the other spices and skip the sauté step.

A quick-to-throw-together chicken soup with a Mexican twist, loaded with chicken, black beans, corn, tomatoes, and salsa. Top with your favorite Mexican cheese, sour cream, crushed tortilla chips, and maybe a jalapeño or two.

2 tablespoons (3 g) dried parsley
1 tablespoon (7 g) onion powder
1 tablespoon (8 g) chili powder
1 teaspoon freshly ground black pepper
1 teaspoon garlic powder
½ teaspoon salt
2 tablespoons (30 ml) olive oil
1 large onion, diced
3 cloves garlic, minced or pressed
4 boneless skinless chicken breasts

2 cans (14.5 fluid ounces, or 429 ml, each) reduced-sodium chicken broth
2 cans (14.5 ounces, or 411 g, each) peeled and diced tomatoes
1 jar (16 ounces, or 454 g) chunky salsa
2 cans (15 ounces, or 425 g, each) black beans, drained and rinsed
1 package (15 ounces, or 425 g) frozen corn
Shredded cheese, sour cream, and tortilla chips, for serving

In a small bowl, mix together the parsley, onion powder, chili powder, pepper, garlic powder, and salt. Set aside.

Select Browning/Sauté and add the olive oil and onion to the pressure cooking pot. Sauté for about 3 minutes, stirring occasionally, until the onion is tender. Add the garlic and cook for 1 minute more. Stir in the chicken, chicken broth, tomatoes, salsa, and spice mixture. Lock the lid in place. Select High Pressure and 8 minutes cook time.

When the cook time ends, turn off the pressure cooker. Let the pressure release naturally for 10 minutes and finish with a quick pressure release. When the valve drops, carefully remove the lid. Remove the chicken from the soup and shred the meat. Return the chicken to the pot and stir in the black beans and corn.

If needed, select Simmer/Sauté and bring the soup to a boil, stirring occasionally until the beans and corn are heated. Serve topped with shredded cheese, sour cream, and tortilla chips, if desired.

Butternut Squash Soup with Chicken and Orzo

YIELD:
8 SERVINGS

TIP: The soup has a richer flavor if you use roasted squash. Roast the cubed squash in a 400°F (200°C, or gas mark 6) oven on a baking sheet for about 20 minutes until it starts to brown and caramelize. If you're in a hurry or just don't want to turn on the oven, a reader of my blog, *Pressure Cooking Today*, suggested browning the squash in the pressure cooker with a little butter or oil, until it gets a nice caramelized coating.

Smooth, creamy, and delicious! The black pepper and red pepper flakes give this soup a bit of heat, and the half-and-half gives it great body and beautiful color. It can stand on its own without the chicken and orzo, but I made the addition since my family prefers a heartier soup. On busy nights, I often use rotesserie chicken.

3 tablespoons (42 g) unsalted butter

1/2 cup (50 g) diced scallions, white and green parts, plus more for serving

1/2 cup (60 g) diced celery

1/2 cup (65 g) diced carrots

1 clove garlic, minced

2 cans (14.5 fluid ounces, or 429 ml, each) reduced-sodium chicken broth

1 can (14.5 ounces, or 411 g) diced tomatoes with juice

1 1/2 pounds (680 g) butternut squash, peeled, cubed, and roasted

1/2 teaspoon Italian seasoning

1/4 teaspoon freshly ground black pepper

1/8 teaspoon red pepper flakes

1/8 teaspoon freshly grated nutmeg

1 cup (140 g) cooked diced chicken

1 cup (about 8 ounces, or 227 g) orzo, cooked

1/2 cup (60 ml) half-and-half, plus more for serving

Scallions, for garnish

Select Browning/Sauté and melt the butter in the pressure cooking pot. Add the scallions, celery, and carrots. Sauté for about 3 minutes until tender. Add the garlic and cook for 1 minute more. Stir in the chicken broth, tomatoes, squash, Italian seasoning, pepper, red pepper flakes, and nutmeg. Lock the lid in place. Select High Pressure and 10 minutes cook time.

When the cook time ends, turn off the pressure cooker. Let the pressure release naturally for 10 minutes and finish with a quick pressure release. When the valve drops, carefully remove the lid. Use an immersion blender to purée the soup until very smooth. (You can also use a standard blender.)

Select Simmer/Sauté. Add the chicken, orzo, and 1/2 cup (120 ml) half-and-half. Heat for about 5 minutes until the chicken is heated through. Serve garnished with scallions and a swirl of half-and-half.

Lighter Zuppa Toscana

....

TIP: When making soups, you don't have to add all the broth at once. The more broth you add, the longer the soup takes to come to pressure. Adding 1 can of broth while pressure cooking, and the remaining 2 cans after pressure cooking, speeds the process and keeps ingredients such as potatoes from being overcooked.

I based this soup on an Italian restaurant's popular offering. This lighter pressure cooker version uses evaporated milk instead of heavy cream—without sacrificing flavor.

6 slices bacon, diced

1 pound (454 g) ground chicken sausage

1 tablespoon (14 g) unsalted butter

1 cup (160 g) diced onion

3 cloves garlic, minced or pressed

3 cans (14.5 fluid ounces, or 429 ml, each) reduced-sodium chicken broth, divided

½ teaspoon salt

½ teaspoon ground black pepper

⅛ teaspoon red pepper flakes

3 large russet potatoes, peeled and cubed

3 tablespoons (24 g) cornstarch

1 can (12 fluid ounces, or 355 ml) evaporated milk

1 cup (80 g) shredded Parmesan cheese, divided

2 cups (60 g) fresh spinach, chopped

Select Browning/Sauté and add the bacon to the pressure cooking pot. Fry for about 5 minutes until crisp, stirring frequently. Transfer to a paper towel–lined plate, leaving the bacon fat in the pot.

Add the sausage to the cooking pot. Cook for about 5 minutes until browned. Transfer to a second paper towel–lined plate.

Add the butter to the cooking pot to melt. Add the onion. Sauté for about 3 minutes, stirring occasionally, until tender. Add the garlic and cook for 1 minute more. Add 1 can (429 ml) chicken broth, the salt, pepper, and red pepper flakes. Put a steamer basket in the cooking pot. Add the potatoes. Lock the lid in place. Select High Pressure and 4 minutes cook time.

When the cook time ends, turn off the pressure cooker. Use a quick pressure release. When the valve drops, carefully remove the lid. Carefully remove the steamer basket with the potatoes from the cooking pot. Set aside. Add the remaining 2 cans (858 ml) chicken broth to the cooking pot.

In a small bowl, whisk the cornstarch in a little evaporated milk until smooth. Add the slurry to the pot along with the remaining evaporated milk. Select Simmer/Sauté and bring the mixture to a boil, stirring often. When the soup thickens, stir in ¾ cup (60 g) Parmesan, the spinach, browned sausage, potatoes, and half the crispy bacon. Serve topped with the remaining Parmesan and bacon.

Quick Turkey Chili

TIP: If you're watching your fat and cholesterol intake. Choose ground turkey made from turkey breasts—it's leaner.

Lean ground turkey is a great alternative to ground beef, and I don't think you'll even miss the beef in this flavorful and quick chili.

1 tablespoon (15 ml) vegetable oil

1½ pounds (680 g) ground turkey

1 cup (160 g) diced onion

3 cloves garlic, minced

1 tablespoon (8 g) chili powder

1 teaspoon ground cumin

½ teaspoon salt, plus more for seasoning

½ teaspoon freshly ground black pepper, plus more for seasoning

1 can (14.5 ounces, or 411 g) diced tomatoes

1 cup (235 ml) reduced-sodium chicken broth

1 can (10 ounces, or 284 g) diced tomatoes and green chilies

2 cans (15 ounces, or 425 g, each) kidney beans, drained and rinsed

1 cup (165 g) frozen corn, thawed

2 tablespoons (14 g) all-purpose flour

Shredded cheese, diced avocado, tortilla chips, fresh cilantro, and sour cream, for serving

Select Browning/Sauté to preheat the pressure cooking pot. When hot, add the vegetable oil. When it begins to sizzle, add the turkey, onion, and garlic. Sauté for about 10 minutes until the meat is no longer pink and the onion is tender. Drain, if needed. Stir in the chili powder, cumin, salt, pepper, diced tomatoes, chicken broth, tomatoes and green chilies, and kidney beans. Lock the lid in place. Select High Pressure and 5 minutes cook time.

When the cook time ends, turn off the pressure cooker. Use a quick pressure release. When the valve drops, carefully remove the lid. Stir in the corn. Sprinkle the flour over the chili and stir to blend. Season with salt and pepper to taste. Serve hot topped with cheese, avocado, tortilla chips, cilantro, and sour cream, if desired.

Chili con Carne

YIELD:
6 SERVINGS

TIP: If you're short on time, replace the dried kidney beans with 2 cans (15 ounces, or 425 g, each) red kidney beans, drained and rinsed. Skip the first step and add the beans with the broth.

This thick, hearty chili is filled with tender bite-size pieces of beef, red beans, and green chilies and thickened with crushed tortilla chips. If you're a chili fanatic, this is a must-try recipe.

1 cup (250 g) dried red kidney beans
1 quart (946 ml) water
Salt and freshly ground black pepper, for seasoning
2 pounds (907 g) beef chuck, trimmed and cut in to 1-inch (2.5 cm) pieces
2 to 4 tablespoons (30 to 60 ml) vegetable oil, plus more as needed
1 cup (160 g) diced onion
2 cloves garlic, minced
1 can (14.5 fluid ounces, or 429 ml) reduced-sodium beef broth

1 can (14.5 ounces, or 411 g) crushed tomatoes
2 cans (4.5 ounces, or 128 g, each) mild green chilies
3 tablespoons (23 g) chili powder
2 tablespoons (32 g) tomato paste
1 teaspoon ground cumin
2/3 cup (about 20 g) finely crushed tortilla chips, plus more for serving
Shredded cheese, fresh cilantro, and sour cream, for serving

Add the beans and 1 quart (946 ml) water to the pressure cooking pot. Lock the lid in place. Select High Pressure and 1 minute cook time. When the cook time ends, turn off the pressure cooker. Let the beans soak in the pot for 1 hour. Drain and set aside.

Season the beef generously with salt and pepper. Select Browning/Sauté and add 2 tablespoons (30 ml) vegetable oil and the beef in small batches. Cook each batch for about 5 minutes to brown, adding more oil as needed and transferring to a plate when done. Continue in small batches, adding more oil as needed, until all the meat is browned.

Add more oil to the cooking pot along with the onion. Sauté for about 3 minutes until tender. Add the garlic and sauté for 1 minute more. Stir in the beef broth, tomatoes, green chilies, chili powder, tomato paste, and cumin. Stir in the browned beef and beans. Lock the lid in place. Select High Pressure and 25 minutes cook time.

When the cook time ends, turn off the pressure cooker. Let the pressure release naturally for 10 minutes and finish with a quick pressure release. When the valve drops, carefully remove the lid. Stir in the tortilla chips and let rest for 10 minutes, uncovered, to thicken. Serve topped with cheese, cilantro, sour cream, and more tortilla chips, as desired.

All-American Beef Stew

YIELD:
6 SERVINGS

TIP: Buying stew meat at the store saves time, but if you cut it yourself, you know what cut of beef you're getting. Chuck roast or rump roast are the best types for stew.

A hearty all-American beef stew loaded with colorful yellow, orange, and green veggies. A perfect meal when you're craving comfort food.

2 pounds (907 g) beef stew meat

Salt and freshly ground black pepper, for seasoning

1 tablespoon (15 ml) vegetable oil, plus more as needed

1 cup (160 g) chopped onion

2 cans (14.5 fluid ounces, or 429 ml, each) reduced-sodium beef broth

1 can (14.5 ounces, or 411 g) crushed tomatoes

2 tablespoons (3 g) dried parsley

2 bay leaves

4 russet potatoes, peeled, cubed, and cut into bite-size pieces

3 large carrots, cut into 1-inch (2.5 cm) pieces

¼ cup (28 g) all-purpose flour

¼ cup (60 ml) cold water

1 cup (165 g) frozen corn, thawed

½ cup (65 g) frozen peas, thawed

Season the beef generously with salt and pepper. Select Browning/Sauté and add the vegetable oil to the pressure cooking pot. When the oil begins to sizzle, brown the meat in batches for about 5 minutes per batch until all the meat is browned—do not crowd the pot. Add more oil as needed. Transfer the browned meat to a plate.

Add the onion to the cooking pot. Sauté for about 3 minutes, stirring frequently, until softened. Stir in the beef broth to deglaze the pot, scraping up any brown bits from the bottom of the pot. Stir in the tomatoes, parsley, bay leaves, salt and pepper, and browned beef with any accumulated juices. Lock the lid in place. Select High Pressure and 10 minutes cook time.

When the cook time ends, let the pressure release naturally for 5 minutes and finish with a quick pressure release. When the valve drops, carefully remove the lid. Add the potatoes and carrots. Replace the lid and cook on High Pressure for 2 minutes more. When the cook time ends, turn off the pressure cooker. Let the pressure release naturally for 5 minutes and finish with a quick pressure release. When the valve drops, carefully remove the lid. Remove and discard the bay leaves.

In a small bowl, whisk the flour and cold water until smooth. Add 1 cup (235 ml) hot broth to the flour mixture and stir to combine. Add the slurry to the pot. Select Simmer/Sauté and bring the sauce to a boil, stirring constantly until it thickens. Stir in the corn and peas. Season with additional salt and pepper to taste.

Hearty Beef and Barley Soup

YIELD:
6 SERVINGS

TIP: Pearl barley is softer and takes less time to cook then hulled barley. Because pearl barley contains fiber throughout the entire kernel and not just in the outer bran layer, it is still a good source of fiber.

A robust, stick-to-your-ribs soup with fun little barley pearls.

1½ pounds (680 g) beef chuck, trimmed and cut into 1-inch (2.5 cm) pieces

Salt and freshly ground black pepper, for seasoning

2 to 4 tablespoons (30 to 60 ml) vegetable oil, divided

1 cup (160 g) diced onion

2 large carrots, diced

1 cup (120 g) diced celery

2 tablespoons (32 g) tomato paste

3 cans (14.5 fluid ounces, or 429 ml, each) reduced-sodium beef broth

1 can (14.5 ounces, or 411 g) diced tomatoes

1 cup (200 g) pearl barley, rinsed and drained

1 bay leaf

¼ cup (15 g) flat-leaf parsley leaves, finely chopped

Season the beef generously with salt and pepper. Select Browning/Sauté to preheat the pressure cooking pot. Add 2 tablespoons (30 ml) vegetable oil and brown the beef in batches for about 5 minutes per batch, transferring the beef to a plate when browned. Add more oil as needed.

Add the remaining 1 tablespoon (15 ml) vegetable oil to the cooking pot along with the onion, carrots, and celery. Sauté for about 3 minutes until tender. Stir in the tomato paste and sauté for 1 minute more. Add the broth, tomatoes, barley, and bay leaf. Stir to combine; stir in the browned beef. Lock the lid in place. Select High Pressure and 25 minutes cook time.

When the cook time ends, turn off the pressure cooker. Let the pressure release naturally for 10 minutes and finish with a quick release. When the valve drops, carefully remove the lid. Remove and discard the bay leaf. Stir in the parsley. Season with additional salt and pepper to taste.

Pasta Fagioli

YIELD:
6 SERVINGS

....

TIP: If you dislike the time-consuming job of mincing garlic, buy a garlic press—you don't even have to peel the garlic when you "mince" it—just one squeeze and you're on your way.

An inexpensive yet filling soup loaded with pasta, tomatoes, vegetables, and two kinds of beans. This soup is quick and easy to make with ingredients you likely keep in your pantry.

1 pound (454 g) ground beef

1 tablespoon (15 ml) olive oil

1 cup (160 g) diced onion

2 large carrots, diced

1 rib celery, diced

4 cloves garlic, minced

2 cans (15 ounces, or 425 g, each) crushed tomatoes with purée

2 cans (14.5 fluid ounces, or 429 ml, each) reduced-sodium chicken broth

2 cups (470 ml) water

1 cup (168 g) ditalini pasta

1 teaspoon Italian seasoning

1½ teaspoons salt, plus more for seasoning

⅛ teaspoon red pepper flakes

1 can (14.5 ounces, or 411 g) red kidney beans, drained and rinsed

1 can (14.5 ounces, or 411 g) Great Northern beans, drained and rinsed

¼ cup (15 g) chopped fresh parsley leaves, or 2 tablespoons (2.6 g) dried parsley

Freshly ground black pepper, for seasoning

Select Browning/Sauté. Add the ground beef to the pressure cooking pot. Sauté for about 5 minutes, stirring occasionally, until browned and crumbled. Transfer to a paper towel–lined plate. Drain any excess fat from the pot.

Add the olive oil and onion. Sauté for 3 minutes, stirring occasionally. Add the carrots, celery, and garlic. Sauté for 2 minutes more. Add the browned beef back to the cooking pot along with the tomatoes, chicken broth, water, ditalini, Italian seasoning, salt, and red pepper flakes. Lock the lid in place. Select High Pressure and 4 minutes cook time.

When the cook time ends, turn off the pressure cooker. Let the pressure release naturally for 5 minutes and finish with a quick pressure release. When the valve drops, carefully remove the lid. Stir in the beans and parsley and season with salt and pepper to taste.

Minestrone Soup

YIELD:
8 SERVINGS

TIP: Adding the third can of chicken broth after pressure cooking allows the soup to come to pressure faster, prevents overfilling the pot, and helps cool the soup so that you can eat it sooner.

A classic Italian soup loaded with veggies, beans, and pasta. This good-for-you soup is a great way to eat more veggies.

1 tablespoon (15 ml) olive oil

1 large onion, finely chopped

2 large carrots, diced

1 rib celery, diced

1 small zucchini, chopped

4 cloves garlic, minced

3 cans (14.5 fluid ounces, or 429 ml, each) reduced-sodium chicken broth, divided

2 cans (14 ounces, or 397 g, each) diced tomatoes

1 can (14 ounces, or 397 g) crushed tomatoes in purée

¾ cup (56 g) small shell pasta

1½ teaspoons Italian seasoning

1 teaspoon salt, plus more as needed

½ teaspoon freshly ground black pepper, plus more as needed

1 can (15 ounces, or 425 g) kidney beans, drained and rinsed

1 can (15 ounces, or 425 g) white navy beans or cannellini beans, drained and rinsed

1 cup (124 g) frozen cut green beans

2 cups (60 g) fresh baby spinach

Parmesan cheese, for serving

Select Browning/Sauté and add the olive oil to the pressure cooking pot. When the oil is hot, add the onion. Sauté for about 3 minutes, stirring occasionally, until the onion is tender. Add the carrots, celery, zucchini, and garlic. Cook for 3 minutes more, stirring occasionally. Stir in 2 cans chicken broth, the tomatoes, pasta, Italian seasoning, salt, and pepper. Stir in the kidney beans, white beans, and green beans. Lock the lid in place. Select High Pressure and 3 minutes cook time.

When the cook time ends, turn off the pressure cooker. Let the pressure release naturally for 5 minutes and finish with a quick pressure release. When the valve drops, carefully remove the lid. Stir in the remaining 1 can chicken broth and the spinach. Season with salt and pepper to taste. Serve topped with Parmesan.

Posole (Pork and Hominy Stew)

YIELD:
6 SERVINGS

TIP: Squeeze a bit of lime juice directly on the avocado after cutting to prevent browning.

Hominy is simply dried corn kernels soaked in lime or lye until soft, swollen, and slightly chewy. If you haven't tried hominy yet, now is the time—it's delicious and a good source of fiber.

2 tablespoons (30 ml) vegetable oil, divided

1 teaspoon salt, plus more as needed

1¼ pounds (567 g) boneless pork shoulder, trimmed and cut into 4-inch (10 cm) pieces

1 medium-size white onion, chopped

4 cloves garlic, minced

2 tablespoons (15 g) chili powder

1 quart (940 ml) reduced-sodium chicken broth, divided

2 tablespoons (16 g) cornstarch

¼ cup (60 ml) cold water

2 cans (29 ounces, or 822 g, each) hominy, drained and rinsed

Diced avocado and lime wedges, for serving

Select Browning/Sauté and add 1 tablespoon (15 ml) vegetable oil to the cooking pot. When the oil is hot, season the pork with salt and add it to the cooking pot. Cook for about 5 minutes until browned on all sides. Transfer to a large bowl.

Add the remaining 1 tablespoon (15 ml) vegetable oil to the cooking pot. When the oil is hot, add the onion, garlic, and chili powder. Sauté for 4 minutes until soft. Stir in 2 cups (470 ml) chicken broth to deglaze the pot, scraping up any browned bits from the bottom with a wooden spoon. Add the remaining 2 cups (470 ml) chicken broth and the pork. Lock the lid in place. Select High Pressure and 30 minutes cook time.

When the cook time ends, turn off the pressure cooker. Let the pressure release naturally for 10 minutes and finish with a quick pressure release. When the valve drops, carefully remove the lid. Transfer the pork back to the large bowl and shred it using 2 forks.

In a small bowl, whisk the cornstarch and cold water until smooth. Add the slurry to the pot. Select Simmer/Sauté and stir until the broth thickens. Stir in the shredded pork and hominy. Season with salt to taste. Serve with avocado and lime.

Creamy Swiss Onion Soup

TIP: French-fried onions are usually found with the canned vegetables. They add a nice crisp contrast to the creamy smooth soup.

Unlike traditional, long-simmered French onion soup, this creamy version comes together in no time. If you like the flavor of onion soup but aren't crazy about the big pieces of onion left at the bottom of the bowl, this soup is for you.

1 tablespoon (14 g) unsalted butter

1 tablespoon (15 ml) olive oil

3 cups (480 g) halved, thinly sliced onions

3 cans (14.5 fluid ounces, or 429 ml, each) reduced-sodium chicken broth

½ teaspoon salt

¼ teaspoon freshly ground black pepper

⅛ teaspoon red pepper flakes

3 tablespoons (24 g) cornstarch

1 can (12 fluid ounces, or 355 ml) evaporated milk, divided

1½ cups (165 g) shredded Swiss cheese

1 package (2.8 ounces, or 80 g) French-fried onions

Select Simmer/Sauté and melt the butter in the pressure cooking pot, then add the olive oil. When the butter melts, add the onions. Sauté for about 8 minutes, stirring occasionally, until tender. Stir in the chicken broth, salt, pepper, and red pepper flakes. Lock the lid in place. Select High Pressure and 4 minutes cook time.

When the cook time ends, turn off the pressure cooker. Use a quick pressure release. When the valve drops, carefully remove the lid. Use an immersion or standard blender to purée the soup until it is very smooth.

In a small bowl, whisk the cornstarch in ¼ cup (60 ml) evaporated milk until smooth. Add the slurry to the pot along with the remaining evaporated milk. Select Simmer/Sauté and bring the soup to a boil, stirring constantly until it thickens slightly. Add the cheese a handful at a time and stir until it melts and the soup is thick and creamy. Serve garnished with French-fried onions. Top with chives and red pepper flakes, if desired.

Broccoli Cheese Soup

YIELD:
6 SERVINGS

TIP: Substitute frozen chopped broccoli in this recipe, if you prefer, without changing the cook time.

My family prefers soups with at least a little texture. So I adapted traditional creamy broccoli cheese soup by leaving pieces of broccoli and carrot in the soup, which also gives it a prettier color. You'll also be pleased at how quick this great-tasting soup is to make and serve!

2 tablespoons (28 g) unsalted butter

1 cup (160 g) diced onion

2 cloves garlic, minced

2 cans (14.5 fluid ounces, or 429 ml, each) reduced-sodium chicken broth

4 cups (284 g) bite-size broccoli florets

1 cup (110 g) matchstick carrots

½ teaspoon salt, plus more as needed

¼ teaspoon freshly ground black pepper, plus more as needed

⅛ teaspoon red pepper flakes

¼ cup (32 g) cornstarch

¼ cup (60 ml) cold water

2 cups (470 ml) half-and-half

2 cups (240 g) grated Cheddar cheese

Select Browning/Sauté to preheat the pressure cooking pot. Add the butter and onion. Sauté for about 3 minutes until tender. Add the garlic and sauté for 1 minute more. Stir in the chicken broth, broccoli, carrots, salt, pepper, and red pepper flakes. Lock the lid in place. Select High Pressure and 1 minute cook time.

When the cook time ends, turn off the pressure cooker. Use a quick pressure release. When the valve drops, carefully remove the lid.

In a small bowl, whisk the cornstarch and cold water until smooth. Select Simmer/Sauté and add the slurry to the pot, stirring constantly until the soup comes to a boil and thickens. Turn off the pressure cooker. Gradually stir in the half-and-half. Add the Cheddar a handful at a time, stirring until it melts. Season with salt and pepper to taste.

Garden Fresh Tomato, Basil, and Parmesan Soup

YIELD:
6 SERVINGS

TIP: If garden-ripe tomatoes aren't available, substitute 2 cans (14.5 ounces, or 411 g, each) diced tomatoes.

Make this soup in the summer with fresh-from-the-garden (or farmers' market) tomatoes and basil. Made in the pressure cooker, you can have it ready to eat in under 30 minutes, and it's so much better than that stuff in a can.

3 tablespoons (42 g) unsalted butter

1 large onion, diced

2 ribs celery, diced

1 large carrot, diced

2 cloves garlic, minced or crushed

2 cans (14.5 fluid ounces, or 429 ml, each) reduced-sodium chicken broth

3 pounds (1.4 kg) fresh tomatoes, cored, peeled, and quartered

¼ cup (9 g) fresh basil leaves

1 tablespoon (16 g) tomato paste

1 teaspoon sugar

½ teaspoon salt

½ teaspoon freshly ground black pepper

½ cup (40 g) shredded Parmesan cheese

1 cup (235 ml) half-and-half

Select Browning/Sauté and melt the butter in the pressure cooking pot. Add the onion, celery, and carrot. Sauté for about 3 minutes until tender. Add the garlic and cook for 1 minute, stirring often. Stir in the chicken broth, tomatoes, basil, tomato paste, sugar, salt, and pepper. Lock the lid in place. Select High Pressure and 5 minutes cook time.

When the cook time ends, turn off the pressure cooker. Let the pressure release naturally for 5 minutes and finish with a quick pressure release. When the valve drops, carefully remove the lid. Use an immersion or standard blender to purée the soup until very smooth. Select Simmer/Sauté, stir in the Parmesan and half-and-half, and simmer until heated through—do not boil.

Chunky Potato Cheese Soup

YIELD:
6 SERVINGS

TIP: If you don't have a steamer basket, cook the potatoes directly in the broth. The potatoes may not hold their shape quite as well, but the flavor will still be amazing.

This perfect potato soup cooks the potatoes in the steamer basket above the onions, broth, and spices, which cooks them without breaking them down. The finished soup is smooth and creamy with firm chunks of potato.

2 tablespoons (28 g) unsalted butter

½ cup (80 g) chopped onion

2 cans (14.5 fluid ounces, or 429 ml, each) reduced-sodium chicken broth, divided

2 tablespoons (3 g) dried parsley

1 teaspoon salt

½ teaspoon freshly ground black pepper

⅛ teaspoon red pepper flakes

4 cups (440 g) peeled and cubed russet potatoes

2 tablespoons (16 g) cornstarch

2 tablespoons (30 ml) cold water

3 ounces (85 g) cream cheese, cubed

1 cup (120 g) shredded Cheddar cheese

2 cups (470 ml) half-and-half

1 cup (165 g) frozen corn

6 slices crisp-cooked bacon, crumbled

Select Browning/Sauté and melt the butter in the pressure cooking pot. Add the onion. Sauté for about 5 minutes, stirring occasionally, until tender. Stir in 1 can chicken broth, the parsley, salt, pepper, and red pepper flakes. Put a steamer basket in the pressure cooking pot. Add the potatoes. Lock the lid in place. Select High Pressure and 4 minutes cook time.

When the cook time ends, turn off the pressure cooker. Let the pressure release naturally for 5 minutes and finish with a quick pressure release. When the valve drops, carefully remove the lid. Remove the steamer basket with the potatoes from the cooking pot.

In a small bowl, whisk the cornstarch and cold water until smooth. Select Simmer/ Sauté and add the slurry to the pot, stirring constantly until the soup thickens. Stir in the cream cheese and Cheddar until they melt. Add the remaining can of chicken broth, the half-and-half, corn, bacon, and cooked potatoes. Stir to combine and heat through—do not bring to a boil—then serve.

Rhode Island Clam Chowder

YIELD:
6 SERVINGS

....

TIP: You can sub-
stitute 1 teaspoon
dried thyme for the
fresh thyme.

If you're a clam chowder aficionado looking for something lighter
and healthier, this Rhode Island Clam Chowder is just the ticket.
With a clear broth loaded with potatoes, celery, bacon, and fresh
herbs, it's a great alternative to the creamier Boston clam chowder.

3 slices bacon, diced

1 cup (160 g) diced onion

2 ribs celery, diced

3 cloves garlic, minced or crushed

**6 red potatoes, diced into bite-size
 pieces**

**4 cans (6.5 ounces, or 184 g, each)
 chopped clams with juice**

**2 cups (470 ml) reduced-sodium
 chicken broth**

3 sprigs fresh thyme

2 bay leaves

**Salt and freshly ground black
 pepper, for seasoning**

**Chopped parsley and oyster
 crackers, for serving**

Select Browning/Sauté and add the bacon
to the pressure cooking pot. Fry for about 5
minutes until crisp, stirring frequently. Transfer
to a paper towel–lined plate, leaving the bacon
fat in the pot.

Add the onion and celery to the cooking pot.
Sauté for about 5 minutes, stirring occasionally,
until tender. Add the garlic and cook for
1 minute more. Stir in the potatoes, clams,
chicken broth, thyme, and bay leaves. Lock the
lid in place. Select High Pressure and 3 minutes
cook time.

When the cook time ends, turn off the pressure
cooker. Use a quick pressure release. When the
valve drops, carefully remove the lid. Remove
and discard the bay leaves and thyme. Season
with salt and pepper to taste. Serve topped
with the bacon. Finish with chopped parsley
and oyster crackers, if desired.

Cabbage Patch Stew

YIELD:
6 TO 8 SERVINGS

TIP: The cabbage core is tough and unpleasant to eat. Remove it before slicing the cabbage.

Growing up, I refused to eat Cabbage Patch Stew because of all the green stuff in it. Now I can't get enough of this good-for-you, flavorful soup.

1 pound (454 g) ground beef

1 tablespoon (15 ml) vegetable oil

1 large onion, diced

3 cloves garlic, minced

2 cans (14.5 fluid ounces, or 429 ml, each) reduced-sodium chicken broth

2 cans (14.5 ounces, or 411 g, each) diced tomatoes

½ head cabbage, cut into bite-size pieces

2 cans (15 ounces, or 425 g, each) kidney beans, drained and rinsed

1 tablespoon (12 g) sugar

1 tablespoon (8 g) chili powder

½ teaspoon salt, plus more as needed

¼ teaspoon freshly ground black pepper, plus more as needed

Select Browning/Sauté to preheat the pressure cooking pot. Add the ground beef and cook for about 5 minutes until browned. Transfer to a paper towel–lined plate. Drain any excess fat from the pot.

Add the vegetable oil and onion to the cooking pot. Sauté for about 3 minutes, stirring occasionally, until tender. Add the garlic and cook for 1 minute more. Stir in the chicken broth, tomatoes, cabbage, kidney beans, sugar, chili powder, salt, pepper, and ground beef. Lock the lid in place. Select High Pressure and 4 minutes cook time.

When the cook time ends, turn off the pressure cooker. Let the pressure release naturally for 15 minutes and finish with a quick pressure release. When the valve drops, carefully remove the lid. Season with additional salt and pepper to taste.

Bean with Bacon Soup

YIELD:
8 SERVINGS

TIP: If you're in a hurry, substitute 3 cans (15 ounces, or 425 g, each) Great Northern beans, drained and rinsed, for the dried beans. Since you don't need to cook canned beans, begin by frying the bacon and add the beans with the broth.

This colorful veggie-filled bean with bacon soup is a mix of smooth and creamy and hearty and chunky.

2 cups dried Great Northern beans, picked over and rinsed
2 quarts (1.9 L) water
10 slices bacon, diced
1 cup (160 g) chopped onion
1 cup (130 g) diced carrots
1 cup (120 g) diced celery
2 cans (14.5 fluid ounces, or 429 ml) reduced-sodium chicken broth
1 can (15 ounces, or 425 g) diced fire-roasted tomatoes
½ teaspoon dried thyme
2 bay leaves
1 teaspoon salt, plus more as needed
½ teaspoon freshly ground black pepper, plus more as needed
Fresh parsley leaves, for serving

Combine the beans with 2 quarts (1.9 L) water in the pressure cooking pot. Lock the lid in place. Select High Pressure and 1 minute cook time. When the cook time ends, turn off the pressure cooker. Let the beans soak for 1 hour, letting the pressure release naturally. Drain the beans and set aside. Discard the soaking water.

Select Browning/Sauté and add the bacon to the pressure cooking pot. Fry for about 5 minutes until crisp, stirring frequently. Transfer to a papertowel lined–plate, leaving the bacon fat in the pot.

Add the onion, carrots, and celery to the cooking pot. Sauté for about 5 minutes, stirring occasionally, until tender. Stir in the chicken broth, tomatoes, thyme, bay leaves, salt, and pepper. Stir in the soaked beans. Lock the lid in place. Select High Pressure and 5 minutes cook time.

When the cook time ends, turn off the pressure cooker. Let the pressure release naturally for 10 minutes and finish with a quick pressure release. When the valve drops, carefully remove the lid. Remove and discard the bay leaves. Test several beans to make sure they're as tender as you like; if they need a little more time, select Simmer/Sauté and simmer until tender.

Transfer 2 cups (470 ml) soup to a large bowl. Use an immersion or regular blender to purée the remaining soup until smooth. Stir in the reserved soup and season with additional salt and pepper to taste. Serve topped with crumbled bacon and fresh parsley.

Creamy Red Lentil Soup

YIELD:
8 SERVINGS

TIP: Puréeing only part of the soup gives the soup a great texture and body. If you prefer a smoother soup, purée all of it.

Lentils are high in fiber and protein, and the red lentils in this recipe give this delicious soup its pretty orange color.

2 tablespoons (30 ml) olive oil

1 cup (160 g) diced onion

1 cup (130 g) diced carrots

½ cup (60 g) diced celery

5 cloves garlic, minced

2 cans (14.5 ounces, or 411 g, each) fire-roasted diced tomatoes

1 quart (946 ml) reduced-sodium vegetable broth

2 cups (470 ml) water

1½ cups (288 g) red lentils, rinsed

1 teaspoon ground cumin

½ teaspoon dried thyme

1 teaspoon salt, plus more as needed

½ teaspoon freshly ground black pepper, plus more as needed

2 cups (60 g) fresh baby spinach, coarsely chopped

1 tablespoon (15 ml) red wine vinegar

Heavy cream, for serving

Select Browning/Sauté and add the olive oil to the pressure cooking pot. When the oil is hot, add the onion, carrots, and celery. Sauté for about 5 minutes until tender. Add the garlic and cook for 1 minute more. Stir in the tomatoes, vegetable broth, water, lentils, cumin, thyme, salt, and pepper. Lock the lid in place. Select High Pressure and 10 minutes cook time.

When the cook time ends, turn off the pressure cooker. Let the pressure release naturally for 10 minutes and finish with a quick pressure release. When the valve drops, carefully remove the lid. Transfer 2 cups (470 ml) soup to a large bowl. Use an immersion or regular blender to purée the soup until smooth. Stir in the reserved soup, spinach, and red wine vinegar. Select Simmer/Sauté and cook for just a few minutes until the spinach wilts. Season with additional salt and pepper, if needed. Ladle the soup into bowls and serve with a swirl of heavy cream.

13-Bean Soup

YIELD:
6 SERVINGS

TIP: Some of the beans in the 13-bean soup mix break down as they cook, helping thicken the soup without using thickeners or blending.

Bean soup mixes from the grocery store are colorful and fun, and they typically include a variety of beans, peas, and lentils. Look for a mix with no seasonings added.

2 cups (about 430 g) 13-bean soup mix

3 quarts (2.8 L) water, divided

2 tablespoons (30 ml) vegetable oil

1 cup (160 g) chopped onion

½ cup (65 g) diced carrots

½ cup (60 g) diced celery

2 cloves garlic, minced

4 teaspoons (27 g) ham base

1 can (15 ounces, or 425 g) crushed tomatoes in purée

1 teaspoon chili powder

1 teaspoon salt, plus more as needed

¼ teaspoon freshly ground black pepper, plus more as needed

1 ham steak (8 ounces, or 227 g), cubed

In the pressure cooking pot, combine the 13-bean soup mix and 2 quarts (1.9 L) water. Lock the lid in place. Select High Pressure and 1 minute cook time.

When the cook time ends, turn off the pressure cooker. Let the beans soak for 1 hour. Drain the beans and set aside. Discard the soaking water.

Select Browning/Sauté. Add the vegetable oil, onion, carrots, and celery to the pot. Sauté for about 3 minutes until tender. Add the garlic and sauté for 1 minute more. Stir in the remaining water, ham base, tomatoes, chili powder, salt and pepper, and the soaked beans. Lock the lid in place. Select High Pressure and 3 minutes cook time.

When the cook time ends, turn off the pressure cooker. Let the pressure release naturally for 10 minutes and finish with a quick pressure release. When the valve drops, carefully remove the lid. Stir in the ham. Season with additional salt and pepper to taste.

Country-Style French Chicken Stew

YIELD:
6 SERVINGS

TIP: You could substitute boneless skinless chicken breasts in this recipe, but if you haven't tried chicken thighs in the pressure cooker, definitely try them. They are more tender and have more flavor than chicken breasts.

This delectable stew tastes like it's been simmering for hours on the stove.

1 tablespoon (15 ml) olive oil

1 cup (160 g) diced onion

½ cup (60 g) diced celery

2 cloves garlic, minced

2 cans (14.5 fluid ounces, or 429 ml, each) reduced-sodium chicken broth

2 pounds (907 g) boneless skinless chicken thighs (about 8), trimmed and cut into bite-size pieces

1½ pounds (680 g) small red potatoes, unpeeled, cut, and quartered

4 carrots, cut into ½-inch (1 cm) pieces

2 sprigs fresh thyme

1 teaspoon salt, plus more as needed

½ teaspoon freshly ground black pepper, plus more as needed

⅛ teaspoon red pepper flakes

1 cup (130 g) frozen peas, thawed

2 tablespoons (8 g) chopped fresh parsley leaves

¼ cup (32 g) cornstarch

¼ cup (60 ml) cold water

1 cup (235 ml) half-and-half

Select Browning/Sauté to preheat the pressure cooking pot. When hot, add the olive oil, onion, and celery. Sauté for 3 minutes, stirring frequently. Add the garlic and sauté for 1 minute more. Stir in the chicken broth, chicken, potatoes, carrots, thyme, salt, pepper, and red pepper flakes. Lock the lid in place. Select High Pressure and 2 minutes cook time.

When the cook time ends, turn off the pressure cooker. Let the pressure release naturally for 5 minutes and finish with a quick pressure release. When the valve drops, carefully remove the lid. Remove and discard the thyme. Stir in the peas and parsley.

In a small bowl, whisk the cornstarch and cold water until smooth. Select Simmer/Sauté and add the slurry to the pot, stirring constantly until the sauce comes to a boil and thickens. Stir in the half-and-half. Season with salt and pepper to taste.

Sausage, Kale, and White Bean Soup

TIP: When cooking beans at high altitude (see page 22), increase the cook time. Many recipes aren't as affected by altitude, but beans really do need the extra time.

Soups made with dried beans don't have to simmer all day—this hearty, good-for-you soup is ready in about an hour.

2 tablespoons (30 ml) vegetable oil, divided

1 pound (454 g) smoked kielbasa sausage, halved lengthwise and cut crosswise into ¼-inch (0.6 cm) slices

1 cup (160 g) chopped onion

2 cloves garlic, minced

2 cans (14.5 fluid ounces, or 429 ml, each) reduced-sodium chicken broth

3 cups (705 ml) water

8 ounces (227 g) dried Great Northern beans

½ teaspoon salt

½ teaspoon freshly ground black pepper

½ teaspoon dried thyme

2 bay leaves

4 carrots, halved lengthwise and cut into ¼-inch (0.6 cm) slices

2 cups (134 g) baby kale leaves, stemmed

Freshly grated Parmesan cheese, for serving

Select Browning/Sauté to preheat the pressure cooking pot. Add 1 tablespoon (15 ml) vegetable oil and the sausage to the cooking pot. Cook for about 5 minutes until browned. Use a slotted spoon to transfer the sausage to a paper towel–lined plate.

If needed, add the remaining 1 tablespoon (15 ml) vegetable oil to the cooking pot. Add the onion. Sauté for about 3 minutes, stirring occasionally, until tender. Add the garlic and cook for 1 minute more. Stir in the chicken broth, water, beans, salt, pepper, thyme, and bay leaves. Lock the lid in place. Select High Pressure and 35 minutes cook time.

When the cook time ends, turn off the pressure cooker. Let the pressure release naturally for 10 minutes and finish with a quick pressure release. When the valve drops, carefully remove the lid. Check several beans to be sure they're tender. If not, relock the lid and cook on High Pressure a few minutes more. Remove and discard the bay leaves. Add the carrots, kale, and sausage. Lock the lid in place. Select High Pressure and 3 minutes cook time.

When the cook time ends, turn off the pressure cooker. Use a quick pressure release. When the valve drops, carefully remove the lid. Serve topped with grated Parmesan.

Italian Wedding Soup

YIELD:

6 TO 8 SERVINGS

TIP: Substitute ground Italian sausage for the ground beef if you like your soup a little spicier.

Italian Wedding Soup is a staple in many Italian restaurants. It's quick and easy to make at home.

FOR MEATBALLS:
½ cup (60 g) dried bread crumbs
½ cup (50 g) grated Parmesan cheese, plus more for serving
2 tablespoons (3 g) dried parsley
1 teaspoon dried oregano
1 teaspoon minced garlic

1 teaspoon salt
½ pound (227 g) extra-lean ground beef
½ pound (227 g) ground pork
⅓ cup (53 g) finely grated onion
1 large egg

FOR SOUP:
10 cups (2.4 L) reduced-sodium chicken broth
2 cups (60 g) spinach or endive, coarsely chopped

½ cup (28 g) acini de pepe pasta
Salt and freshly ground black pepper, for seasoning
Parmesan cheese, for serving

TO MAKE THE MEATBALLS: In a large bowl, combine the bread crumbs, Parmesan, parsley, oregano, garlic, and salt. Add the ground beef, ground pork, onion, and egg. Mix thoroughly. Form the mixture into 1-inch (2.5 cm) balls. Set aside.

TO MAKE THE SOUP: In the pressure cooking pot, stir together the chicken broth, spinach, and pasta. Add the meatballs. Lock the lid in place. Select High Pressure and 2 minutes cook time.

When the cook time ends, turn off the pressure cooker. Let the pressure release naturally for 15 minutes and finish with a quick pressure release. When the valve drops, carefully remove the lid.

Season with salt and pepper to taste. Served topped with a sprinkle of Parmesan.

Cheeseburger Soup

TIP: Turn this soup into bacon cheese-burger soup by adding bacon bits when serving.

If you crave cheeseburgers, try this hearty, cheesy beef and vegetable soup.

1 pound (454 g) ground beef

2 tablespoons (30 ml) vegetable oil

1 cup (160 g) chopped onion

1 cup (130 g) diced carrots

1 cup (120 g) diced celery

2 cans (14.5 fluid ounces, or 429 ml, each) reduced-sodium chicken broth

4 cups (440 g) peeled and diced potatoes

1 tablespoon (1 g) dried parsley

1 teaspoon dried basil

1 teaspoon salt

½ teaspoon freshly ground black pepper

2 tablespoons (16 g) cornstarch

2 tablespoons (30 ml) cold water

2 cups (225 g) shredded Cheddar cheese

1 cup (235 ml) milk

½ cup (120 ml) heavy cream

Select Browning/Sauté to preheat the pressure cooking pot. When hot, add the ground beef. Cook for about 5 minutes, stirring frequently, until browned and crumbled. Transfer to a paper towel–lined plate.

Add the vegetable oil and onion to the cooking pot. Sauté for 3 minutes, stirring occasionally. Add the carrots and celery. Sauté for 2 minutes more. Stir in the chicken broth, potatoes, parsley, basil, salt, and pepper. Stir in the browned beef. Lock the lid in place. Select High Pressure and 3 minutes cook time.

When the cook time ends, turn off the pressure cooker. Use a quick pressure release. When the valve drops, carefully remove the lid.

In a small bowl, whisk the cornstarch and cold water until smooth. Select Simmer/Sauté and add the slurry to the pot, stirring constantly. Add the Cheddar a handful at a time and stir until the cheese melts. Stir in the milk and heavy cream and heat through—do not bring to a boil.

Asian Chicken Noodle Soup

YIELD:
6 SERVINGS

This fabulous soup features Asian-flavored chicken broth with cabbage, mushrooms, scallions, and fun-to-eat curly ramen noodles.

TIP: Some pressure cookers let you select a cook time of 0 minutes, essentially bringing the pressure cooker to pressure and then switching to the Keep Warm setting as soon as pressure is achieved. If your pressure cooker doesn't offer this, select High Pressure and allow the pressure cooker to come to pressure. Cancel the cooking cycle once the pressure has been reached and the timer starts to count down.

2 tablespoons (30 ml) vegetable oil

1 cup (130 g) diced carrots

4 cloves garlic, minced

1 teaspoon grated peeled fresh ginger

2 pounds (907 g) boneless skinless chicken tenders, frozen

3 cans (14.5 fluid ounces, or 429 ml, each) reduced-sodium chicken broth

3 tablespoons (45 ml) low-sodium soy sauce

2 tablespoons (30 ml) mirin (rice wine)

2 tablespoons (30 ml) rice vinegar

1 teaspoon Sriracha

1 tablespoon (15 ml) sesame oil

2 packages (3 ounces, or 85 g, each) dry ramen noodles (discard the seasoning packets)

3 cups (270 g) slightly packed chopped napa cabbage

6 ounces (170 g) cremini mushrooms, sliced

1 tablespoon (15 ml) fresh lime juice

3 scallions, white and green parts, sliced, for serving

Select Browning/Sauté and add the vegetable oil to the pressure cooking pot. When the oil is hot, add the carrots. Sauté for about 3 minutes, stirring occasionally, until tender. Add the garlic and ginger and sauté for 1 minute more. Stir in the chicken, chicken broth, soy sauce, mirin, rice vinegar, Sriracha, and sesame oil. Lock the lid in place. Select High Pressure and 2 minutes cook time.

When the cook time ends, turn off the pressure cooker. Use a quick pressure release. When the valve drops, carefully remove the lid. Use a slotted spoon and kitchen shears to cut the chicken tenders into bite-size pieces in the cooking pot. Break the ramen noodles in half and stir them into the soup. Stir in the cabbage and mushrooms. Lock the lid in place. Select High Pressure and 0 minutes cook time (see Tip).

When the cook time ends, turn off the pressure cooker. Use a quick pressure release. When the valve drops, carefully remove the lid. Stir with a fork to separate the noodles. Stir in the lime juice. Serve garnished with scallions.

Chicken Noodle Soup with Homemade Chicken Stock

YIELD:
6 TO 8 SERVINGS

....

TIP: Refrigerate the chicken stock (bone broth) for up to 1 week, or freeze it in 1-cup (235 ml) portions for up to 6 months.

My local market often has chicken legs and wings on sale for 99 cents per pound (454 g). The legs and wings are a good mix for chicken soup because there's plenty of meat to make the soup, and the wings make a thick, delicious bone broth.

FOR HOMEMADE CHICKEN STOCK:

2 quarts (1.9 L) water, divided

4 pounds (1.8 kg) chicken legs

2 pounds (907 g) chicken wings

1 large onion, diced

5 sprigs fresh parsley

3 sprigs fresh thyme

1 tablespoon (18.5 g) kosher salt

½ teaspoon peppercorns

1 bay leaf

FOR CHICKEN NOODLE SOUP:

1 tablespoon (14 g) unsalted butter

1 large onion, diced

4 carrots, cut into ¼-inch-thick (0.6 cm) rounds

1 rib celery, diced

2 quarts (1.9 L) homemade chicken stock

2 cups diced chicken

2 tablespoons (8 g) finely chopped fresh parsley leaves

Salt and freshly ground black pepper, for seasoning

1 package (12 ounces, or 340 g) egg noodles, cooked according to package directions

TO MAKE THE HOMEMADE CHICKEN STOCK: Add 1 quart (946 ml) water to the pressure cooking pot along with the chicken legs and wings, onion, parsley, thyme, salt, peppercorns, and bay leaf. Lock the lid in place. Select High Pressure and 5 minutes cook time.

When the cook time ends, turn off the pressure cooker. Let the pressure release naturally. When the valve drops, carefully remove the lid. Remove the chicken legs from the pot and take the meat from the bones. Refrigerate until ready to use. Return the chicken leg bones to the cooking pot and add the remaining 1 quart (946 ml) water. Lock the lid in place. Select High Pressure and 60 minutes cook time.

When the cook time ends, turn off the pressure cooker. Let the pressure release naturally. When the valve drops, carefully remove the lid. Pour the stock through a fine-mesh strainer set over a large pot. Discard the solids. Skim the fat from the surface of the stock and set aside.

TO MAKE THE CHICKEN SOUP: Select Browning/Sauté and melt the butter in the cooking pot. Add the onion, carrots, and celery. Sauté for 3 minutes stirring occasionally. Stir in the chicken stock, chicken, and parsley. Lock the lid in place. Select High Pressure and 3 minutes cook time.

When the cook time ends, turn off the pressure cooker. Let the pressure release naturally for 5 minutes and finish with a quick pressure release. When the valve drops, carefully remove the lid. Season with salt and pepper to taste. Serve the soup spooned over the cooked noodles.

Pumpkin, Chorizo, and Black Bean Soup

YIELD:
6 TO 8 SERVINGS

....

TIP: If you don't have time or prefer to use canned black beans, substitute 2 cans (15 ounces, or 425 g, each) for the dried black beans. Since canned beans don't need to be cooked, begin by seasoning the beef and add the beans with the broth.

The pumpkin gives this soup its cheery color, great texture, and good-for-you fiber, and the pumpkin flavor is really subtle. The chorizo, Mexican oregano, and cumin are the flavors that stand out in this recipe.

1 cup (250 g) dried black beans

1 quart (946 ml) water

1 tablespoon (15 ml) vegetable oil

1 pound (454 g) chorizo sausage

1 cup (160 g) diced onion

2 cloves garlic, chopped

2 cans (14.5 fluid ounces, or 429 ml, each) reduced-sodium chicken broth

1 can (15 ounces, or 425 g) diced tomatoes

1 can (15 ounces, or 425 g) pumpkin purée

1 teaspoon dried Mexican oregano

½ teaspoon ground cumin

¼ cup (60 ml) heavy cream

Salt and freshly ground black pepper, for seasoning

¼ cup (4 g) fresh cilantro leaves, chopped, for serving

In the pressure cooking pot, combine the black beans and 1 quart (946 ml) water. Lock the lid in place. Select High Pressure and 1 minute cook time.

When the cook time ends, turn off the pressure cooker. Let the beans soak for 1 hour. Drain the beans and set aside. Discard the soaking water.

Select Browning/Sauté to preheat the cooking pot. When hot, add the vegetable oil. Add the chorizo and onion. Sauté for about 3 minutes, stirring occasionally, until the onion is tender. Add the garlic and cook for 1 minute more. Stir in the chicken broth, tomatoes, pumpkin, oregano, and cumin. Stir in soaked beans. Lock the lid in place. Select High Pressure and 5 minutes cook time.

When the cook time ends, turn off the pressure cooker. Let the pressure release naturally for 10 minutes and finish with a quick pressure release. When the valve drops, carefully remove the lid. Stir in the heavy cream. Season with salt and pepper to taste. Serve topped with cilantro.

Ratatouille Soup

YIELD:
6 SERVINGS

TIP: When an eggplant is small, the nutrient-rich skin is tender and can be left on when dicing.

Ratatouille is a French vegetable stew loaded with colorful, nutrient-rich ingredients. Puréeing half the soup gives this dish a creamy texture without adding any cream.

2 tablespoons (30 ml) olive oil

1 large onion, diced

4 cloves garlic, minced or pressed

2 cups (470 ml) reduced-sodium chicken broth or vegetable broth

1 can (28 ounces, or 794 g) crushed tomatoes

1 small eggplant, diced

1 small zucchini, diced

1 yellow bell pepper, diced

¼ cup (9 g) fresh basil leaves, chopped, plus more for serving

1 teaspoon Italian seasoning

1½ teaspoons salt, plus more as needed

½ teaspoon freshly ground black pepper, plus more as needed

¼ teaspoon red pepper flakes

Fresh basil, for serving

Select Browning/Sauté and add the olive oil to the pressure cooking pot. Add the onion. Sauté for about 3 minutes, stirring occasionally, until tender. Add the garlic and cook for 1 minute more. Stir in the chicken broth, tomatoes, eggplant, zucchini, yellow bell pepper, basil, Italian seasoning, salt, pepper, and red pepper flakes. Lock the lid in place. Select High Pressure and 2 minutes cook time.

When the cook time ends, turn off the pressure cooker. Let the pressure release naturally for 5 minutes and finish with a quick pressure release. When the valve drops, carefully remove the lid. Transfer 3 cups (705 ml) soup to a large bowl. Use an immersion or standard blender to purée the remaining soup until smooth. Stir in the reserved soup. Season with salt and pepper to taste. Serve garnished with fresh basil.

Sue's Hearty Taco Soup

YIELD:
6 TO 8 SERVINGS

....

TIP: If you don't use lean ground beef in this recipe, drain any excess fat from the pot before adding the onion and seasonings.

This recipe was adapted from a slow cooker recipe that is a family favorite of my next-door neighbor, Sue. Whenever she cooks it, she changes it up based on what she has on hand.

1 pound (454 g) lean ground beef
¼ cup (14 g) dried onion
1 package (1.3 ounces, or 36 g) taco seasoning mix
1 teaspoon chili powder
1 teaspoon salt
1 quart (946 ml) water
1 can (14.5 ounces, or 411 g) diced tomatoes
1 can (15 fluid ounces, or 444 ml) tomato sauce
2 cans (15 ounces, or 425 g, each) black beans, drained and rinsed
1 can (15 ounces, or 425 g) pinto beans, drained and rinsed
1 can (15 ounces, or 425 g) corn, with liquid
1 can (4 ounces, or 113 g) diced green chilies, with liquid
Corn chips, sour cream, and shredded cheese, for serving

Select Browning/Sauté to preheat the pressure cooking pot. When hot, add the ground beef. Cook for about 5 minutes, stirring frequently, until browned and crumbled. Stir in the onion, taco seasoning mix, chili powder, and salt. Add the water, tomatoes, tomato sauce, black beans, pinto beans, corn, and green chilies. Stir to combine. Lock the lid in place. Select High Pressure and 5 minutes cook time.

When the cook time ends, turn off the pressure cooker. Let the pressure release naturally for 10 minutes and finish with a quick pressure release. When the valve drops, carefully remove the lid. Serve topped with your favorite toppings, such as corn chips, sour cream, or shredded cheese.

Creamy Golden Mushroom Soup

YIELD:
6 SERVINGS

....

TIP: While you can use white button mushrooms in this recipe, cremini mushrooms have a bolder flavor.

Mushroom soup is a classic soup that's perfect any time of the year. The addition of tomatoes to mushroom soup gives it a richer, darker color and great flavor.

¼ cup (56 g) unsalted butter
1 cup (160 g) diced onion
1 pound (454 g) cremini mushrooms, thinly sliced
½ cup (120 ml) dry white wine
2 cups (470 ml) reduced-sodium beef broth
1 can (14.5 ounces, or 411 g) diced tomatoes, undrained
1 tablespoon (16 g) tomato paste
½ teaspoon salt
¼ teaspoon freshly ground black pepper
½ cup (120 ml) heavy cream

Select Browning/Sauté and melt the butter in the pressure cooking pot. Add the onion. Sauté for about 3 minutes, stirring occasionally, until tender. Add the mushrooms. Sauté for 3 minutes until they start to sweat. Add the white wine and cook for 1 minute more. Stir in the beef broth, tomatoes, tomato paste, salt, and pepper. Lock the lid in place. Select High Pressure and 4 minutes cook time.

When the cook time ends, turn off the pressure cooker. Use a quick pressure release. When the valve drops, carefully remove the lid. Use an immersion or regular blender to purée the soup until smooth. Stir in the heavy cream and serve.

Ham and Split Pea Soup

YIELD:
6 TO 8 SERVINGS

TIP: No ham bone? Substitute 2 meaty ham hocks. Make sure there is enough meat to get the 2 cups diced ham you need for the recipe.

Save that leftover ham bone from the holidays to make this stick-to-your ribs creamy split pea soup.

2 tablespoons (30 ml) vegetable oil
1 large onion, finely chopped
½ cup (60 g) diced celery
½ cup (65 g) diced carrots
2 cloves garlic, minced or pressed
2 cans (14.5 fluid ounces, or 429 ml, each) reduced-sodium chicken broth
2 cups (470 ml) water

1 package (1 pound, or 454 g) split peas, rinsed and sorted
¼ teaspoon red pepper flakes
1 ham bone
½ cup (115 g) sour cream
2 cups (300 g) diced ham
Salt and freshly ground black pepper, for seasoning

Select Browning/Sauté to preheat the pressure cooking pot. When hot, add the vegetable oil, onion, celery, and carrots. Sauté for about 5 minutes until tender. Add the garlic and cook for 1 minute more. Stir in the chicken broth, water, split peas, and red pepper flakes. Add the ham bone. Lock the lid in place. Select High Pressure and 10 minutes cook time.

When the cook time ends, turn off the pressure cooker. Let the pressure release naturally for 10 minutes and finish with a quick pressure release. When the valve drops, carefully remove the lid. Remove the ham bone from the pressure cooking pot and discard it.

For a smooth, creamy soup, use an immersion or regular blender to purée the soup until smooth. For a chunky soup, transfer 2 cups (470 ml) soup to a separate bowl, purée the remaining soup, and return the reserved soup to the pot.

In a small bowl, whisk the sour cream with 1 cup puréed soup. Stir this into the pressure cooking pot. Stir in the ham and, if needed, heat the soup until warm. Season with salt and pepper to taste.

Home-Style Vegetable Beef Soup

YIELD:
6 TO 8 SERVINGS

....

TIP: Don't skip the 5-minute natural pressure release after cooking the beef. The 5-minute time allows the liquid inside the pot to stop boiling so that you don't have liquid coming out of the pressure cooking valve when you use a quick pressure release.

Growing up, my mom made us vegetable beef soup with tender bite-size pieces of beef and lots of hearty root vegetables. Now I make it for my family, and it's always a hit.

1 pound (454 g) beef chuck, trimmed and cut into 1-inch (2.5 cm) pieces

1 teaspoon salt, plus more for seasoning

½ teaspoon freshly ground black pepper, plus more for seasoning

2 to 4 tablespoons (30 to 60 ml) vegetable oil

1 large onion, diced

1 rib celery, chopped

3 cloves garlic, finely chopped or pressed

2 cans (14.5 fluid ounces, or 429 ml, each) reduced-sodium beef broth

1 can (14 ounces, or 397 g) diced tomatoes

2 cups (470 ml) tomato juice

2 tablespoons (3 g) dried parsley

1 tablespoon (4 g) Italian seasoning

2 russet potatoes, peeled and diced into 1-inch (2.5 cm) pieces

2 carrots, sliced into thin coins

Season the beef generously with salt and pepper. Select Browning/Sauté and add the vegetable oil to the cooking pot. When the oil begins to sizzle, add the meat in batches and brown each batch for about 5 minutes until all the meat is browned—do not crowd the pot. Add more oil as needed and transfer the browned meat to a plate.

Add the onion and celery. Sauté for about 3 minutes, stirring frequently, until the onion softens. Add the garlic and cook for 1 minute more. Stir in the beef broth to deglaze the pot, scraping up any browned bits from the bottom. Add the tomatoes, tomato juice, parsley, Italian seasoning, additional salt and pepper to taste, and browned beef with any accumulated juices. Lock the lid in place. Select High Pressure and 14 minutes cook time.

When the cook time ends, turn off the pressure cooker. Let the pressure release naturally for 5 minutes and finish with a quick release. When the valve drops, carefully remove the lid. Add the potatoes and carrots. Lock the lid in place. Select High Pressure and 1 minute cook time.

When the cook time ends, turn off the pressure cooker. Let the pressure release naturally for 5 minutes and finish with a quick pressure release. When the valve drops, carefully remove the lid.

Chapter 4

Shortcut Dinners

Readers of my blog, *Pressure Cooking Today*, have asked me why most pressure cooker recipes in cookbooks aren't like the super simple recipes they see in the infomercials selling electric pressure cookers. If you were drawn to the electric pressure cooker by the ease of using a few simple, premade ingredients to get you out of the kitchen fast, these recipes are for you.

"Baked" Cheese Ravioli

YIELD:
4 SERVINGS

....

TIP: There are only four ingredients in this dish, so be sure to choose a flavorful marinara sauce.

I often buy refrigerated ravioli for those days when I don't feel like cooking but don't want to go out. This recipe is so easy that it doesn't even feel like you're cooking.

2 cups (470 ml) marinara sauce (store-bought or homemade)
1 package (1 pound, or 454 g) refrigerated cheese ravioli
¼ cup (25 g) freshly grated Parmesan cheese
½ to 1 cup (60 to 115 g) shredded mozzarella cheese

Spray a metal 7-inch (18 cm) cake pan or a 1½-quart (1.4 L) baking dish with nonstick cooking spray.

Put a trivet in the pressure cooking pot and add 1 cup (235 ml) water.

Add the marinara and ravioli to the prepared dish and stir to combine. Use a sling to carefully lower the pasta-filled pan onto the trivet. Lock the lid in place. Select High Pressure and 5 minutes cook time.

When the cook time ends, turn off the pressure cooker. Use a quick pressure release. When the valve drops, carefully remove the lid. Sprinkle the Parmesan and mozzarella over the top of the ravioli. Place the lid back on the pressure cooker and let rest, covered, for 5 minutes or until the cheese melts.

Ready-When-You-Are Spaghetti with Ragù

YIELD:
8 SERVINGS

....

TIP: Brown 1 pound (454 g) sausage and freeze half for a busy day.

There are lots of tasty marinara sauces at the market, but it's harder to find a hearty ragù sauce with chunks of meat in it. Fortunately, it's easy to add your own meat to your favorite store-bought marinara and, in the pressure cooker, you can cook the pasta while you heat the sauce.

½ pound (227 g) ground beef or ground Italian sausage
½ teaspoon onion powder
½ teaspoon garlic powder
2½ teaspoons (15 g) salt, divided
¼ teaspoon freshly ground black pepper
5 cups (1.2 L) water, plus more as needed

2 tablespoons (30 ml) vegetable oil
1 package (1 pound, or 454 g) spaghetti, broken in half
1 jar (28 fluid ounces, or 828 ml) marinara sauce
2 tablespoons (5 g) chopped fresh basil, optional
Freshly grated Parmesan cheese, for serving

Select Browning/Sauté. Add the ground beef to the pressure cooking pot. Sprinkle in the onion powder, garlic powder, ½ teaspoon salt, and the pepper. Sauté for about 5 minutes, stirring occasionally, until the beef is browned and crumbled. Transfer to a paper towel–lined plate. Drain any excess fat from the pot.

Add the water, remaining 2 teaspoons (12 g) salt, vegetable oil, and spaghetti to the pot. If needed, add more water to just cover the spaghetti—do not stir. Place a rack directly on the spaghetti.

In a 7-inch (18 cm) round cake pan, combine the browned beef and marinara sauce. Use a sling to carefully place the pan on the rack. Lock the lid in place. Select High Pressure and 4 minutes cook time.

When the cook time ends, turn off the pressure cooker. Use a quick pressure release or, if necessary, use an intermittent pressure release. Remove the pan and rack from the cooking pot. Ladle off any excess water from the spaghetti. Pour the sauce into the cooking pot over the spaghetti, add the basil, and stir to combine. Serve topped with Parmesan.

Anytime Spaghetti and Meatballs

YIELD:
8 SERVINGS

TIP: If you prefer to make your own marinara sauce, use the quick marinara sauce recipe with the Marinara Chicken with Melted Mozzarella (page 169), or your favorite home-made recipe.

I made several versions of this recipe trying to perfect it, and my boys came to love having leftover spaghetti and meatballs in the fridge for a quick lunch or late-night dinner. When I stopped testing the recipe, my son asked me to teach him to make it so that he could have it whenever he wanted.

2 tablespoons (30 ml) olive oil
3 cloves garlic, finely chopped
¼ teaspoon red pepper flakes
1 pound (454 g) fully cooked Italian-style meatballs
   (½-ounce, or 15 g, size)
1 teaspoon salt
1 package (1 pound, or 454 g) spaghetti, broken in half
1 to 1½ quarts (946 ml to 1.4 L) water
1 jar (28 fluid ounces, or 828 ml) marinara sauce
2 tablespoons (5 g) chopped fresh basil leaves, optional
Freshly grated Parmesan cheese, for serving

Select Browning/Sauté. Add the olive oil, garlic, and red pepper flakes to the pressure cooking pot. Sauté for 1 minute. Add the meatballs in an even layer on the bottom of the pot. Sprinkle with salt and top with the spaghetti. Pour in enough water to just cover the spaghetti—do not stir. Lock the lid in place. Select High Pressure and 4 minutes cook time.

When the cook time ends, turn off the pressure cooker. Use a quick pressure release, or, if necessary, use an intermittent pressure release. When the valve drops, carefully remove the lid. Check for excess water and remove it with a ladle. Stir in the sauce and fresh basil. Serve topped with Parmesan.

San Francisco Treat Chicken

YIELD:
6 SERVINGS

TIP: You can use frozen chicken breasts in this recipe without increasing the time, but frozen meat doesn't brown well, so skip the browning step.

If you grew up eating Rice-A-Roni, you're going to savor this time-saving recipe that cooks the chicken and rice at the same time.

6 large boneless skinless chicken breasts
Salt and freshly ground black pepper, for seasoning
2 tablespoons (30 ml) olive oil, divided
¼ cup (56 g) unsalted butter

2 packages (6.9 ounces, or 196 g, each) chicken-flavored Rice-A-Roni
1 quart (946 ml) water
1 tablespoon (15 ml) fresh lemon juice

Season the chicken with salt and pepper. Select Browning/Sauté to preheat the pressure cooking pot. When hot, add 1 tablespoon (15 ml) olive oil and 3 chicken breasts; cook on one side for about 3 minutes to brown and transfer to a plate. Add the remaining 1 tablespoon (15 ml) olive oil and brown the remaining breasts.

Add the butter to the cooking pot and scrape up any browned bits on the bottom as the butter melts. Add the Rice-A-Roni. Sauté, stirring frequently, until the vermicelli browns. Stir in the water and Rice-A-Roni seasoning packets. Arrange the chicken on the rice. Lock the lid in place. Select High Pressure and 7 minutes cook time.

When the cook time ends, turn off the pressure cooker. Let the pressure release naturally for 5 minutes and finish with a quick pressure release. When the valve drops, carefully remove the lid. Transfer the chicken to a serving platter. Drizzle the lemon juice over the rice and stir with a fork to combine.

Cheesy Salsa-Lime Chicken

YIELD:
4 SERVINGS

TIP: My large chicken breasts took 12 minutes to cook from frozen. If you have smaller chicken breasts, reduce the cook time. If using thawed chicken breasts, set the cook time to 5 to 6 minutes, depending on the size.

I always have a large bag of chicken breasts in the freezer and often don't think about defrosting the chicken until it's time to start dinner. Luckily you don't have to thaw the chicken first when pressure cooking it.

1 cup (260 g) salsa, mild or medium
1 cup (245 g) tomato sauce
4 large boneless skinless chicken breasts, frozen
½ teaspoon salt
¼ teaspoon freshly ground black pepper
Juice of 2 limes
1 cup (150 g) grated mozzarella cheese

In the pressure cooking pot, combine the salsa, tomato sauce, chicken, salt, pepper, and lime juice. Lock the lid in place. Select High Pressure and 12 minutes cook time.

When the cook time ends, turn off the pressure cooker. Use a quick pressure release. When the valve drops, carefully remove the lid. Use an instant-read thermometer to make sure the chicken is cooked to 165°F (74°C). If not, return the lid and cook at High pressure for a few more minutes.

Preheat the broiler and spray a small glass casserole dish with nonstick cooking spray. Remove the chicken from the pot and transfer it to the prepared dish. Select Simmer/Sauté and cook the sauce, stirring frequently, until it reaches your desired consistency. Spoon the sauce over the chicken. Sprinkle the mozzarella on top and put the dish under the broiler for about 5 minutes, or until the cheese melts and starts to brown—watch it carefully because the cheese browns quickly.

Barbecue Chicken Legs

YIELD:
6 SERVINGS

TIP: Pressure cook the chicken legs early in the day, refrigerate them until you're ready to serve, and finish them on the grill to warm them and caramelize the sauce.

This recipe is so quick and easy, you'll make it again and again, all summer long.

1 teaspoon chili powder
½ teaspoon salt
¼ teaspoon freshly ground black pepper
12 chicken legs
1 cup (250 g) barbecue sauce

In a small bowl, mix the chili powder, salt, and pepper. Place the chicken legs on a rimmed baking sheet and sprinkle with the seasoning.

Place a rack in the pressure cooking pot. Add 1 cup (235 ml) water and place the seasoned chicken legs on the rack, stacking them crosswise on top of each other. Lock the lid in place. Select High Pressure and 4 minutes cook time.

When the cook time ends, turn off the pressure cooker. Let the pressure release naturally for 10 minutes and finish with a quick pressure release. When the valve drops, carefully remove the lid. Remove the chicken legs to a rimmed baking sheet and coat with the barbecue sauce.

Preheat a grill to medium heat. Place the chicken on the grill and cook for 3 to 5 minutes per side until the sauce is caramelized and sticky. Baste with more sauce as desired. Alternatively, finish in a very hot oven or under the broiler, watching carefully to prevent burning.

Shortcut Homemade Chicken Noodle Soup

YIELD:
6 TO 8 SERVINGS

TIP: I like to make a big pot of soup and freeze it in individual servings in freezer zipper bags. Many soups freeze well, but soups with noodles, potatoes, or rice freeze better if you freeze the noodles, potatoes, or rice in separate single-serving bags and reheat the two separately.

I often like to buy a roasted chicken at the grocery store. I dice the meat and use half for something like Chicken Fettuccine Alfredo (page 195) and use the bones and the other half of the meat to make a homemade soup with tons of flavor.

1 large fully cooked rotisserie
   chicken

FOR CHICKEN BROTH:

1 large onion, coarsely chopped with
   the skin on

2 large carrots, roughly chopped

2 ribs celery, roughly chopped

3 cloves garlic, smashed

1 bay leaf

1 teaspoon dried thyme

½ teaspoon peppercorns

2 quarts (1.9 L) water

FOR CHICKEN SOUP:

1 tablespoon (14 g) unsalted butter

1 large onion, diced

1 rib celery, diced

4 carrots, cut into ¼-inch-thick
   (0.6 cm) rounds

1 tablespoon (1 g) dried parsley

2 teaspoons salt, plus more as
   needed

½ teaspoon freshly ground black
   pepper, plus more as needed

1 package (12 ounces, or 340 g) egg
   noodles, cooked according to
   package directions

Remove the meat from the rotisserie chicken and dice it into bite-size pieces. Save the bones, meat, and skin and refrigerate until ready to use.

TO MAKE THE CHICKEN BROTH: Put chicken bones and skin in the pressure cooking pot. Add the onion, carrots, celery, garlic, bay leaf, thyme, peppercorns, and water. Lock the lid in place. Select High Pressure and 20 minutes cook time.

When the cook time ends, turn off the pressure cooker. Let the pressure release naturally until completely released. (If you're short on time, let the pressure release naturally for 10 minutes and finish with a quick pressure release.) When the valve drops, carefully remove the lid. Pour the stock through a strainer set over a very large bowl or pot. Discard the bones, skin, vegetables, and herbs. If time permits, let cool and remove the fat from the top.

TO MAKE THE SOUP: Select Browning/Sauté and melt the butter in the pressure cooking pot. Add the onion and celery. Sauté for about 3 minutes, stirring occasionally, until tender. Stir in your homemade chicken broth, the diced chicken, carrots, parsley, salt, and pepper. Lock the lid in place. Select High Pressure and 4 minutes cook time.

When the cook time ends, turn off the pressure cooker. Let the pressure release naturally for 5 minutes and finish with a quick pressure release. When the valve drops, carefully remove the lid. Season with additional salt and pepper to taste. Serve the soup spooned over the cooked noodles.

No-Slice Au Gratin Potatoes

YIELD:
4 SERVINGS

....

TIP: For a one-pot
meal, stir in ½ cup
(75 g) diced ham
and 1 cup (130 g)
frozen peas.

Occasionally, my *Pressure Cooking Today* blog readers comment
on my recipe for au gratin potatoes asking if they can use a package
of dried au gratin potatoes instead of slicing fresh potatoes themselves. Absolutely!

1 tablespoon (14 g) unsalted butter
1½ cups (360 ml) water
1 package (4.7 ounces, or 133 g) au gratin potatoes with sauce packet
½ cup (120 ml) milk
Dash cayenne pepper

Select Browning/Sauté and melt the butter in the pressure cooking pot. Stir in
the water and potatoes. Lock the lid in place. Select High Pressure and 5 minutes
cook time.

When the cook time ends, turn off the pressure cooker. Use a quick pressure release.
When the valve drops, carefully remove the lid. Stir in the milk, sauce packet, and
cayenne. Select Simmer/Sauté and gently stir until the sauce reaches your desired
consistency.

Pot Stickers with Spicy Orange Dipping Sauce

YIELD:
4 SERVINGS

TIP: For a restaurant-quality look, brown the pot stickers after pressure cooking. Reduce the High Pressure cook time to 1 minute. After the quick pressure release, add 1 tablespoon (15 ml) vegetable oil to a preheated skillet and place the pot stickers in a single layer. Cook for about 1 minute until golden-brown.

These pot stickers are perfect for a quick appetizer when guests are coming, or they can be part of an easy lunch or dinner any night of the week.

2 tablespoons (38 g) orange marmalade
1 tablespoon (15 g) packed light brown sugar
2 teaspoons low-sodium soy sauce
1 teaspoon rice wine vinegar
¼ teaspoon chili-garlic sauce
¼ teaspoon sesame oil
12 frozen pot stickers

In a small bowl, whisk the orange marmalade, brown sugar, soy sauce, vinegar, chili-garlic sauce, and sesame oil. Set aside until ready to serve.

Put a steamer basket in the pressure cooking pot and add 1 cup (235 ml) water. Spray the steamer basket with nonstick cooking spray. Add the pot stickers in a single layer. Lock the lid in place. Select High Pressure and 2 minutes cook time.

When the cook time ends, turn off the pressure cooker. Use a quick pressure release. When the valve drops, carefully remove the lid. Serve the pot stickers with the dipping sauce.

Short-Order Buffalo Wings with Blue Cheese Dip

YIELD:
6 TO 8 SERVINGS

....

TIP: If you prefer, take a shortcut with the dip and buy prepared blue cheese salad dressing.

The pressure cooker makes short work of buffalo wings. Pressure cook them early and finish them under the broiler before the big game!

FOR BLUE CHEESE DIP:
½ cup (115 g) sour cream
½ cup (115 g) mayonnaise
½ cup (60 g) crumbled blue cheese
3 scallions, white and green parts, finely chopped

1 tablespoon (1 g) dried parsley
1 tablespoon (15 ml) lemon juice
¼ teaspoon garlic salt
¼ teaspoon ground black pepper

FOR WINGS:
¼ cup (60 ml) water
1 cup (235 ml) Frank's RedHot Buffalo sauce, divided
1 tablespoon (8 g) paprika

3 pounds (1.4 kg) chicken wings, split at the joints
2 tablespoons (40 g) honey

TO MAKE THE BLUE CHEESE DIP: In a medium-size bowl, stir together the sour cream, mayonnaise, blue cheese, scallions, dried parsley, lemon juice, garlic salt, and pepper until well blended. Cover and refrigerate until ready to serve.

TO MAKE THE BUFFALO WINGS: In the pressure cooking pot, stir together the water, ¼ cup (60 ml) buffalo sauce, and paprika. Add the wings. Lock the lid in place. Select High Pressure and 6 minutes cook time.

When the cook time ends, turn off the pressure cooker. Let the pressure release naturally for 10 minutes and finish with a quick pressure release. When the valve drops, carefully remove the lid.

In a large bowl, mix the remaining ¾ cup (175 ml) buffalo sauce with the honey. Use a slotted spoon to remove the wings from the cooking pot and add them to the bowl. Stir to coat the wings with the sauce. Preheat the broiler.

Line a rimmed baking sheet with aluminum foil. Place a wire rack on the prepared sheet. With tongs, place the coated wings on the rack. Place the wings under the broiler for 3 to 5 minutes until they start to brown. Remove from the oven and turn the wings over. Broil the second side for 3 to 5 minutes more until they start to brown. Watch them closely so that they don't burn. Serve with the blue cheese dip.

Grand-Slam Ballpark Chili Dogs

YIELD:
8 SERVINGS

TIP: Load your chili dogs with diced red onion, diced tomatoes, jalapeños, and sour cream.

We don't often have hot dogs at our house, so when we do, my husband likes them loaded with chili and cheese—just like you'd get at the ballpark. This shortcut version cooks the chili and hot dogs at the same time in one pot.

1 can (15 ounces, or 425 g) chili
8 hot dogs
8 hot dog buns
Shredded Cheddar cheese, for serving

Pour 1 cup (235 ml) water into the pressure cooking pot and place a trivet in the bottom. Spoon the chili into a 7 × 3-inch (18 × 7.5 cm) round cake pan and place it on the trivet. Stack a second trivet on the cake pan and place the hot dogs on it. Lock the lid in place. Select High Pressure and 1 minute cook time.

When the cook time ends, turn off the pressure cooker. Use a quick pressure release. When the valve drops, carefully remove the lid. To serve, put a hot dog in each bun and top with chili and Cheddar.

Blue Box Mac and Cheese

YIELD:
4 SERVINGS

....

TIP: This recipe can be doubled without increasing the cook time.

Most kids are fond of that orangey, boxed macaroni and cheese—even my college-age "kids" will buy a box and make it for themselves. It's even more convenient in the pressure cooker since there's no need to watch the stove to keep your pot from boiling over.

¼ cup (56 g) unsalted butter
1¼ cups (295 ml) water
**1 (7.25 ounces, or 206 g) package Kraft Macaroni
  & Cheese Dinner, or your favorite brand**
¼ cup (60 ml) milk
Dash cayenne pepper (optional)

Select Simmer/Sauté and melt the butter in the pressure cooking pot. Stir in the water and macaroni. Lock the lid in place. Select High Pressure and 3 minutes cook time.

When the cook time ends, turn off the pressure cooker. Use a quick pressure release. When the valve drops, carefully remove the lid. Stir in the milk, cheese packet, and cayenne (if desired). Select Simmer/Sauté and gently stir the macaroni until the sauce reaches your desired consistency.

Presto Italian Meatball Sandwiches

YIELD:
4 SERVINGS

....

TIP: If you prefer to make your own sauce, you can use a 28-ounce (794 g) can crushed tomatoes in purée, 1½ teaspoons garlic powder, 1 teaspoon dried basil, ¼ teaspoon red pepper flakes, and ¼ teaspoon salt instead, or your favorite recipe.

A tasty meatball sub doesn't have to take all day to make. This shortcut recipe uses frozen ready-to-use meatballs and jarred marinara sauce—it's hot, delicious, and ready in minutes.

**1 bag (24 ounces, or 680 g) frozen fully cooked
    beef Italian meatballs
1 jar (28 fluid ounces, or 828 ml) marinara sauce
4 crusty sub rolls, toasted
2 cups (230 g) shredded mozzarella cheese**

Add 1 cup (235 ml) water to the pressure cooking pot. Place a steamer basket in the pot and add the frozen meatballs. Lock the lid in place. Select High Pressure and 5 minutes cook time.

When the cook time ends, turn off the pressure cooker. Use a quick pressure release. When the valve drops, carefully remove the lid. Carefully remove the steamer basket and meatballs from the cooking pot. Discard the cooking water. Place the meatballs directly in the cooking pot. Add the marinara and stir to combine. Select Simmer/Sauté and heat until the sauce starts to boil. Switch to the Keep Warm setting until ready to serve.

Pile the meatballs and sauce onto the sub rolls. Top with the mozzarella and place under the preheated broiler to melt the cheese, if desired.

Better-than-Take-Out Sweet-and-Sour Chicken

YIELD:
6 SERVINGS

TIP: If needed, add a little water to the pineapple juice to equal ½ cup (120 ml).

A perennial favorite. This colorful dish can be on the table in less than 15 minutes.

4 large boneless skinless chicken breasts, cut into 1-inch (2.5 cm) pieces
1 can (8 ounces, or 227 g) pineapple chunks, juice drained and reserved
1 green bell pepper, cut into 1-inch (2.5 cm) chunks
1 red bell pepper, cut into 1-inch (2.5 cm) chunks
2 tablespoons (16 g) cornstarch
2 tablespoons (30 ml) cold water
1 jar (12 fluid ounces, or 355 ml) sweet-and-sour sauce
¼ cup (25 g) sliced scallions, white and green parts
Cooked rice, for serving

In the pressure cooking pot, combine the chicken, pineapple juice, and bell peppers. Lock the lid in place. Select High Pressure and 3 minutes cook time.

When the cook time ends, turn off the pressure cooker. Use a quick pressure release. When the valve drops, carefully remove the lid.

In a small bowl, whisk the cornstarch and cold water until smooth. Add the slurry to the pot. Select Simmer/Sauté and simmer, stirring constantly, until the liquid thickens. Stir in the sweet-and-sour sauce and pineapple chunks. Garnish with scallions and serve over rice.

Chicken Tikka Masala and Rice

YIELD:
4 SERVINGS

TIP: Jarred sauces often contain thickeners that can settle to the bottom of the pressure cooking pot and cause problems with the cooker achieving proper pressure. Eliminate this problem by adding jarred sauces after you finish pressure cooking.

If you're an Indian food enthusiast and have a favorite jarred sauce, this recipe will become a favorite in your menu rotation!

½ cup (120 ml) reduced-sodium chicken broth
4 large boneless skinless chicken breasts
1¾ cups (410 ml) water
1½ cups (278 g) long-grain white rice, rinsed
½ teaspoon salt
1 jar (15 fluid ounces, or 444 ml) tikka masala sauce
½ cup (120 ml) heavy cream
Fresh chopped cilantro leaves, for garnish (optional)

In the pressure cooking pot, combine the chicken broth and chicken. Put a trivet on the chicken. Place a 7 × 3-inch (18 × 7.5 cm) round cake pan on the trivet and add the water, rice, and salt to it. Lock the lid in place. Select High Pressure and 5 minutes cook time.

When the cook time ends, turn off the pressure cooker. Wait 10 minutes. Use a quick pressure release. When the valve drops, carefully remove the lid. Remove the cake pan and trivet from the cooking pot and fluff the rice with a fork. Cover the rice to keep it warm until ready to serve.

Use a slotted spoon to transfer the chicken from the cooking pot to a cutting board. Cut the chicken into bite-size pieces. Stir the tikka masala sauce into the broth in the pot. Stir in the diced chicken and heavy cream. Serve over rice, if desired, garnished with cilantro.

Quick-Cooking Chicken and Pierogi Dumplings

YIELD:
4 SERVINGS

TIP: Look for potato-and-Cheddar pierogies in the frozen vegetable section of your grocery store.

Chicken and dumplings is classic comfort food! This shortcut version uses quick-cooking bite-size chicken and frozen, ready-made pierogies instead of traditional dumplings.

1 tablespoon (15 ml) olive oil
1 cup (160 g) diced onion
½ cup (60 g) diced celery
½ cup (65 g) diced carrots
2 cans (14.5 fluid ounces, or 429 ml, each) reduced-sodium chicken broth
4 large boneless skinless chicken breasts, cut into bite-size pieces
1 tablespoon (1 g) dried parsley
1 teaspoon salt

½ teaspoon dried thyme
¼ teaspoon freshly ground black pepper
¼ cup (32 g) cornstarch
¼ cup (60 ml) cold water
⅓ cup (78 ml) half-and-half
12 frozen potato-and-Cheddar pierogies (1 pound, or 454 g, package)

Select Browning/Sauté to preheat the pressure cooking pot. When hot, add the olive oil, onion, celery, and carrots. Sauté for 3 minutes, stirring frequently. Stir in the chicken broth, chicken, parsley, salt, thyme, and pepper. Lock the lid in place. Select High Pressure and 3 minutes cook time.

When the cook time ends, turn off the pressure cooker. Use a quick pressure release. When the valve drops, carefully remove the lid.

In a small bowl, whisk the cornstarch and cold water until smooth. Select Simmer/Sauté and add the slurry to the pot, stirring constantly until the sauce comes to a boil and thickens. Stir in the half-and-half. Stir in the pierogies and simmer for 6 minutes, or until they are warmed through.

Jazzy New Orleans-Style Red Beans, Rice, and Sausage

YIELD:
4 SERVINGS

TIP: To really jazz this up, serve this red beans and rice with some Louisiana Hot Sauce.

Red beans and rice is a New Orleans staple, but sometimes you just don't have time to make it from scratch. Use this shortcut recipe next time you have a craving but are short on time.

2 tablespoons (28 g) unsalted butter
6 ounces (170 g) andouille sausage,
   halved lengthwise and cut crosswise into
   ¼-inch -thick (0.6 cm) slices
2½ cups (590 ml) water
1 package (8 ounces, or 227 g) red beans and rice

Select Browning/Sauté and melt the butter in the pressure cooking pot. Add the sausage. Sauté for about 3 minutes until it starts to brown. Stir in the water and red beans and rice. Lock the lid in place. Select High Pressure and 13 minutes cook time.

When the cook time ends, turn off the pressure cooker. Let the pressure release naturally for 10 minutes and finish with a quick pressure release. When the valve drops, carefully remove the lid. Stir with a fork and let sit for 5 minutes, uncovered, before serving.

Easy Pork Chops in Mushroom Gravy

YIELD:
4 SERVINGS

....

TIP: Serve over
Creamy Mashed
Potatoes (page 248)
for an old-fashioned
comfort food meal.

This recipe is adapted from a stovetop recipe my mother-in-law made for my husband growing up. These scrumptious, fall-off-the-bone pork chops in a creamy mushroom gravy have become a favorite on my blog, *Pressure Cooking Today*.

4 bone-in 1-inch-thick (2.5 cm) pork chops
Lemon pepper or your favorite spice blend, for seasoning
2 tablespoons (30 ml) vegetable oil
1½ cups (360 ml) water
1 can (10.5 ounces, or 298 g) condensed cream of mushroom soup
3 tablespoons (45 ml) cold water (optional)
2 tablespoons (14 g) all-purpose flour (optional)

Pat the pork chops dry and season liberally with lemon pepper. Select Browning/Sauté and add the vegetable oil to the pressure cooking pot. When the oil begins to sizzle, add 2 chops and brown for about 3 minutes per side. Transfer to a platter and repeat with the remaining 2 chops.

Add the water to deglaze the pot, scraping up any browned bits from the bottom. Stir in the mushroom soup. Add the pork chops and any accumulated juices. Lock the lid in place. Select High Pressure and 18 minutes cook time.

When the cook time ends, turn off the pressure cooker. Let the pressure release naturally for 10 minutes and finish with a quick pressure release. When the valve drops, carefully remove the lid. Transfer the chops to a large serving bowl.

If you prefer a thicker gravy, select Simmer/Sauté and whisk 3 tablespoons (45 ml) cold water with 2 tablespoons (14 g) all-purpose flour until smooth. Add 1 cup (235 ml) gravy to the flour mixture and stir until well combined. Slowly stir this mixture into the gravy in the cooking pot. Pour the gravy over the chops to serve.

Pork Teriyaki Rice Bowls

YIELD:
6 SERVINGS

TIP: Cut the veggies into similar-size pieces so that they all cook in the same amount of time. If desired, substitute a frozen stir-fry vegetable blend.

A local restaurant serves a teriyaki rice bowl that my boys always order. This quick pressure cooker version is loaded with colorful vegetables, tender pork, and drizzled with sweet teriyaki sauce.

1 tablespoon (30 ml) vegetable oil
2 carrots, diced
1 small zucchini, diced into small cubes
1 cup (71 g) chopped broccoli florets
1 cup (235 ml) teriyaki sauce
½ cup (120 ml) water
1¼ pounds (567 g) pork tenderloin
2 tablespoons (16 g) cornstarch
3 tablespoons (45 ml) cold water
Cooked white rice or coconut rice, for serving

Select Browning/Sauté to preheat the pressure cooking pot. When hot, add the vegetable oil, carrots, zucchini, and broccoli. Sauté the vegetables for about 5 minutes until crisp-tender. Transfer to a plate and cover to keep warm.

Combine the teriyaki sauce and water in the pressure cooking pot. Add the pork tenderloin. Lock the lid in place. Select High Pressure and 5 minutes cook time.

When the cook time ends, turn off the pressure cooker. Let the pressure release naturally for 5 minutes and finish with a quick pressure release. When the valve drops, carefully remove the lid. Transfer the tenderloin to a work surface and cut it into bite-size pieces.

In a small dish, whisk the cornstarch and cold water until smooth. Add the slurry to the pot. Select Simmer/Sauté and simmer, stirring constantly, until the sauce thickens. Stir in the diced tenderloin and sautéed vegetables. Serve in bowls over white rice or coconut rice.

Weeknight Chocolate Cake

YIELD:
6 TO 8 SERVINGS

A half-size Bundt pan fits perfectly in a 6-quart (5.7 L) electric pressure cooker. This shortcut version is quick and easy to make, and no one will know it started with a mix.

8 ounces (227 g) chocolate cake mix
2 large eggs
½ cup (120 ml) water
¼ cup (60 ml) vegetable oil
¼ cup (60 g) sour cream
Chocolate ganache (page 284) and sprinkles, for decorating

Spray a half-size Bundt pan with nonstick cooking spray.

In a large bowl, stir together the cake mix, eggs, water, vegetable oil, and sour cream for 2 minutes. Spoon the batter into the prepared Bundt pan. Cover the pan with a paper towel and cover the paper towel completely with aluminum foil, crimped around the edges to seal.

Pour 1 cup (235 ml) water into the pressure cooking pot and place a trivet in the bottom. Center the Bundt pan on a sling and lower it onto the trivet. Lock the lid in place. Select High Pressure and 20 minutes cook time.

When the cook time ends, turn off the pressure cooker. Let the pressure release naturally for 10 minutes and finish with a quick pressure release. When the valve drops, carefully remove the lid.

Use the sling to transfer the Bundt pan to a wire rack. Remove the foil and paper towel. Cool for 5 minutes, uncovered. Gently loosen the edges, remove the cake from the pan, and cool completely on a wire rack.

If desired, decorate the cake with chocolate ganache and sprinkles.

{ Chapter 5 }

30-Minute Meals

When the pressure's on to get dinner on the table in a hurry, turn to these 30-minute meals. All recipes in this section are quick and easy to make. Many are faster and easier than going out—and they're definitely better tasting and better for you.

Easy Peasy Chicken Potpie

YIELD:
6 SERVINGS

TIP: Make the filling earlier in the day, let it come to room temperature, refrigerate, and finish the last step when it's time for dinner.

Chicken potpie is classic comfort food. This updated recipe uses the pressure cooker to cook the filling, so it's ready in a fraction of the time.

1 tablespoon (15 ml) vegetable oil
½ cup (80 g) diced onion
1 rib celery, chopped
½ cup (120 ml) reduced-sodium chicken broth
2 large (about 1 pound, or 454 g) boneless skinless chicken breasts, diced into bite-size pieces
1 large russet potato, cut into 1-inch (2.5 cm) cubes
2 carrots, cut into ¼-inch (0.6 cm) slices

½ teaspoon salt
¼ teaspoon dried thyme
¼ teaspoon freshly ground black pepper
½ cup (65 g) frozen peas, thawed
⅓ cup (75 g) unsalted butter
⅓ cup (37 g) all-purpose flour
½ cup (120 ml) milk, plus more as needed
1 homemade or store-bought piecrust

Preheat the oven to 425°F (220°C, or gas mark 7). Spray a deep-dish pie plate with non-stick cooking spray and set aside.

Select Browning/Sauté to preheat the pressure cooking pot. When hot, add the vegetable oil, onion, and celery. Sauté for about 3 minutes, stirring occasionally, until the onion is tender. Stir in the chicken broth, chicken, potato, carrots, salt, thyme, and pepper. Lock the lid in place. Select High Pressure and 3 minutes cook time.

When the cook time ends, turn off the pressure cooker. Use a quick pressure release. When the valve drops, carefully remove the lid. Stir in the peas.

In a small saucepan over medium heat, melt the butter. Whisk in the flour. Cook for 2 to 3 minutes, stirring constantly until smooth and bubbly. Gradually add the milk, stirring constantly for about 2 minutes until the sauce is thick and smooth. Add this to the pressure cooking pot and stir until the sauce is thick and creamy. Add more milk, if needed, to achieve your desired consistency. Pour the potpie filling into the prepared pie plate. Top with the piecrust and bake for 10 minutes, or until the crust is golden-brown and the filling is hot.

Braised Chicken and Mushrooms with Creamy Polenta

TIP: Don't substitute instant or finely-ground polenta as these will give the food a pasty texture and will cook too quickly.

Juicy chicken thighs in a rich tomato-based sauce with mushrooms and thyme served over Parmesan-flavored polenta. The polenta cooks at the same time as the chicken, so dinner can be on the table in a flash.

FOR CHICKEN AND MUSHROOMS:

2 pounds (907 g) boneless skinless chicken thighs, well trimmed

Salt and freshly ground black pepper, for seasoning

2 tablespoons (30 ml) vegetable oil, divided

2 tablespoons (28 g) unsalted butter, divided

¼ cup (60 ml) white wine

1 tablespoon (16 g) tomato paste

½ cup (120 ml) reduced-sodium chicken broth

3 sprigs fresh thyme, or 1 teaspoon dried thyme

8 ounces (227 g) sliced mushrooms

2 tablespoons (16 g) cornstarch

3 tablespoons (45 ml) cold water

2 tablespoons (8 g) chopped fresh parsley leaves

FOR POLENTA:

3 cups (705 ml) water

1 cup (140 g) coarse polenta

⅓ cup (33 g) grated Parmesan cheese

½ teaspoon salt

Pinch freshly ground black pepper

1 tablespoon (14 g) butter

TO MAKE THE CHICKEN: Season the chicken generously with salt and pepper. Select Browning/Sauté and add 1 tablespoon (15 ml) vegetable oil and 1 tablespoon (14 g) butter to the pressure cooking pot. When the butter melts, add the chicken in batches. Cook for about 3 minutes to brown well on one side. Transfer the browned chicken to a platter.

Add the white wine to deglaze the pot, scraping up any browned bits from the bottom. Cook for about 5 minutes, or until reduced by half. Whisk in the tomato paste. Stir in the chicken broth, thyme, and browned chicken along with any juices. Set aside.

TO MAKE THE POLENTA: Spray a 7 × 3-inch (18 × 7.5 cm) round cake pan with nonstick cooking spray. Add the water, polenta, Parmesan, salt, and pepper. Stir to combine. Place a rack on the chicken in the pressure cooking pot and carefully place the cake pan on the rack. Lock the lid in place. Select High Pressure and 8 minutes cook time.

TO MAKE THE MUSHROOMS: While the chicken and polenta cook, heat a large sauté pan over medium-high heat until hot. Add the remaining 1 tablespoon (15 ml) vegetable oil and 1 tablespoon (14 g) butter. When the butter melts, add the mushrooms and cook for 3 to 5 minutes until golden. Season with salt and pepper.

When the cook time ends, turn off the pressure cooker. Use a natural release for 10 minutes and finish with a quick pressure release. When the valve drops, carefully remove the lid. Remove the polenta and rack from the cooking pot and stir in the butter. Set aside. Remove and discard the thyme from the cooking pot.

In a small bowl, whisk the cornstarch and cold water until smooth. Push the chicken to one side of the pot, and add the slurry to the sauce in the pot, stirring constantly. Select Simmer/Sauté and bring the mixture to a boil, stirring constantly until the sauce thickens. Stir in the mushrooms and parsley. Season with additional salt and pepper to taste. Serve the polenta in bowls topped with chicken and mushrooms.

Chicken Cordon Bleu "Bake"

YIELD:
6 SERVINGS

....

TIP: Stir in some thawed frozen peas or vegetables along with the ham to make this a one-pot meal.

An easy-to-make, easy-to-serve deconstructed chicken cordon bleu—chicken, ham, and cheese served casserole-style and topped with crunchy bread crumbs.

5 tablespoons (70 g) unsalted butter, plus more for greasing the baking dish

2 large boneless skinless chicken breasts, cut into bite-size pieces

1 cup (235 ml) reduced-sodium chicken broth

1 teaspoon dry mustard

½ teaspoon salt

⅛ teaspoon cayenne pepper

4 medium-size russet potatoes, peeled and cubed

1 cup (50 g) panko bread crumbs

¼ cup (20 g) shredded Parmesan cheese

½ cup (115 g) sour cream

1 cup (110 g) shredded Swiss cheese

8 ounces (227 g) deli ham, diced

Grease a 9 × 13-inch (23 × 33 cm) ovenproof dish with butter and set aside.

Select Browning/Sauté and add 2 tablespoons (28 g) butter to the pressure cooking pot to melt. Add the chicken. Sauté for 3 minutes, stirring occasionally. Stir in the chicken broth, dry mustard, salt, and cayenne.

Put a steamer basket in the cooking pot on the chicken. Add the potatoes to the basket. Lock the lid in place. Select High Pressure and 4 minutes cook time. While the chicken cooks, preheat the broiler.

In a small bowl, mix the panko and Parmesan with 3 tablespoons (42 g) melted butter. Set aside.

When the cook time ends, turn off the pressure cooker. Use a quick pressure release. When the valve drops, carefully remove the lid. Remove the steamer basket and potatoes from the pot.

Add the sour cream and Swiss cheese to the cooking pot and stir until the cheese melts. Stir in the potatoes and ham. Pour the mixture into the prepared dish. Top with the panko mixture. Broil for 1 to 2 minutes until golden-brown—watch closely so that it doesn't burn.

Chicken Enchilada Pasta

YIELD:
6 SERVINGS

TIP: To make your own taco seasoning, mix 2 teaspoons chili powder, ½ teaspoon ground cumin, ½ teaspoon garlic powder, 1 teaspoon onion powder, and a dash of cayenne.

This zesty dish is a fusion of Tex-Mex and Italian. It's a quick one-pot meal that's perfect for a busy weeknight.

1 tablespoon (15 ml) vegetable oil

1 cup (160 g) diced onion

2 cloves garlic, minced or pressed

1 can (19 fluid ounces, or 562 ml) enchilada sauce

1 can (10 ounces, or 284 g) diced tomatoes and green chilies

1¼ cups (295 ml) water

1 package (1.25 ounces, or 36 g) taco seasoning mix

2 large boneless skinless chicken breasts (about 1 pound, or 454 g), diced into bite-size pieces

3 cups (12 ounces, or 340 g) dried rotini pasta

2 cups (225 g) shredded Mexican cheese

Scallions, olives, diced tomatoes, and fresh cilantro, for serving

Spray an 8 × 8-inch (20 × 20 cm) ovenproof baking dish with nonstick cooking spray. Set aside.

Select Browning/Sauté and add the vegetable oil to the pressure cooking pot. When the oil is hot, add the onion. Sauté for about 3 minutes until tender. Add the garlic and sauté for 1 minute more. Stir in the enchilada sauce, tomatoes and green chilies, water, and taco seasoning mix. Add the diced chicken and pasta. Lock the lid in place. Select High Pressure and 4 minutes cook time.

When the cook time ends, turn off the pressure cooker. Use a quick pressure release. When the valve drops, carefully remove the lid. Select Simmer/Sauté and cook for about 1 minute, stirring often, until the pasta is tender. Turn off the pressure cooker and pour the pasta into the prepared dish. Sprinkle the cheese on top. Place the dish under the preheated broiler and broil until the cheese melts and starts to brown. Served topped with scallions, olives, diced tomatoes, and cilantro, as desired.

Thai Chicken Thighs

YIELD:
6 SERVINGS

TIP: Don't worry about trimming all the fat from the chicken thighs— just what you can cut away quickly. During pressure cooking, the fat melts away from the chicken, leaving tender, juicy meat.

Fork-tender boneless skinless chicken thighs in a delicious Thai peanut sauce. I adapted this recipe from a slow cooker recipe, so you get that luxurious slow-cooked flavor in a fraction of the time. This is my son-in-law's favorite pressure cooker meal.

2 tablespoons (30 ml) vegetable oil, divided
2 pounds (907 g) boneless skinless chicken thighs, trimmed
½ cup (120 ml) reduced-sodium chicken broth
¼ cup (65 g) peanut butter
¼ cup (60 ml) low-sodium soy sauce
¼ teaspoon cayenne pepper
1 teaspoon grated peeled fresh ginger
1 tablespoon (1 g) chopped fresh cilantro leaves
2 tablespoons (30 ml) fresh lime juice
¼ cup (36 g) chopped peanuts

Select Browning/Sauté and add 1 tablespoon (15 ml) vegetable oil to the pressure cooking pot. When the oil is hot, add the chicken thighs in small batches to brown, about 3 minutes per batch. Do not crowd the pot. Transfer the browned chicken to a platter and repeat until all the chicken is browned.

Stir in the chicken broth to deglaze the pot, scraping up any browned bits from the bottom. Add the peanut butter, soy sauce, cayenne, and ginger. Stir to combine. Add the browned chicken to the pot, along with any accumulated juices. Lock the lid in place. Select High Pressure and 9 minutes cook time.

When the cook time ends, turn off the pressure cooker. Use a quick pressure release. When the valve drops, carefully remove the lid. Stir in the cilantro and lime juice. Serve garnished with chopped peanuts.

Thai Chicken Rice Bowl

YIELD:
6 SERVINGS

TIP: I prefer a fairly mild curry flavor; if you like it hot, double the red curry powder in this recipe.

The contrasting colors of the red bell peppers and green cilantro in the flavorful yellow coconut curry sauce make a pretty presentation.

3 large (about 1½ pounds, or 227 g)
   boneless skinless chicken breasts, cut into bite-size pieces
Salt and freshly ground black pepper, for seasoning
2 tablespoons (30 ml) olive oil
2 cloves garlic, minced or pressed
1 can (14 fluid ounces, or 414 ml) unsweetened coconut milk
1½ teaspoons red curry powder
1 red bell pepper, thinly sliced and halved
1 can (15 ounces, or 425 g) chickpeas (garbanzo beans), drained and rinsed
2 tablespoons (16 g) cornstarch
2 tablespoons (30 ml) cold water
¼ cup (4 g) fresh cilantro leaves, chopped
Cooked rice, for serving

Generously season the chicken with salt and pepper. Select Browning/Sauté to preheat the pressure cooking pot. When hot, add the olive oil and chicken. Sauté for 3 minutes, stirring occasionally. Add the garlic and sauté for 30 seconds more. Stir in the coconut milk and curry powder. Add the red bell pepper and chickpeas. Stir to combine. Lock the lid in place. Select High Pressure and 3 minutes cook time.

When the cook time ends, turn off the pressure cooker. Use a quick pressure release. When the valve drops, carefully remove the lid.

In a small bowl, whisk the cornstarch and cold water until smooth. Add the slurry to the pot. Select Simmer/Sauté and cook, stirring constantly, until the sauce thickens. Turn off the pressure cooker and stir in the cilantro. Serve over rice.

Honey-Sesame Chicken

YIELD:
6 SERVINGS

TIP: If you dice the chicken when you bring it home from the store—before you freeze it—it's recipe ready. Freeze the diced chicken flat, not in one big clump.

Heavenly bite-size chunks of chicken in a sticky sweet sauce. A meal the whole family will cheer for.

4 large (about 2 pounds, or 907 g)
   boneless skinless chicken breasts, diced into bite-size pieces
Salt and freshly ground black pepper, for seasoning
1 tablespoon (15 ml) vegetable oil
½ cup (80 g) diced onion
2 cloves garlic, minced
½ cup (120 ml) low-sodium soy sauce
¼ cup (60 g) ketchup
¼ teaspoon red pepper flakes
2 teaspoons sesame oil
½ cup (170 g) honey
2 tablespoons (16 g) cornstarch
3 tablespoons (45 ml) cold water
2 scallions, white and green parts, chopped
Cooked rice and toasted sesame seeds, for serving

Season the chicken with salt and pepper. Select Browning/Sauté to preheat the pressure cooking pot. When hot, add the vegetable oil, onion, garlic, and chicken to the pot. Sauté for about 3 minutes, stirring occasionally, until the onion softens. Stir in the soy sauce, ketchup, and red pepper flakes. Lock the lid in place. Select High Pressure and 3 minutes cook time.

When the cook time ends, turn off the pressure cooker. Use a quick pressure release. When the valve drops, carefully remove the lid. Add the sesame oil and honey to the pot and stir to combine.

In a small bowl, whisk the cornstarch and cold water until smooth. Add the slurry to the pot. Select Simmer/Sauté and simmer, stirring constantly, until the sauce thickens. Stir in scallions. Serve over rice and sprinkle with toasted sesame seeds, if desired.

Spicy Orange Chicken

YIELD:
6 SERVINGS

TIP: Serve this dish over white rice or, for a lower-carb version, over zucchini and carrot noodles made with a spiral vegetable slicer.

The orange marmalade adds a bright, concentrated orange flavor to this sweet, spicy dish.

4 large (about 2 pounds, or 907 g)
   boneless skinless chicken breasts, diced into bite-size pieces
¼ cup (60 ml) low-sodium soy sauce
¼ cup (60 ml) water
2 tablespoons (30 g) packed light brown sugar
1 tablespoon (15 ml) rice wine vinegar
1 teaspoon sesame oil
¼ teaspoon chili-garlic sauce
½ cup (150 g) orange marmalade
3 tablespoons (24 g) cornstarch
3 tablespoons (45 ml) cold water
2 scallions, white and green parts, chopped for serving
Red pepper flakes, for seasoning for serving

In the pressure cooking pot, combine the chicken, soy sauce, water, brown sugar, rice wine vinegar, sesame oil, and chili-garlic sauce. Stir to combine. Lock the lid in place. Select High Pressure and 3 minutes cook time.

When the cook time ends, turn off the pressure cooker. Use a quick pressure release. When the valve drops, carefully remove the lid. Stir in the marmalade.

In a small bowl, whisk the cornstarch and cold water until smooth. Add the slurry to the pot. Select Simmer/Sauté and simmer, stirring constantly, until the sauce is thick and syrupy. Serve topped with scallions and red pepper flakes.

Indian Butter Chicken

YIELD:

6 SERVINGS

TIP: If you're in a hurry, brown only one side of the chicken thighs. The chicken will still have an appetizing color and the sauce will still have the flavor of browning, but you'll get out of the kitchen more quickly.

This classic dish at Indian restaurants is easy to make at home. The combination of tender chicken thighs in a rich, creamy, buttery, tomato sauce is my daughter's favorite—she makes it almost weekly.

2 cans (14.5 ounces, or 411 g, each) diced tomatoes with juice

2 jalapeño peppers, seeded and chopped

2 tablespoons (12 g) chopped peeled fresh ginger

1 tablespoon (8 g) paprika

1 tablespoon (7 g) ground cumin

2 teaspoons garam masala

2 teaspoons kosher salt

½ cup (1 stick, or 113 g) unsalted butter

9 boneless skinless chicken thighs

2 tablespoons (16 g) cornstarch

2 tablespoons (30 ml) cold water

¾ cup (175 ml) heavy cream

¾ cup (180 g) plain Greek yogurt

¼ cup (4 g) fresh cilantro leaves, finely chopped

Cooked basmati rice and naan, for serving

In a blender, combine the tomatoes, jalapeños, ginger, paprika, cumin, garam masala, and salt. Blend to a fine purée. Set aside.

Select Browning/Sauté and melt the butter in the pressure cooking pot. Add 3 chicken thighs to the pot and sear briefly on both sides. Transfer to a cutting board and add another 3 thighs to the pot. Repeat until all the thighs are browned. Add the tomato purée to the cooking pot and turn off the pressure cooker.

Slice the chicken into large bite-size pieces and add it and any accumulated juices to the pot and stir to combine. Lock the lid in place. Select High Pressure and 5 minutes cook time.

When the cook time ends, turn off the pressure cooker. Use a quick pressure release. When the valve drops, carefully remove the lid.

In a small bowl, whisk the cornstarch and cold water until smooth. Add the slurry to the pot. Select Simmer/Sauté and bring the liquid to a boil. Turn off the pressure cooker and stir in the heavy cream, yogurt, and cilantro. Serve with basmati rice and naan, if desired.

Creamy Chicken Pesto Pasta

YIELD:
6 TO 8 SERVINGS

....

TIP: If you're using larger asparagus spears, blanch them briefly in boiling water before adding to the pasta.

I'm crazy about this one-pot meal. It's colorful, packed with flavor, creamy, and rich (but not too high in calories) and has lean protein and fresh veggies.

2 tablespoons (28 g) unsalted butter

3 cloves garlic, minced

2 large (about 1 pound, or 454 g) boneless skinless chicken breasts, cut into bite-size pieces

2 cups (470 ml) reduced-sodium chicken broth

2 cups (470 ml) water

1 package (14 ounces, or 397 g) rotini pasta

1 teaspoon salt, plus more as needed

½ teaspoon freshly ground black pepper, plus more as needed

4 ounces (113 g) cream cheese, cubed

¼ cup (60 ml) milk

2 tablespoons (30 g) prepared pesto

12 thin asparagus spears, cut into 2-inch (5 cm) pieces

1½ cups (270 g) quartered grape tomatoes

2 tablespoons (5 g) finely chopped fresh basil leaves, or parsley leaves (8 g), for serving

Freshly grated Parmesan cheese, for serving

Select Browning/Sauté and melt the butter in the pressure cooking pot. Stir in the garlic and cook for 30 seconds. Add the chicken and sauté for 3 minutes, stirring occasionally. Stir in the chicken broth, water, rotini, salt, and pepper. Lock the lid in place. Select High Pressure and 4 minutes cook time.

When the cook time ends, turn off the pressure cooker. Let the pressure release naturally for 3 minutes and finish with a quick pressure release. When the valve drops, carefully remove the lid. Stir the cream cheese into the hot pasta until melted. Stir in the milk and pesto until blended. Stir in the asparagus and cover the pot to steam for 2 minutes, or until the asparagus is crisp-tender. Mix in the tomatoes and season with salt and pepper to taste. Serve topped with basil or parsley and fresh Parmesan.

Chicken Tetrazzini

YIELD:
6 TO 8 SERVINGS

TIP: Use leftover turkey meat to make a Turkey Tetrazzini.

This classic, colorful, one-pot meal features chunks of juicy chicken and vegetables in a rich, creamy sauce, finished with a crisp, cheesy crumb topping.

FOR CHICKEN:

2 tablespoons (28 g) unsalted butter

3 carrots, split lengthwise and chopped

3 ribs celery, chopped

1 cup (160 g) chopped onion

2 cloves garlic, minced

2 cups (470 ml) reduced-sodium chicken broth

2 cups (470 ml) water

2 large (about 1 pound, or 454 g) boneless skinless chicken breasts, cut into bite-size pieces

1½ teaspoons salt

½ teaspoon dried marjoram

½ teaspoon freshly ground black pepper

1 package (12 ounces, or 340 g) rotini noodles

2 tablespoons (16 g) cornstarch

½ cup (120 ml) half-and-half

½ cup (65 g) frozen petite peas

FOR TOPPING:

1 cup (50 g) panko bread crumbs

½ cup (58 g) shredded Cheddar cheese

¼ cup (20 g) shredded Parmesan cheese

3 tablespoons (42 g) butter, melted

TO MAKE THE CHICKEN: Select Browning/Sauté and melt the butter in the pressure cooking pot. Add the carrots, celery, and onion. Sauté for about 3 minutes, stirring occasionally, until tender. Stir in the garlic and cook for 1 minute more. Add the chicken broth, water, diced chicken, salt, marjoram, and pepper. Stir in the rotini noodles. Lock the lid in place. Select High Pressure and 4 minutes cook time.

TO MAKE THE TOPPING: In a small bowl, stir together the panko, Cheddar, Parmesan, and melted butter. Set aside.

When the cook time ends, turn off the pressure cooker. Use a quick pressure release. When the valve drops, carefully remove the lid.

Preheat the broiler. Spray a 9 × 13-inch (23 × 33 cm) ovenproof dish with nonstick cooking spray. Set aside.

In a small bowl, whisk the cornstarch and half-and-half until smooth. Add the slurry to the pot. Select Simmer/Sauté and bring the liquid to a boil, stirring constantly. When the sauce thickens, stir in the peas to coat with the sauce. Pour the mixture into the prepared dish. Top with the panko mixture and broil for 3 to 5 minutes, or until golden-brown.

Braised Paprika Chicken

TIP: In the United States, most Hungarian paprika has a deep red color and a mild, sweet flavor.

...s quick weeknight meal combines chicken and a sweet paprika s...e and is served over egg noodles.

2½ ...nds (1 kg) boneless skinless ch...n thighs

1 tabl... ...on (8 g) sweet Hungarian papr... ...divided

2 tables... ...s (30 ml) canola oil

1 tablesp... (14 g) unsalted butter

1 large or... diced

1 can (14.5... ...ces, or 411 g) diced tomatoes, ...drained

½ cup (120 ... reduced-sodium chicken broth

1 teaspoon dried marjoram

1 teaspoon salt

½ teaspoon freshly ground black pepper

⅛ teaspoon red pepper flakes

2 tablespoons (16 g) cornstarch

2 tablespoons (30 ml) cold water

½ cup (115 g) sour cream

Cooked egg noodles, for serving

2 tablespoons (8 g) finely minced fresh parsley leaves, for serving

Season the chicken with 1 teaspoon paprika. Select Browning/Sauté to preheat the pressure cooking pot. When hot, add the canola oil and butter. When the butter melts, add 3 chicken thighs and sear briefly. Transfer to a cutting board and add another 3 thighs to the pot. Repeat until all the thighs are browned.

Add the onion to the cooking pot. Sauté for about 3 minutes until tender. Stir in the tomatoes, chicken broth, remaining 2 teaspoons paprika, marjoram, salt, pepper, and red pepper flakes.

Slice the chicken thighs into large bite-size pieces. Add the chicken and any accumulated juices to the pot and stir to combine. Lock the lid in place. Select High Pressure and 4 minutes cook time.

When the cook time ends, turn off the pressure cooker. Use a quick pressure release. When the valve drops, carefully remove the lid.

In a small bowl, whisk the cornstarch and cold water until smooth. Add the slurry to the pot. Select Simmer/Sauté and bring the sauce to a boil, stirring constantly until it thickens. Turn off the pressure cooker and stir in the sour cream. Serve over hot egg noodles and sprinkle with parsley.

Creamy Chicken and Broccoli over Rice

YIELD:
4 SERVINGS

TIP: This recipe can generally be made with frozen chicken breasts without adding any extra High Pressure cook time. Simply dice the chicken after you've released the pressure and return it to the pot to Simmer/Sauté for 1 to 3 minutes more until cooked through. Add the cornstarch slurry and continue as directed.

Chicken and broccoli in a creamy cheese sauce, served over fluffy white rice. This cheesy, family-friendly dish is a great way to get kids (and grown-ups) to eat their broccoli.

2 large (about 1 pound, or 454 g) boneless skinless chicken breasts

½ teaspoon salt, plus more for seasoning

½ teaspoon freshly ground black pepper, plus more for seasoning

1 tablespoon (15 ml) olive oil

1 tablespoon (14 g) unsalted butter

½ cup (80 g) chopped onion

1 can (14.5 fluid ounces, or 429 ml) reduced-sodium chicken broth

⅛ teaspoon red pepper flakes

1 tablespoon (1 g) dried parsley

2 tablespoons (16 g) cornstarch

2 tablespoons (30 ml) cold water

½ cup (4 ounces, or 113 g) light cream cheese, cubed

1 cup (115 g) shredded Cheddar cheese, plus more for serving

3 cups (213 g) chopped broccoli, lightly steamed

3 cups (495 g) prepared white rice, for serving

Season the chicken with salt and pepper to taste. Select Browning/Sauté and add the olive oil and butter to the pressure cooking pot. When the butter melts, add the chicken and sauté for 3 minutes, stirring occasionally. Transfer to a plate.

Add the onion to the cooking pot. Sauté for about 3 minutes, stirring occasionally, until the onion is tender. Stir in the chicken broth, salt, pepper, red pepper flakes, and parsley. Add the browned chicken. Lock the lid in place. Select High Pressure and 5 minutes cook time.

When the cook time ends, turn off the pressure cooker. Use a quick pressure release. When the valve drops, carefully remove the lid. Transfer the chicken to a cutting board and cut it into bite-size pieces.

In a small bowl, whisk the cornstarch and cold water until smooth. Select Simmer/Sauté and add the slurry to the pot, stirring constantly. Add the cream cheese and Cheddar, stirring until the cheese melts. Stir in the diced chicken and steamed broccoli. Serve over rice and garnish with more Cheddar, if desired.

Marinara Chicken with Melted Mozzarella

YIELD:
4 SERVINGS

....

TIP: This recipe is super quick to make. If you're serving it with pasta, have your pasta water boiling before you start the recipe.

A reader of my blog, *Pressure Cooking Today*, requested this marinara chicken recipe. Since I prefer homemade sauce, I include my own quick marina in this recipe. If you'd rather, substitute your favorite jarred sauce for the tomatoes and spices in the recipe.

4 large (about 2 pounds, or 907 g) boneless skinless chicken breasts
Salt, and freshly ground black pepper, for seasoning
1 tablespoon (15 ml) olive oil, plus more as needed
2 cloves garlic, minced or pressed

1 cup (235 ml) water
1 can (14.5 ounces, or 411 g) crushed tomatoes in purée
1 teaspoon dried basil
¼ teaspoon red pepper flakes
1 cup (150 g) grated low-fat mozzarella cheese

Season the chicken with salt and pepper. Select Browning/Sauté and add the olive oil to the pressure cooking pot. When the oil is hot, brown the chicken breasts in 2 batches for about 3 minutes per side. Transfer the browned chicken to a plate.

Add more oil, if needed, and the garlic. Sauté for 1 minute. Stir in the water, tomatoes, basil, and red pepper flakes. Add the chicken breasts to the cooking pot. Lock the lid in place. Select High Pressure and 5 minutes cook time.

When the cook time ends, turn off the pressure cooker. Use a quick pressure release. When the valve drops, carefully remove the lid. Use an instant-read thermometer to make sure the chicken is cooked to 165°F (74°C). If not, return the lid and cook on High Pressure for a few minutes more.

Preheat the broiler and spray a small glass casserole dish with nonstick cooking spray. Transfer the chicken from the cooking pot to the prepared casserole dish. Set aside.

Select Simmer/Sauté and cook the sauce until it reaches your desired consistency. Pour the sauce over the chicken. Sprinkle the mozzarella over the top and put the dish under the broiler until the cheese melts and starts to brown lightly. (Watch it closely—once it starts to brown, it will go quickly.)

Lemon-Rosemary Chicken

YIELD:
6 SERVINGS

TIP: My family likes the strong lemon flavor in this meal; if you prefer a lighter lemon flavor, adjust the ratio of lemon juice and chicken broth. Some lemons are juicer than others, but, typically, 1 lemon yields 3 tablespoons (45 ml) juice. There are 8 tablespoons in ½ cup (120 ml) lemon juice.

Chicken breasts quickly cooked in the pressure cooker are finished in a skillet to give it a golden color. It's draped with a light, lemon-herb sauce created from the cooking juices.

6 large boneless skinless chicken breasts (about 3 pounds, or 1.4 g)
Salt and freshly ground black pepper, for seasoning
2 tablespoons (30 ml) olive oil
2 cloves garlic, minced
½ cup (120 ml) reduced-sodium chicken broth

½ cup (120 ml) fresh lemon juice
1 tablespoon (2 g) minced fresh rosemary leaves, or 1 teaspoon (1 g) dried rosemary, crushed
2 tablespoons (16 g) cornstarch
3 tablespoons (45 ml) cold water
1 tablespoon (15 ml) vegetable oil
2 tablespoons (28 g) unsalted butter

Season the chicken generously with salt and pepper. Set aside. Select Browning/ Sauté to preheat the pressure cooking pot. When hot, add the olive oil and garlic. Sauté for 1 minute. Stir in the chicken broth, lemon juice, and rosemary. Add the chicken to the cooking pot. Lock the lid in place. Select High Pressure and 3 minutes cook time.

When the cook time ends, turn off the pressure cooker. Let the pressure release naturally for 5 minutes and finish with a quick pressure release. When the valve drops, carefully remove the lid. Transfer the chicken to a plate.

In a small bowl, whisk the cornstarch and cold water until smooth. Add the slurry to the pot. Select Simmer/Sauté and simmer, stirring constantly, until the sauce thickens. Salt and pepper to taste. Set aside.

In a large skillet or sauté pan over high heat, heat the vegetable oil and melt the butter. Add the chicken and fry for about 3 minutes per side until brown and the center of the chicken reads 165°F (74°C) on an instant-read thermometer. Serve the chicken with the lemon-rosemary sauce on top.

Southwestern Chicken Taco Bowls

YIELD:
6 SERVINGS

TIP: Quickly thaw frozen corn in a strainer by running cold water over it.

These taco bowls taste just like chicken tacos loaded with your favorite toppings—without the carbs from the tortillas.

1 tablespoon (15 ml) vegetable oil

1 large onion, diced

4 cloves garlic, minced or pressed

1 teaspoon chili powder

½ teaspoon ground cumin

½ teaspoon salt

¼ teaspoon freshly ground black pepper

2 large boneless skinless chicken breasts (about 1 pound, or 454 g), cut into 1-inch (2.5 cm) pieces

2 cans (10 ounces, or 284 g, each) diced tomatoes and green chilies

½ cup (120 ml) water

½ cup (93 g) long-grain white rice

1 cup (165 g) frozen corn, thawed

1 can (15 ounces, or 425 g) black beans, drained and rinsed

1 tablespoon (15 ml) fresh lime juice

2 tablespoons (2 g) chopped fresh cilantro leaves

Avocado, shredded cheese, and crushed tortilla chips, for serving

Select Browning/Sauté and add the vegetable oil to the pressure cooking pot. When the oil is hot, add the onion. Sauté for about 3 minutes until softened. Add the garlic and cook for 1 minute more.

In a large zipper bag, combine the chili powder, cumin, salt, and pepper. Add the chicken and toss to coat. Put the chicken in the cooking pot and sauté for 3 minutes, stirring occasionally. Stir in the tomatoes and green chilies, water, and rice. Lock the lid in place. Select High Pressure and 3 minutes cook time.

When the cook time ends, turn off the pressure cooker. Let the pressure release naturally for 7 minutes and finish with a quick pressure release. When the valve drops, carefully remove the lid. Select Simmer/Sauté and stir in the corn and black beans. Cook for about 3 minutes until the corn and beans are heated. Add the lime juice and cilantro. Season with salt and pepper to taste. Serve with your choice of toppings.

Bruschetta Chicken

YIELD:
4 SERVINGS

TIP: The main ingredients in Italian seasoning are basil, oregano, rosemary, and thyme. If you don't have Italian seasoning available, substitute ¼ teaspoon each.

Grape tomatoes are sweet and juicy year-round, so don't wait for summer to serve this dish.

FOR CHICKEN:

4 large boneless skinless chicken breasts (about 2 pounds, or 907 g)

Salt and freshly ground black pepper, for seasoning

2 tablespoons (30 ml) extra-virgin olive oil

3 cloves garlic, minced

½ cup (120 ml) reduced-sodium chicken broth

1 teaspoon Italian seasoning

¼ cup (25 g) grated Parmesan cheese

Balsamic vinegar, to taste

1 French baguette, thinly sliced, toasted

FOR BRUSCHETTA:

1 pint red grape tomatoes, quartered

2 tablespoons (30 ml) olive oil

2 tablespoons (5 g) fresh basil leaves, minced

2 cloves garlic, minced

¼ teaspoon salt

⅛ teaspoon freshly ground black pepper

TO MAKE THE CHICKEN: Season the chicken generously with salt and pepper. Select Browning/Sauté to preheat the pressure cooking pot. When hot, add the olive oil. Brown the chicken in 2 batches, cooking each batch for about 3 minutes per side. Transfer the browned chicken to a plate.

Add the garlic to the cooking pot and sauté for 1 minute. Stir in the chicken broth, Italian seasoning, and browned chicken. Lock the lid in place. Select High Pressure and 7 minutes cook time.

TO MAKE THE BRUSCHETTA: While the chicken cooks, in a large bowl, lightly toss the tomatoes, olive oil, basil, garlic, salt, and pepper. Cover and refrigerate until serving.

When the cook time ends, turn off the pressure cooker. Let the pressure release naturally for 5 minutes and finish with a quick pressure release. When the valve drops, carefully remove the lid. Transfer the chicken to a serving plate. Top each piece with some bruschetta, Parmesan, and a drizzle of balsamic vinegar. Serve with toasted baguette slices.

Beef and Broccoli

YIELD:
6 SERVINGS

TIP: You can use the pressure cooker two different ways to steam the broccoli for this recipe. Before browning the beef, place the broccoli in a steamer basket over 1 cup (235 ml) water. Lock the lid in place. Select High Pressure and 0 minutes cook time—the pressure cooker will come to pressure and then immediately release. Or, if you prefer, add the broccoli to the pot after pressure cooking and let it steam in the sauce with the lid on and with the cooker on the Keep Warm setting.

Thin-sliced beef and broccoli in a rich sauce that is salty and sweet—with a little heat from the red pepper flakes. Cooking inexpensive beef chuck in the pressure cooker tenderizes the meat, so it's not tough and chewy like stir-fried beef and broccoli can often be. This recipe also works well with flank steak or London broil.

1½ pounds (680 g) boneless beef chuck roast, well trimmed and sliced into thin strips

Salt and freshly ground black pepper, for seasoning

1 tablespoon (15 ml) vegetable oil

1 medium-size onion, finely chopped

4 cloves garlic, minced

¾ cup (175 ml) reduced-sodium beef broth

½ cup (120 ml) low-sodium soy sauce

⅓ cup (75 g) packed light brown sugar

2 tablespoons (30 ml) sesame oil

⅛ teaspoon red pepper flakes

3 tablespoons (24 g) cornstarch

3 tablespoons (45 ml) cold water

3 cups (213 g) chopped broccoli, lightly steamed

Cooked rice and toasted sesame seeds, for serving

Season the beef with salt and pepper. Select Browning/Sauté to preheat the pressure cooking pot. When hot, add the vegetable oil. In batches, quickly brown one side of the beef strips. Transfer the browned meat to a plate.

Add the onion to the pot. Sauté for 3 minutes until it starts to soften. Add the garlic and sauté for 1 minute more. Stir in the beef broth, soy sauce, brown sugar, sesame oil, and red pepper flakes, stirring until the sugar dissolves. Add the browned beef and any accumulated juices. Lock the lid in place. Select High Pressure and 12 minutes cook time.

When the cook time ends, turn off the pressure cooker. Use a quick pressure release. When the valve drops, carefully remove the lid.

In a small bowl, whisk the cornstarch and cold water until smooth. Select Simmer/Sauté and add the slurry to the pot, stirring constantly until the sauce comes to a boil and thickens. Stir in the steamed broccoli. Serve over hot, cooked rice and garnish with toasted sesame seeds, if desired.

Mongolian Beef

YIELD:
6 SERVINGS

TIP: You can also brown the beef whole and then thinly slice it to save time browning.

A pressure cooker version of a popular beef dish—thinly sliced flank steak cooked in a sweet, savory sauce until it's melt-in-your-mouth amazing. This is one of the most popular recipes on my blog, *Pressure Cooking Today*.

2 pounds (907 g) flank steak, cut into ¼-inch (0.6 cm) strips

Salt and freshly ground black pepper, for seasoning

1 tablespoon (15 ml) vegetable oil

4 cloves garlic, minced

½ cup (120 ml) low-sodium soy sauce

½ cup (120 ml) water

⅔ cup (150 g) packed light brown sugar

½ teaspoon minced peeled fresh ginger

2 tablespoons (16 g) cornstarch

3 tablespoons (45 ml) cold water

3 scallions, white and green parts, sliced into 1-inch (2.5 cm) pieces

Cooked rice, for serving

Season the steak with salt and pepper. Select Browning/Sauté to preheat the pressure cooking pot. When hot, add the vegetable oil. In batches, quickly brown one side of the steak strips. Transfer the browned meat to a plate.

Add the garlic and sauté for 1 minute. Stir in the soy sauce, water, brown sugar, and ginger, scraping up any browned bits from the bottom of the pot. Add the browned beef and any accumulated juices. Lock the lid in place. Select High Pressure and 12 minutes cook time.

When the cook time ends, turn off the pressure cooker. Use a quick pressure release. When the valve drops, carefully remove the lid.

In a small bowl, whisk the cornstarch and cold water until smooth. Add the slurry to the pot. Select Simmer/Sauté and bring the liquid to a boil, stirring constantly until the sauce thickens. Stir in the scallions. Serve over cooked rice.

Tamale Pie

TIP: If you don't have corn muffin mix on hand, make your own: Mix ¾ cup (84 g) all-purpose flour, ⅓ cup (47 g) cornmeal, 2 tablespoons (24 g) sugar, 1 tablespoon (14 g) baking powder, ¼ teaspoon salt, and 2 tablespoons (30 ml) vegetable oil.

This upside-down tamale pie is super easy to make using ingredients you probably have on hand.

1 package (8.5 ounces, or 241 g) corn muffin mix
½ cup (120 ml) milk
1 large egg
1 pound (454 g) lean ground beef
1 tablespoon (15 ml) vegetable oil
½ cup (80 g) finely chopped onion
1 teaspoon garlic powder
1 teaspoon chili powder

1 teaspoon ground cumin
½ teaspoon salt
1 can (14.5 ounces, or 411 g) diced tomatoes, drained
1 can (4.5 ounces, or 128 g) chopped green chilies, drained
1 cup (165 g) frozen corn
1 cup (115 g) shredded Cheddar cheese

Spray a 1½-quart (1.4 L) baking dish or a 7-inch (18 cm) round cake pan with nonstick cooking spray. In a large bowl, stir together the muffin mix, milk, and egg until just blended. Spoon the batter into the prepared pan and set aside.

Select Browning/Sauté and when hot, add the ground beef. Cook for about 5 minutes, stirring occasionally, until the meat is crumbled and no longer pink. Transfer to a paper towel–lined plate. Drain any excess fat from the pot.

Add the vegetable oil and onion to the cooking pot. Sauté for about 3 minutes until tender. Add the ground beef, garlic powder, chili powder, cumin, and salt. Sauté for 1 minute more. Turn off the pressure cooker and stir in the tomatoes, green chilies, and corn. Gently spoon the mixture over the cornbread batter.

Wipe out the cooking pot. Pour 1 cup (235 ml) water into the pot and place a trivet in the bottom. Center the pan on a sling and carefully lower the pan onto the trivet. Lock the lid in place. Select High Pressure and 10 minutes cook time.

When the cook time ends, turn off the pressure cooker. Let the pressure release naturally for 5 minutes and finish with a quick pressure release. When the valve drops, carefully remove the lid. Sprinkle the Cheddar on top of the tamale pie. Put the lid back on the pressure cooker until the cheese melts, about 3 minutes. Carefully remove pan from the pressure cooker and serve immediately.

Stuffed Green Pepper Casserole

YIELD:
6 SERVINGS

TIP: If you prefer
not to dirty 2 dishes,
sprinkle the cheese
on the casserole in
the pressure cooking
pot. Put the lid on
and let the steam
from the hot casse-
role melt the cheese.

This casserole has all the flavors of stuffed green peppers. My sweet
friend Genene and I adapted this recipe from one that takes more
than an hour to make in the oven.

1 pound (454 g) lean ground beef
½ cup (80 g) chopped onion
2 cloves garlic, minced
2 large green bell peppers, chopped
Handful fresh spinach, coarsely chopped
1 can (14.5 ounces, or 411 g) diced tomatoes with juices
1 can (8 fluid ounces, or 235 ml) tomato sauce
½ cup (120 ml) reduced-sodium beef broth
½ cup (93 g) long-grain white rice
1 tablespoon (15 ml) Worcestershire sauce
½ teaspoon salt
¼ teaspoon freshly ground black pepper
1 cup (115 g) shredded mozzarella cheese

Select Browning/Sauté to preheat the pressure cooking pot. When hot, add the
ground beef and onion. Sauté for about 5 minutes, stirring occasionally, until the
beef is crumbled and browned. Add the garlic and sauté for 1 minute more. Stir in
the bell peppers, spinach, tomatoes, tomato sauce, beef broth, rice, Worcestershire
sauce, salt, and pepper. Lock the lid in place. Select High Pressure and 4 minutes
cook time.

When the cook time ends, turn off the pressure cooker. Use a natural release for
10 minutes and finish with a quick pressure release. When the valve drops, carefully
remove the lid. Pour the casserole into an ovenproof baking dish. Sprinkle the
mozzarella on top and broil until the cheese melts and starts to brown.

Creamy Sausage Tortellini

YIELD:
6 SERVINGS

....

TIP: I use cheese
tortellini, but, really,
almost any flavor
works.

Recipe-ready frozen tortellini is the key ingredient in this easy, yet
impressive, one-pot pasta meal.

1 pound (454 g) country-style sausage
½ cup (120 ml) reduced-sodium chicken broth
2 cans (14.5 ounces, or 411 g, each) diced tomatoes
1 teaspoon dried basil
½ teaspoon garlic salt
½ teaspoon onion powder
2 cups (60 g) fresh baby spinach
1 package (19 ounces, or 540 g) frozen tortellini
2 tablespoons (16 g) cornstarch
2 tablespoons (30 ml) cold water
4 ounces (113 g) cream cheese, cut into 1-inch (2.5 cm) cubes

Select Browning/Sauté to preheat the pressure cooking pot. When hot, add the
sausage. Cook for 3 to 5 minutes until browned and crumbled. Transfer to a paper
towel–lined plate. Set aside. Drain any excess fat from the pot.

Add the chicken broth to deglaze the pot, scraping up any browned bits from the
bottom. Stir in the tomatoes, basil, garlic salt, and onion powder. Add the browned
sausage, spinach, and tortellini. Stir to combine. Lock the lid in place. Select High
Pressure and 2 minutes cook time.

When the cook time ends, turn off the pressure cooker. Use a quick pressure release.
When the valve drops, carefully remove the lid.

In a small bowl, whisk the cornstarch and cold water until smooth. Select Simmer/
Sauté and add the slurry to the pot, stirring constantly. Add the cream cheese and
stir until it melts.

Linguine and Clam Sauce

YIELD:
6 SERVINGS

TIP: Don't skip the Parmesan at the end; it really pulls the dish together.

My family loves clams in a creamy white sauce. I keep canned clams in the pantry so that I can make this recipe on those nights when I need something in a hurry without a lot of fuss.

2 tablespoons (28 g) unsalted butter
1 tablespoon (15 ml) olive oil
2 tablespoons (20 g) minced garlic
1/8 teaspoon red pepper flakes
2 cans (6.5 ounces, or 184 g, each) chopped clams in juice, strained, juice reserved
2 cups (470 ml) water, plus more as needed
1 pound (454 g) linguine, broken in half
1 cup (235 ml) heavy cream
2 tablespoons (8 g) chopped fresh parsley leaves
Salt and freshly ground black pepper, for seasoning
Freshly grated Parmesan cheese, for serving

Select Browning/Sauté and add the butter and olive oil to the pressure cooking pot. When the butter melts, add the garlic and red pepper flakes. Sauté for 1 minute. Stir in the reserved clam juice and water. Add the linguine. If needed, add more water to just cover the linguine—do not stir. Lock the lid in place. Select High Pressure and 5 minutes cook time.

When the cook time ends, turn off the pressure cooker. Let the pressure release naturally for 2 minutes and finish with a quick pressure release. When the valve drops, carefully remove the lid. Stir the linguine with a fork to separate the strands. Taste for doneness. If needed, select Simmer/Sauté and cook for a few minutes more until the desired tenderness. Turn off the pressure cooker.

Stir in the heavy cream, clams, and parsley. Season with salt and pepper to taste. Serve topped with the Parmesan.

Bow Tie Pasta with Sausage

YIELD:
6 SERVINGS

....

TIP: If you don't have bow tie pasta on hand, or if you'd like to use whole-wheat or gluten-free pasta, you'll need to adjust the cook time. Pressure cook the pasta for 1 minute less than half of the cook time listed on the package.

This filling pasta dish is the perfect busy weeknight meal—quick, easy, and delicious! It's a one-pot meal you'll make again and again.

1 tablespoon (15 ml) olive oil

1 pound (454 g) lean ground sausage

1 small onion, finely chopped

2 cloves garlic, minced or pressed

1 can (28 ounces, or 794 g) crushed tomatoes in purée

1 teaspoon dried basil

¼ teaspoon salt, plus more as needed

⅛ teaspoon red pepper flakes

3½ cups (840 ml) water

1 package (1 pound, or 454 g) bow tie pasta (also called farfalle)

Freshly ground black pepper, for seasoning

Select Browning/Sauté and add the olive oil to the pressure cooking pot. When the oil is hot, add the sausage, onion, and garlic. Sauté for about 10 minutes until the meat is no longer pink and the onion is tender. Drain, if needed. Stir in the tomatoes, basil, salt, red pepper flakes, water, and pasta.

Lock the lid in place. Select High Pressure and 5 minutes cook time.

When the cook time ends, turn off the pressure cooker. Use a quick pressure release. When the valve drops, carefully remove the lid and stir the mixture. Select Simmer/Sauté and, if needed, cook for 2 to 5 minutes more, stirring often, until the pasta is tender. Season with salt and pepper to taste.

Monterey Chicken Pasta

YIELD:

6 TO 8 SERVINGS

TIP: Fusili pasta is a fun, cork-screw shaped pasta. It's great for this dish because the ridges hold the sauce well, giving you more flavor in each bite, but if you don't have it on-hand, feel free to use a different type of pasta.

Chicken, bacon, barbecue sauce, and Monterey Jack cheese make this a tangy pasta version of a popular restaurant sandwich.

8 slices bacon, diced
1 small onion, finely chopped
1 teaspoon minced garlic
1 can (14.5 fluid ounces, or 429 ml)
  reduced-sodium chicken broth
1/3 cup (85 g) barbecue sauce
3 tablespoons (60 g) honey
3 tablespoons (45 ml) low-sodium soy sauce
2 large boneless skinless chicken breasts (about 1 pound, or 454 g),
  cut into bite-size pieces
1 package (1 pound, or 454 g) fusilli pasta
1 quart (946 ml) water
2 cups (230 g) shredded Monterey Jack cheese
1/4 cup (15 g) fresh parsley leaves, chopped
Salt and freshly ground black pepper, for seasoning

Select Browning/Sauté and add the bacon to the pressure cooking pot. Fry for about 5 minutes until crisp, stirring frequently. Transfer the bacon to a paper towel–lined plate, leaving the bacon fat in the pot.

Add the onion. Sauté for 3 minutes. Add the garlic and sauté for 1 minute more. Stir in the chicken broth, barbecue sauce, honey, and soy sauce. Add the chicken and pasta and stir to combine. Add enough water to cover the pasta, about 1 quart (946 ml). Lock the lid in place. Select High Pressure and 5 minutes cook time.

When the cook time ends, turn off the pressure cooker. Use a quick pressure release, or if necessary, use an intermittent release to prevent liquid from coming out of the valve. When the valve drops, carefully remove the lid. Stir the mixture and taste for doneness. If needed, select Simmer/Sauté and cook for 2 to 5 minutes more, stirring often, until the pasta is tender. Stir in the Monterey Jack a little at a time until it melts. Stir in the bacon and parsley. Season with salt and pepper to taste.

Pasta Primavera

YIELD:
6 TO 8 SERVINGS

TIP: Add halved red and yellow cherry tomatoes for an extra pop of color and burst of flavor.

This fresh-tasting pasta primavera pairs pasta and spring vegetables in a creamy lemon-Parmesan sauce. It is a great meatless meal, though my husband views it as a perfect side for grilled chicken.

3 tablespoons (45 ml) vegetable oil, divided

1 pound (454 g) thin asparagus spears, cut into 1-inch (2.5 cm) pieces

1 large onion, diced

2 cloves garlic, minced

5 cups (1.2 L) reduced-sodium chicken broth

1 package (1 pound, or 454 g) bow tie pasta

½ teaspoon salt, plus more for seasoning

¼ teaspoon freshly ground black pepper, plus more for seasoning

1 cup (130 g) frozen peas

1 tablespoon (8 g) cornstarch

½ cup (120 ml) half-and-half

1 tablespoon (6 g) lemon zest

2 tablespoons (8 g) chopped fresh parsley leaves

½ cup (50 g) grated Parmesan cheese, plus more for serving

Select Browning/Sauté to preheat the pressure cooking pot. When hot, add 1 tablespoon (15 ml) vegetable oil. When the oil is hot, add the asparagus. Sauté for about 2 minutes, stirring frequently, until the asparagus starts to get tender. Transfer the asparagus to a plate and cover with aluminum foil to keep warm.

Add the remaining 2 tablespoons (30 ml) vegetable oil and the onion to the pot. Sauté for about 3 minutes until tender. Add the garlic and sauté for 1 minute more. Stir in the chicken broth, pasta, salt, and pepper. Lock the lid in place. Select High Pressure and 5 minutes cook time.

When the cook time ends, turn off the pressure cooker. Let the pressure release naturally for 2 minutes and finish with a quick pressure release. When the valve drops, carefully remove the lid. Select Simmer/Sauté and add the peas. Cook for about 1 minute, stirring often, until the peas are hot and pasta is tender.

In a small bowl, whisk the cornstarch and half-and-half until smooth. Add the slurry to the pot. Cook, stirring constantly, until the sauce thickens. Mix in the lemon zest, parsley, Parmesan, and cooked asparagus. Season with salt and pepper to taste and top with additional Parmesan.

Pepperoni Pizza Pasta

YIELD:
6 TO 8 SERVINGS

TIP: Feel free to include your favorite pizza toppings, such as diced green bell peppers, Canadian bacon, or sausage.

The whole family will come to the table for this fun mash-up of pizza and pasta (with a few hidden veggies inside).

2 tablespoons (30 ml) olive oil, divided
8 ounces (227 g) sliced mushrooms
1 cup (160 g) diced onion
2 cloves garlic, diced
3 cups (720 ml) water
1 can (15 fluid ounces, or 444 ml) tomato sauce
1 can (14.5 ounces, or 411 g) diced tomatoes
½ cup (55 g) finely shredded carrots

½ teaspoon Italian seasoning
½ teaspoon salt
Dash red pepper flakes
1 package (1 pound, or 454 g) medium-size shell pasta
½ cup (80 g) sliced black olives
3 ounces (85 g) sliced pepperoni
1 (8-ounce, or 227 g) package shredded mozzarella cheese
½ cup (50 g) grated Parmesan cheese

Spray a 9 × 13-inch (23 × 33 cm) baking dish with nonstick cooking spray. Set aside. Preheat the broiler.

Select Browning/Sauté and, when hot, add 1 tablespoon (15 ml) olive oil. Add half the mushrooms and sauté for about 5 minutes until browned. Transfer the mushrooms to a plate and cover. Repeat with the remaining mushrooms.

Add the remaining 1 tablespoon (15 ml) olive oil and the onion to the cooking pot. Sauté for about 3 minutes until tender. Add the garlic and sauté for 1 minute more. Stir in the water, tomato sauce, tomatoes, carrots, Italian seasoning, salt, and red pepper flakes. Add the pasta. Lock the lid in place. Select High Pressure and 3 minutes cook time. When the cook time ends, turn off the pressure cooker. Use a quick pressure release. When the valve drops, carefully remove the lid.

Select Simmer/Sauté. Add the mushrooms and the olives and pepperoni. Cook for about 1 minute, stirring often, until the pasta is tender. Turn off the pressure cooker and pour the pasta into the prepared dish. Sprinkle the mozzarella and Parmesan over the top. Broil until the cheeses melt and start to brown.

Italian Sausage and Spinach Risotto

YIELD:
8 SERVINGS

TIP: Arborio rice is an Italian short-grain rice with a higher starch content, making it creamy as it cooks.

A creamy, one-pot risotto loaded with sausage, tomatoes, and spinach—but not a drop of cream.

1 pound (454 g) mild Italian sausage, casings removed
1 tablespoon (15 ml) olive oil
½ cup (80 g) finely diced onion
2 cloves garlic, minced
2 cups (384 g) arborio rice
1 can (14.5 ounces, or 411 g) diced tomatoes
5 cups (1.2 L) reduced-sodium chicken broth, divided
1 teaspoon dried basil
⅓ cup (33 g) grated Parmesan cheese, plus more for serving
1 package (6 ounces, or 170 g) fresh baby spinach, coarsely chopped
Salt and freshly ground black pepper, for seasoning

Select Browning/Sauté to preheat the pressure cooking pot. When hot, add the sausage. Cook for about 5 minutes, breaking it up as it cooks, until browned and cooked through. Transfer the sausage to a paper towel–lined plate. Drain any excess fat from the pot.

Add the olive oil and onion to the cooking pot. Sauté for about 3 minutes until tender. Add the garlic and sauté for 1 minute more. Stir in the rice and cook for about 2 minutes, stirring frequently, until opaque. Add the sausage. Stir in the tomatoes, 4 cups (946 ml) chicken broth, and the basil. Lock the lid in place. Select High Pressure and 6 minutes cook time.

When the cook time ends, turn off the pressure cooker. Use a quick pressure release. When the valve drops, carefully remove the lid. Select Simmer/Sauté and stir in the remaining 1 cup (235 ml) chicken broth. Check the rice for doneness; if needed, continue simmering and stirring until tender. Stir in the Parmesan and spinach. Cook for about 1 minute until wilted. Season with salt and pepper to taste. Serve topped with more Parmesan.

Cheeseburger Macaroni Casserole

YIELD:

8 SERVINGS

TIP: If you prefer to use dried parsley, add it with the ingredients before pressure cooking. You can also mix up the cheese—my family prefers this dish with mozzarella, though it's a little messier to eat.

This family-size casserole is great to feed a crowd in a hurry, and you can't beat the flavor!

2 pounds (907 g) ground beef
2 tablespoons (30 ml) vegetable oil
1 cup (160 g) diced onion
2 cloves garlic, minced
3 cups (720 ml) reduced-sodium beef broth
2 cups (470 ml) water
1 pound (454 g) elbow macaroni, uncooked
1 teaspoon salt, plus more as needed
½ teaspoon freshly ground black pepper, plus more as needed
Dash cayenne pepper
½ cup (120 ml) milk
4 cups (460 g) shredded Colby Jack cheese
2 tablespoons (8 g) chopped fresh parsley leaves

Select Browning/Sauté to preheat the pressure cooking pot. When hot, add the ground beef. Cook for about 5 minutes, stirring occasionally, until the meat is crumbled and no longer pink. Transfer the beef to a paper towel–lined plate. Drain any excess fat from the pot.

Add the vegetable oil and onion to the cooking pot. Sauté for about 3 minutes until tender. Add the garlic and sauté for 1 minute more. Stir in the beef broth, water, ground beef, macaroni, salt, pepper, and cayenne. Lock the lid in place. Select High Pressure and 4 minutes cook time.

When the cook time ends, turn off the pressure cooker. Use a quick pressure release. When the valve drops, carefully remove the lid. Stir the mixture. Select Simmer/Sauté and add the milk and Colby Jack 1 cup (115 g) at a time, stirring until the cheese melts before adding the next cup. Stir until the pasta is tender, about 2 minutes. Stir in the parsley. Season with salt and pepper to taste.

Asian Beef, Snow Peas, and Mushrooms

YIELD:
6 SERVINGS

TIP: Look for chili-garlic sauce in the Asian section at the market, usually with a bright green lid. It's a chili sauce similar to Sriracha, but chunkier and more scoopable with a stronger garlic flavor.

A lightly sweet, not-too-spicy Asian beef dish loaded with vegetables. Adjust the spice level with more or less chili-garlic sauce.

¼ cup (60 ml) vegetable oil, divided

1 pound (454 g) snow peas

1 package (8 ounces, or 227 g) white mushrooms, sliced

1 pound (454 g) top sirloin steak, cut into ¼-inch -thick (0.6 cm) slices

Freshly ground black pepper, for seasoning

½ cup (120 ml) low-sodium soy sauce

½ cup (120 ml) reduced-sodium beef broth

2 tablespoons (30 g) packed light brown sugar

1 tablespoon (8 g) grated peeled fresh ginger

1½ teaspoons chili-garlic sauce

2 tablespoons (16 g) cornstarch

2 tablespoons (30 ml) cold water

Cooked rice and toasted sesame seeds, for serving

Select Browning/Sauté to preheat the pressure cooking pot. When hot, add 2 tablespoons (30 ml) vegetable oil, the snow peas, and mushrooms. Stir-fry for 5 to 7 minutes until tender. Transfer the vegetables to a paper towel–lined plate.

Lightly season the steak with pepper. Add the remaining 2 tablespoons (30 ml) vegetable oil to the pot. Working in batches, brown one side of the beef strips. Transfer the browned meat to a plate.

Add the soy sauce, beef broth, brown sugar, ginger, and chili-garlic sauce to the cooking pot. Stir in the browned beef and any accumulated juices. Lock the lid in place. Select High Pressure and 12 minutes cook time.

When the cook time ends, turn off the pressure cooker. Use a quick pressure release. When the valve drops, carefully remove the lid.

In a small bowl, whisk the cornstarch and cold water until smooth. Select Simmer/Sauté and add the slurry to the pot, stirring constantly until the sauce comes to a boil and thickens. Stir in the snow peas and mushrooms. Serve over rice and garnish with toasted sesame seeds, if desired.

Game Day Potatoes

YIELD:
6 SERVINGS

TIP: The potatoes cook best when they're in cut into uniform sizes. I first halve the potato lengthwise and cut each half into thirds lengthwise—similar in shape to large steak fries.

These potatoes are perfect to serve for the big game—or any day you're craving something cheesy and delicious.

1 pound (454 g) extra-lean ground beef
2 teaspoons chili powder
1 teaspoon onion powder
½ teaspoon garlic powder
½ teaspoon ground cumin
¼ teaspoon salt
Dash cayenne pepper
6 medium-size russet potatoes, cut into wedges
3 cups (340 g) shredded Cheddar cheese
Sour cream, scallions, olives, and hot sauce, for topping

Select Browning/Sauté to preheat the pressure cooking pot. When hot, add the ground beef. Cook for about 5 minutes, stirring occasionally, until the meat is crumbled and no longer pink. Add the chili powder, onion powder, garlic powder, cumin, salt, and cayenne. Cook for 1 minute more. Transfer the beef to a bowl.

Wipe out the pressure cooking pot. Pour 1 cup (235 ml) water into the pot and place a steamer basket in it. Add the potato wedges. Lock the lid in place. Select High Pressure and 5 minutes cook time.

When the cook time ends, turn off the pressure cooker. Use a quick pressure release. When the valve drops, carefully remove the lid. Check the potatoes to make sure they're tender; if they need more time, put the lid back on and let them steam for 1 to 2 minutes more.

Preheat the broiler.

Spread the potatoes into a single layer on an aluminum foil-lined baking sheet. Sprinkle the seasoned ground beef evenly on top. Sprinkle the Cheddar evenly on top of the meat. Broil until the cheese melts and starts to brown. Serve topped with sour cream, scallions, olives, and hot sauce, if desired.

Chicken Lo Mein

YIELD:
6 SERVINGS

....

TIP: I use only a small amount of Sriracha in this recipe to keep things mild. Those of us who like things a little hotter can sprinkle more on our individual servings.

Kids don't always like Chinese food, but it's a hit when you add long slurp-y noodles. When I made this for my grandson, he told me he liked it even better than the lo mein from our favorite restaurant.

2 large boneless skinless chicken breasts (about 1 pound, or 454 g)

1 package (1 pound, or 454 g) uncooked spaghetti, broken in half

¼ cup (60 ml) vegetable oil, divided

1½ quarts (1.4 L) water

1 large onion, diced

1 large carrot, split lengthwise and sliced

1 large rib celery, split lengthwise and sliced

2 cloves garlic, minced

1 cup (235 ml) reduced-sodium chicken broth

⅓ cup (78 ml) low-sodium soy sauce

2 tablespoons (30 g) packed light brown sugar

½ teaspoon ground ginger

¼ teaspoon Sriracha

1 can (14 ounces, or 397 g) mixed Chinese vegetables, drained

2 tablespoons (16 g) cornstarch

3 tablespoons (45 ml) cold water

2 scallions, white and green parts, chopped, for serving

Add the chicken to the pressure cooking pot and top it with the spaghetti. Add 2 tablespoons (30 ml) vegetable oil and the water to cover the spaghetti. Lock the lid in place. Select High Pressure and 4 minutes cook time.

When the cook time ends, turn off the pressure cooker. Let the pressure release naturally for 4 minutes and finish with a quick pressure release. When the valve drops, carefully remove the lid. Transfer the chicken to a cutting board and cut it into bite-size pieces. Drain the spaghetti.

Heat a wok, stir-fry pan, or large skillet over medium-high heat. Add the remaining 2 tablespoons (30 ml) vegetable oil and the onion. Sauté for about 3 minutes until the onion starts to soften. Add the carrot, celery, and garlic. Sauté for 3 minutes more. Stir in the chicken broth, soy sauce, brown sugar, ginger, and Sriracha. Stir in the chicken and Chinese vegetables.

In a small bowl, whisk the cornstarch and cold water until smooth. Stir the slurry into the wok and simmer until the sauce is thick and syrupy. Add the spaghetti and mix with the chicken, vegetables, and sauce. Serve topped with scallions.

Cashew Chicken

YIELD:
6 SERVINGS

TIP: I like to use cashew halves in this recipe so that you get a cashew in every bite. If you have whole cashews, break them in half.

My boys are crazy about cashews, so they love the crunchy cashews mixed with the juicy chicken in a sweet, not-too-spicy sauce.

1½ pounds (680 g) boneless skinless chicken breasts, diced into bite-size peices
Freshly ground black pepper, for seasoning
1 tablespoon (15 ml) vegetable oil
¼ cup (60 ml) reduced-sodium chicken broth
¼ cup (60 ml) low-sodium soy sauce
3 tablespoons (60 g) honey
2 tablespoons (30 ml) rice vinegar
½ teaspoon chili-garlic sauce
2 tablespoons (16 g) cornstarch
2 tablespoons (30 ml) cold water
½ cup (68 g) roasted cashew halves
Prepared rice, for serving
4 scallions, white and green parts, sliced, for serving

Lightly season the chicken with pepper. Select Browning/Sauté to preheat the pressure cooking pot. When hot, add the vegetable oil and chicken. Sauté for about 3 minutes. Stir in the chicken broth, soy sauce, honey, rice vinegar, and chili-garlic sauce. Lock the lid in place. Select High Pressure and 3 minutes cook time.

When the cook time ends, turn off the pressure cooker. Use a quick pressure release. When the valve drops, carefully remove the lid.

In a small bowl, whisk the cornstarch and cold water until smooth. Gradually add the slurry to the pot. Select Simmer/Sauté and simmer, stirring constantly, until the sauce thickens. Stir in the cashews and simmer for 2 minutes more. Serve over rice, if desired, and garnish with scallions.

Kung Pao Chicken

YIELD:
6 SERVINGS

....

TIP: I keep a container of dry-roasted salted peanuts in the pantry for snacks and use those in this recipe; if you prefer, use unsalted peanuts.

A slightly spicy Kung Pao Chicken with colorful vegetables, red pepper flakes, and crunchy peanuts. Substitute whole dried chilies for the red pepper flakes for an extra pop of color and heat.

1 tablespoon (15 ml) sesame oil

3 large cloves garlic, minced

2 teaspoons grated peeled fresh ginger

½ teaspoon red pepper flakes

⅓ cup (78 ml) low-sodium soy sauce

½ cup (120 ml) reduced-sodium chicken broth

2 tablespoons (30 ml) seasoned rice vinegar

2 teaspoons sugar

3 boneless skinless chicken breasts (about 1½ pound, or 680 g), diced into bite-size pieces

3 tablespoons (24 g) cornstarch

3 tablespoons (45 ml) cold water

1 cup (130 g) sliced carrots

1½ cups (93 g) snow peas

6 scallions, white and green parts, chopped

½ cup (75 g) roasted peanuts, chopped

Cooked rice or noodles, for serving

Select Browning/Sauté and add the sesame oil, garlic, ginger, and red pepper flakes to the pressure cooking pot. Stir-fry for 30 seconds, stirring constantly. Stir in the soy sauce, chicken broth, rice vinegar, and sugar. Add the chicken and stir to combine. Lock the lid in place. Select High Pressure and 3 minutes cook time.

When the cook time ends, turn off the pressure cooker. Use a quick pressure release. When the valve drops, carefully remove the lid.

In a small bowl, whisk the cornstarch and cold water until smooth. Add the slurry to the pot. Select Simmer/Sauté and simmer, stirring constantly, until the sauce thickens. Stir in the carrots and snow peas and simmer for about 5 minutes until tender. Stir in the scallions, leaving a few for garnishing, and the peanuts. Serve over rice or noodles, if desired, and top with the remaining scallions.

Chicken Fettuccine Alfredo

YIELD:
6 SERVINGS

TIP: When browning meat, it's important to pat the meat dry with paper towels so the meat browns and doesn't steam.

When we go out to an Italian restaurant, my boys always order Chicken Fettuccine Alfredo. With this pressure cooker version, I can make it at home for a fraction of the cost of eating out.

2 large boneless skinless chicken breasts (about 1 pound, or 454 g)
1 teaspoon salt, plus more for seasoning
Freshly ground black pepper, for seasoning
¼ cup (56 g) unsalted butter
3 cloves garlic, minced
4 cups (955 ml) water, divided

1 pound (454 g) fettuccine
1 cup (100 g) grated Parmesan cheese, plus more for serving
1 cup (235 ml) heavy cream
¼ cup (15 g) chopped fresh flat-leaf parsley leaves (optional)
3 tablespoons (24 g) cornstarch
3 tablespoons (45 ml) cold water

Generously season the chicken with salt and pepper. Select Browning/Sauté to preheat the pressure cooking pot. When hot, add the butter to melt. Add the chicken. Cook for about 3 minutes per side until browned. Transfer the chicken to a plate.

Add the garlic to the pot and sauté for 1 minute. Add 1 cup (235 ml) water to deglaze the pot, scraping up any browned bits from the bottom. Stir in the salt. Add the chicken to the pot. Place the fettuccine on the chicken and add enough of the remaining 3 cups (720 ml) water to just cover the pasta. Lock the lid in place. Select High Pressure and 5 minutes cook time.

When the cook time ends, turn off the pressure cooker. Use a quick pressure release. When the valve drops, carefully remove the lid. Transfer the chicken to a cutting board and cut it into strips. Stir the pasta. If needed, select Simmer/Sauté and continue to cook, stirring often, until the fettuccine is tender. Stir in the Parmesan a little at a time until melted. Stir in the heavy cream and parsley.

In a small bowl, whisk the cornstarch and cold water until smooth. Select Simmer/Sauté and add the slurry to the pot, stirring constantly until the sauce thickens. Stir in the sliced chicken and season with additional salt and pepper to taste.

Lemon Chicken Scaloppini

YIELD:
6 SERVINGS

TIP: If you prefer, you can buy recipe-ready chicken cutlets at the grocery store or ask the butcher to cut the breasts into cutlets for you.

This dish features a flavorful lemon, caper, white wine sauce that is lick-your-plate delicious!

3 large boneless skinless chicken breasts (about 1½ pounds, or 680 g), halved horizontally into 6 thin cutlets

Salt and freshly ground black pepper, for seasoning

2 tablespoons (28 g) unsalted butter, divided

2 tablespoons (30 ml) olive oil, divided

¼ cup (60 ml) white wine

1¼ cups (295 ml) reduced-sodium chicken broth

1 tablespoon (8 g) cornstarch

2 tablespoons (30 ml) cold water

2 tablespoons (17 g) capers, drained

1 small lemon, thinly sliced

2 tablespoons (8 g) finely chopped fresh parsley leaves

Cooked angel hair pasta or spaghetti, for serving

Generously season the chicken with salt and pepper. Select Browning/Sauté to preheat the pressure cooking pot. When hot, add 1 tablespoon (14 g) butter and 1 tablespoon (15 ml) olive oil. When the butter melts, add 3 chicken breast cutlets. Cook for about 3 minutes to brown on one side. Transfer to a plate. Repeat with the remaining butter, olive oil, and chicken breast cutlets.

Add the white wine to the cooking pot to deglaze, scraping up any browned bits from the bottom. Let the wine simmer until reduced by half. Add the chicken broth and browned chicken along with any accumulated juices to the pot. Lock the lid in place. Select High Pressure and 2 minutes cook time.

When the cook time ends, turn off the pressure cooker. Use a quick pressure release. When the valve drops, carefully remove the lid. Transfer the chicken to a plate.

In a small bowl, whisk the cornstarch and cold water until smooth. Add the slurry to the pot. Select Simmer/Sauté and bring the sauce to a boil, stirring constantly until it thickens. Stir in the capers and lemon slices. Return the chicken to the pot and stir to coat with the sauce. Season with salt and pepper to taste. Serve over angel hair pasta or spaghetti, if desired, garnished with chopped parsley.

Spicy-Cheesy Chicken Spaghetti

YIELD:
6 SERVINGS

....

TIP: I prefer using Ro-Tel mild diced tomatoes and green chilies, but if you prefer it even milder, reduce the chili powder. If you like things a little spicier, use Ro-Tel Original.

A flavorful fusion of Italian and Mexican. This recipe is super easy. You cook the spaghetti, chicken, and cheesy, delicious sauce all in one pot!

3 cups (720 ml) reduced-sodium chicken broth

1 can (10 ounces, or 284 g) diced tomatoes and green chilies

2 tablespoons (30 ml) vegetable oil

1 teaspoon chili powder

1 teaspoon garlic powder

1 teaspoon salt

2 large boneless skinless chicken breasts (about 1 pound, or 454 g)

1 pound (454 g) spaghetti, broken in half

1 package (8 ounces, or 227 g) cream cheese, cut into small cubes

1 cup (225 g) shredded Mexican cheese blend

2 tablespoons (2 g) chopped fresh cilantro leaves

In the pressure cooking pot, stir together the chicken broth, tomatoes and green chilies, vegetable oil, chili powder, garlic powder, and salt. Add the chicken and top with the spaghetti. Lock the lid in place. Select High Pressure and 4 minutes cook time.

When the cook time ends, turn off the pressure cooker. Let the pressure release naturally for 2 minutes and finish with a quick pressure release. When the valve drops, carefully remove the lid. Transfer the chicken to a cutting board and cut it into bite-size pieces. Return the chicken to the pot and stir to combine.

Add the cream cheese to the spaghetti and stir until melted. Add the Mexican cheese a handful at a time and stir until melted. Serve topped with cilantro.

Tuscan Garlic Chicken Fettuccine

YIELD:
6 SERVINGS

TIP: I use sundried tomatoes in oil for this recipe. You could use dry-packed sundried tomatoes if you prefer. Hydrate in a little warm water to plump them before chopping.

You'll enjoy this tempting chicken dish in a rich, colorful, creamy garlic-Parmesan sauce served over fettuccine.

3 large boneless skinless chicken breasts (about 1½ pounds, or 680 g), cut into bite-size pieces

Salt and freshly ground black pepper, for seasoning

2 tablespoons (30 ml) olive oil

1 tablespoon (10 g) minced or pressed garlic (about 8 cloves)

1½ cups (360 ml) reduced-sodium chicken broth

½ teaspoon dried basil

½ teaspoon Italian seasoning

⅛ teaspoon red pepper flakes

2 tablespoons (16 g) cornstarch

2 tablespoons (30 ml) cold water

1 cup (100 g) grated Parmesan cheese

½ cup (120 ml) heavy cream

2 cups (60 g) fresh spinach

¼ cup (14 g) sun-dried tomatoes packed in oil, chopped

1 pound (454 g) fettuccine, prepared according to package directions

Select Browning/Sauté to preheat the pressure cooking pot. Generously season the chicken with salt and pepper. Add the olive oil and chicken to the cooking pot. Sauté for 3 minutes, stirring occasionally. Add the garlic and sauté for 30 seconds more. Stir in the chicken broth, basil, Italian seasoning, and red pepper flakes. Lock the lid in place. Select High Pressure and 3 minutes cook time.

When the cook time ends, turn off the pressure cooker. Use a quick pressure release. When the valve drops, carefully remove the lid.

In a small bowl, whisk the cornstarch and cold water until smooth. Add the slurry to the pot. Select Simmer/Sauté and bring the sauce to a boil, stirring constantly until it thickens. Turn off the pressure cooker. Stir in the Parmesan until melted. Stir in the heavy cream, spinach, and sun-dried tomatoes.

Add the fettuccine to the cooking pot and toss to combine. Serve immediately.

Penne and Quick Homemade Marinara Sauce

YIELD:
6 SERVINGS

TIP: If your pasta isn't as tender as you'd like after pressure cooking, select Simmer/Sauté and simmer until it reaches your desired tenderness.

Homemade sauce in the time it takes to cook the pasta? Yes. And you're going to love it.

1 quart (946 ml) water, plus more as needed
2 tablespoons (30 ml) vegetable oil
2¼ teaspoons salt, divided
1 pound (454 g) penne pasta
1 can (28 ounces, or 794 g) crushed tomatoes in purée
1½ teaspoons garlic powder
1 teaspoon dried basil
¼ teaspoon red pepper flakes
Freshly grated Parmesan cheese, for serving

In the pressure cooking pot, stir together the water, vegetable oil, 2 teaspoons salt, and penne. Make sure the water covers the penne. Place a rack on the penne.

In a 7-inch (18 cm) round cake pan, stir together the tomatoes, garlic powder, basil, red pepper flakes, and remaining ¼ teaspoon salt. Use a sling to carefully lower the pan onto the rack. Lock the lid in place. Select High Pressure and 4 minutes cook time.

When the cook time ends, turn off the pressure cooker. Use a quick pressure release, or, if necessary, use an intermittent pressure release. When the valve drops, carefully remove the lid. Remove the pan and rack from the cooking pot. Ladle off any excess water from the penne. Stir in the marinara. Taste and adjust the seasoning. Serve topped with Parmesan.

Spaghetti Squash Matrichana

YIELD:
6 SERVINGS

....

TIP: You can use regular bacon in this recipe, but you'll need to double the amount of pepper.

The pressure cooker is the best way to cook spaghetti squash. This matrichana sauce recipe was given to me by my Spanish teacher—it's a flavorful sauce made with tomatoes simmered with onion, garlic, and bacon, and spiced with plenty of black pepper.

8 slices peppered bacon, diced
1 large onion, diced
1 tablespoon (10 g) minced garlic
2 cans (28 ounces, or 794 g, each) diced tomatoes, undrained
½ cup (120 ml) water
1 teaspoon salt, plus more as needed
¼ teaspoon freshly ground black pepper, plus more as needed
1 medium spaghetti squash (about 3 pounds, or 1.4 g), stem end removed, halved lengthwise then crosswise into 4 pieces, seeds and pulp removed

Select Browning/Sauté and add the bacon to the pressure cooking pot. Fry for about 5 minutes until crisp, stirring frequently. Transfer the bacon to a paper towel–lined plate, leaving the bacon fat in the pot.

Add the onion. Sauté for about 3 minutes, stirring frequently, until the onion softens and begins to brown. Add the garlic and sauté for 1 minute more. Stir in the tomatoes, water, salt, and pepper. Place the squash pieces in the cooking pot with the sauce. Lock the lid in place. Select High Pressure and 7 minutes cook time.

When the cook time ends, turn off the pressure cooker. Use a quick pressure release. When the valve drops, carefully remove the lid. Use tongs and a large fork to carefully remove the squash from the cooking pot.

Select Simmer/Sauté and simmer the sauce to thicken. Stir in the bacon. Season with salt and pepper to taste.

When the squash is cool enough to handle, use a fork to scrape the flesh into strands. Serve topped with the sauce.

Sweet Teriyaki Pork Tenderloin

YIELD:
4 SERVINGS

TIP: Pork tenderloin is generally sold with two tenderloins in a package. If you prefer, cook both at the same time without changing the cook time or sauce ingredients.

Pork tenderloin is a long, thin strip of pork that's very tender and cooks quickly in the pressure cooker. I've paired it with a flavorful sweet teriyaki sauce that's perfect served over rice.

1¼ pounds (567 g) pork tenderloin
Salt and freshly ground black pepper, for seasoning
1 tablespoon (15 ml) vegetable oil
½ cup (120 ml) reduced-sodium chicken broth
½ cup (120 ml) teriyaki sauce
¼ cup (60 g) packed light brown sugar

2 tablespoons (30 ml) white vinegar
Pinch red pepper flakes
2 tablespoons (16 g) cornstarch
2 tablespoons (30 ml) cold water
Cooked white rice, chopped scallions, toasted sesame seeds, for serving

Generously season the tenderloin with salt and pepper. Select Browning/Sauté and add the vegetable oil to the cooking pot. When the oil is hot, add the tenderloin and brown for about 3 minutes per side. Transfer to a platter.

Stir in the chicken broth to deglaze the pot, scraping up any browned bits from the bottom. Add the teriyaki sauce, brown sugar, white vinegar, and red pepper. Stir to combine.

Slice the tenderloin into 2-inch -thick (5 cm) medallions. Add the medallions and any accumulated juices to the pot. Lock the lid in place. Select High Pressure and 1 minute cook time.

When the cook time ends, turn off the pressure cooker. Let the pressure release naturally for 10 minutes and finish with a quick pressure release. When the valve drops, carefully remove the lid.

In a small bowl, whisk the cornstarch and cold water until smooth. Add the slurry to the pot. Select Simmer/Sauté and bring the sauce to a boil, stirring constantly until it thickens. Serve over white rice, if desired, garnished with scallions and sesame seeds.

Korean Beef Rice Bowl

YIELD:
4 TO 6 SERVINGS

TIP: Serve drizzled with Go Chu Jang Korean Chili Sauce or Sriracha if you like a little more heat.

Turn inexpensive ground beef into a flavorful Asian-inspired meal.

2 tablespoons (30 ml) vegetable oil, divided
1 pound (454 g) ground beef
1 cup (160 g) diced onion
3 cloves garlic, minced
¼ cup (60 ml) low-sodium soy sauce
¼ cup (60 ml) reduced-sodium beef broth
⅓ cup (75 g) packed light brown sugar
2 teaspoons sesame oil
¼ teaspoon red pepper flakes
¼ teaspoon ground ginger
1¾ cups (410 ml) water
1½ cups (278 g) long-grain white rice, rinsed
½ teaspoon salt
2 tablespoons (16 g) cornstarch
2 tablespoons (30 ml) cold water
3 scallions, white and green parts, sliced

Select Browning/Sauté to preheat the pressure cooking pot. When hot, add 1 tablespoon (15 ml) vegetable oil and the ground beef. Cook for about 5 minutes, stirring frequently, until the beef is browned and crumbled. Transfer to a paper towel–lined plate. Drain any excess fat from the pot.

Add the remaining 1 tablespoon (15 ml) vegetable oil and the onion to the cooking pot. Sauté for about 3 minutes, stirring occasionally, until tender. Add the garlic and cook for 1 minute more. Stir in the soy sauce, beef broth, brown sugar, sesame oil, red pepper flakes, and ginger. Stir in the browned beef.

Place a trivet on the beef in the cooking pot. Place a 7 × 3-inch (18 × 7.5 cm) round cake pan or other flat-bottomed dish on the trivet and add the water, rice, and salt. Lock the lid in place. Select High Pressure and 5 minutes cook time.

When the cook time ends, turn off the pressure cooker. Let the pressure release naturally for 10 minutes and finish with a quick pressure release. When the valve drops, carefully remove the lid. Remove the cake pan and trivet from the cooking pot. Fluff the rice with a fork and cover it to keep warm until ready to serve.

In a small bowl, whisk the cornstarch and 2 tablespoons (30 ml) cold water until smooth. Add the slurry to the pot. Select Simmer/Sauté and bring the sauce to a boil, stirring constantly until it thickens. Serve the beef over the rice garnished with scallions.

{ Chapter 6 }

Sunday Suppers

On Sunday, my mom always cooked a hot, homemade meal. While she reserved these wonderful meals for Sunday, making them in a pressure cooker allows you to enjoy them any night of the week that you have a little extra time.

Beef Stroganoff

YIELD:
6 SERVINGS

TIP: You can quickly turn a cheap round steak into a tender, flavorful meal in the pressure cooker, but much of the flavor in this dish comes from the browning stage—don't skip it! While it does take time to brown the beef, it adds a rich, caramelized flavor to the gravy that you just can't get any other way.

My family loves this braised beef with golden mushrooms and flavorful, creamy gravy, served over egg noodles.

2 pounds (907 g) beef round steak, cut into 1-inch (2.5 cm) pieces
Salt and freshly ground black pepper, for seasoning
2 tablespoons (30 ml) vegetable oil, divided, plus more as needed
1 medium-size onion, chopped
2 cloves garlic, minced or pressed
2 tablespoons (32 g) tomato paste
1½ cups (360 ml) reduced-sodium beef broth
1 tablespoon (14 g) unsalted butter
1 package (12 ounces, or 340 g) white mushrooms, sliced
2 tablespoons (16 g) cornstarch
3 tablespoons (45 ml) cold water
⅓ cup (77 g) sour cream
Cooked egg noodles, for serving

Season the beef generously with salt and pepper. Select Browning/Sauté to preheat the pressure cooking pot. When hot, add 1 tablespoon (15 ml) vegetable oil. Brown the meat in batches, about 3 minutes per batch, until all the meat is browned. Add more oil as needed. Do not crowd the pot. Transfer the browned meat to a plate.

Add the onion to the cooking pot. Sauté for about 3 minutes, stirring frequently, until soft and beginning to brown. Add the garlic and tomato paste. Sauté for 1 minute. Stir in the beef broth to deglaze the pot, scraping up any brown bits from the bottom. Add the browned beef and any accumulated juices. Lock the lid in place. Select High Pressure and 18 minutes cook time.

While the beef cooks, heat a large skillet or sauté pan over medium-high heat until hot. Add the remaining 1 tablespoon (15 ml) vegetable oil and butter. When the butter melts, add the mushrooms. Cook for about 5 minutes until golden. When the cook time ends, turn off the pressure cooker. Let the pressure release naturally for 10 minutes and finish with a quick pressure release. When the valve drops, carefully remove the lid.

In a small bowl, whisk the cornstarch and cold water until smooth. Add the slurry to the pot. Select Simmer/Sauté and bring the gravy to a boil, stirring constantly until it thickens. In a separate bowl, combine ⅓ cup (78.3 ml) gravy with the sour cream and mix well. Add the sour cream mixture to the cooking pot and stir until well blended. Serve over egg noodles.

Fork-Tender Beef Brisket

YIELD:
6 SERVINGS

TIP: You may have to cut the brisket in half to fit it in the cooking pot. If this happens, try to fit the pieces side by side rather than stacking one on top of the other. If serving a crowd, shred the brisket and serve it on rolls, pulled-pork style.

My sister made beef brisket for a family party, and it was so tender and flavorful I asked her for the recipe so I could adapt for the pressure cooker. This brisket marinates overnight but has only 1 hour cook time in the pressure cooker, compared to the usual 6 to 8 hours in the oven.

¼ **teaspoon celery salt**
¼ **teaspoon seasoned salt**
¼ **teaspoon garlic salt**
3 pounds (1.4 kg) beef brisket, fat trimmed to ¼ inch (0.6 cm)
2 tablespoons (30 ml) liquid smoke
1 tablespoon (15 ml) Worcestershire sauce
1 cup (250 g) barbecue sauce, plus more for serving
½ **cup (120 ml) water**

In a small bowl, combine the celery salt, seasoned salt, and garlic salt. Rub the spices into the brisket and place it in a large, heavy-duty zipper bag. Add the liquid smoke and Worcestershire sauce. Seal the bag and refrigerate to marinate overnight.

In the pressure cooking pot, stir together the barbecue sauce and water. Add the brisket and any accumulated juices. Lock the lid in place. Select High Pressure and 55 minutes cook time.

When the cook time ends, turn off the pressure cooker. Let the pressure release naturally for 15 minutes and finish with a quick pressure release. When the valve drops, carefully remove the lid. Carefully transfer the brisket to a large platter and slice the meat across the grain.

In a small bowl, stir together a little cooking liquid with some additional barbecue sauce and drizzle it over the meat just before serving.

Barbecue Bacon Meat Loaf

YIELD:
8 SERVINGS

TIP: If you've shaped your meat loaf tall instead of wide, or if you've customized the ingredients, your meat loaf may need a few minutes more to cook. Check it on the instant-read thermometer!

This meat loaf is covered in smoky bacon and smothered in tangy barbecue sauce. If you haven't tried meat loaf since you were a kid, give this barbecue bacon version a try.

½ cup (120 ml) milk

3 slices bread, torn into small pieces

2 pounds (907 g) ground beef

¾ cup (75 g) grated Parmesan cheese

2 tablespoons (3 g) dried parsley

1 teaspoon salt

¼ teaspoon seasoned salt

3 large eggs, beaten

Freshly ground black pepper, for seasoning

8 slices thinly sliced precooked bacon

½ cup (130 g) barbecue sauce, divided

In a large bowl, pour the milk over the bread pieces and let soak for several minutes. Add the ground beef, Parmesan, parsley, salt, seasoned salt, and eggs. Season with pepper to taste. Using clean hands, mix just until well blended.

Fold a sheet of aluminum foil into a 16 × 7-inch (40.5 × 18 cm) sling. Place the meat mixture on the center of the sling and shape it into a wide 8 × 7-inch (20 × 18 cm) loaf, leaving 4 inches (10 cm) of foil on each side as handles. Lay the bacon over the top, tucking the ends underneath the loaf. Spread ¼ cup (65 g) barbecue sauce over the bacon.

Put a trivet into the cooking pot and add 2 cups (470 ml) water. Use the handles on the sling to carefully lower the meat loaf onto the trivet. Lock the lid in place, making sure the foil does not interfere with locking the lid. Select High Pressure and 20 minutes cook time.

When the cook time ends, turn off the pressure cooker. Use a quick pressure release. When the valve drops, carefully remove the lid. Use an instant-read thermometer to check that the center of the meat has reached 155°F (68°C). If needed, relock the lid and cook at High Pressure for a few minutes more.

Preheat the broiler.

Carefully remove the meat loaf from the pressure cooker and place it on a broiler pan. Spread the remaining ¼ cup (65 g) barbecue sauce over the meat loaf. Broil for about 5 minutes until the sauce starts to caramelize.

Bone-In Beef Short Ribs

YIELD:
4 SERVINGS

TIP: Short ribs release a lot of fat when they cook, which keeps the meat tender and juicy. An easy way to get rid of most of the fat is to make the short ribs the day before you serve them and chill them overnight. Just before serving, remove the layer of fat that has accumulated on top and reheat.

These fall-off-the-bone beef short ribs are my favorite special-occasion dish. Cooking them in the pressure cooker is so much faster that you can make any day a special occasion.

4 large bone-in beef short ribs
Salt and freshly ground black
    pepper, for seasoning
2 tablespoons (30 ml) vegetable oil
2 slices bacon, finely chopped
1 large onion, finely chopped
3 cloves garlic, minced or pressed
½ cup (120 ml) red wine, such as
    Zinfandel

1 cup (235 ml) reduced-sodium beef
    broth
2 tablespoons (32 g) tomato paste
1 tablespoon (8 g) cornstarch
1 tablespoon (15 ml) cold water
Creamy mashed potatoes (page 248)
    or noodles, for serving

Generously season the short ribs with salt and pepper. Select Browning/Sauté and add the vegetable oil to the pressure cooking pot. When the oil is hot, brown the short ribs for 3 to 5 minutes in small batches. Do not crowd the pot. Transfer the browned ribs to a plate.

Add the bacon to the cooking pot. Fry for about 5 minutes until crisp, stirring frequently. Add the onion. Sauté for about 3 minutes until tender. Add the garlic and cook for 1 minute more. Add the red wine to deglaze the pot, scraping up any browned bits from the bottom. Stir in the beef broth and tomato paste. Add the short ribs and the accumulated juices. Lock the lid in place. Select High Pressure and 40 minutes cook time.

When the cook time ends, turn off the pressure cooker. Use a natural pressure release. When the valve drops, carefully remove the lid. Using tongs, transfer the ribs to a platter and cover with aluminum foil to keep warm. Use a fat separator to separate the fat from the juices. Return the juices to the cooking pot.

In a small bowl, whisk the cornstarch and cold water until smooth. Add the slurry to the pot. Select Simmer/Sauté and bring the juices to a boil, stirring constantly until they thicken. Turn off the pressure cooker. Return the short ribs to the cooking pot and stir to coat with the sauce. Put the lid back on the pressure cooker and let the ribs rest for about 10 minutes to absorb some of the sauce, stirring occasionally. Serve over Creamy Mashed Potatoes (page 248) or noodles, if desired.

Corned Beef and Cabbage

YIELD:
6 SERVINGS

TIP: Corned beef is a salt-cured beef brisket. It's called "corned" because the brisket is pre-served in large-grain rock salt, which is known as salt corns. Don't skip rinsing the corned beef under cold water or your finished dish will be very salty.

Everybody's Irish on St. Patrick's Day. Celebrate with a good old-fashioned Irish meal—cooked faster in the pressure cooker.

3 pounds (1.4 kg) flat-cut corned beef brisket with seasoning packet
1 quart (946 ml) reduced-sodium beef broth
1 large onion, quartered
8 cloves garlic

18 small red potatoes
6 large carrots, each cut into 3 pieces
1 small head cabbage, cut into 6 wedges

Rinse the corned beef under cold water to remove excess salt and gel. In the pressure cooking pot, combine the seasoning packet, beef broth, onion, and garlic. Put a rack in the cooking pot and place the corned beef on the rack. Lock the lid in place. Select High Pressure and 90 minutes cook time.

When the cook time ends, turn off the pressure cooker. Let the pressure release naturally for 10 minutes and finish with a quick pressure release. When the valve drops, carefully remove the lid. Transfer the corned beef to a serving plate and cover with aluminum foil until ready to serve.

Remove the rack from the pressure cooking pot. Add the potatoes, carrots, and cabbage to the liquid in the pot. Lock the lid in place. Select High Pressure and 3 minutes cook time.

When the cook time ends, turn off the pressure cooker. Use a quick pressure release. When the valve drops, carefully remove the lid. Check the potatoes to see if they're tender; if needed, select Simmer/Sauté and cook until they reach your desired tenderness. Serve immediately.

Salisbury Steak with Mushroom Gravy

YIELD:
4 SERVINGS

TIP: Remove the patties from the cooking pot before adding the flour slurry if you prefer.

Despite its name, Salisbury steak is actually made with hamburger mixed with other ingredients, shaped like a steak, and served with a flavorful mushroom gravy.

1 pound (454 g) lean ground beef
⅓ cup (38 g) dried bread crumbs
1 egg, beaten
1 teaspoon onion powder
1 teaspoon garlic powder
1 teaspoon salt, plus more as needed
½ teaspoon freshly ground black pepper, plus more as needed
½ teaspoon Worcestershire sauce
2 tablespoons (30 ml) vegetable oil, plus more as needed

½ cup (80 g) chopped onion
1 cup (70 g) sliced mushrooms
1 can (14.5 fluid ounces, or 429 ml) reduced-sodium beef broth
3 tablespoons (21 g) all-purpose flour
¼ cup (60 ml) water
Creamy Mashed Potatoes (page 248), for serving

In a large bowl, mix the ground beef, bread crumbs, egg, onion powder, garlic powder, salt, pepper and Worcestershire sauce until just combined. Shape the mixture into 4 patties, each about 1 inch (2.5 cm) thick.

Select Browning/Sauté to preheat the pressure cooking pot. When hot, add the vegetable oil. Brown the patties, 2 at a time, for about 3 minutes per side. Transfer to a plate.

If needed, add more oil to the pot along with the onion. Sauté for about 3 minutes until tender. Add the mushrooms and sauté for 2 minutes more. Stir in the beef broth to deglaze the pot, scraping up any browned bits from the bottom. Add the browned patties to the pot. Lock the lid in place. Select High Pressure and 2 minutes cook time.

When the cook time ends, turn off the pressure cooker. Use a quick pressure release. When the valve drops, carefully remove the lid.

In a small bowl, whisk the flour and water until smooth. Move the patties to one side of the pot. Gradually whisk the slurry into the pot. Select Simmer/Sauté and bring the sauce to a boil, stirring constantly until it thickens. Season with salt and pepper to taste. Serve over Creamy Mashed Potatoes (page 248), if desired.

Shepherd's Pie

YIELD:
8 SERVINGS

TIP: Ground lamb is traditional in shepherd's pie, but ground beef is less expensive and easier to find. This recipe is delicious either way.

Creamy, cheesy mashed potatoes swirled over a rich, flavorful ground lamb and vegetable stew—Shepherd's Pie is pure comfort food. Perfect any time you need a great, hearty meal.

2 tablespoons (30 ml) vegetable oil, plus more for greasing the baking dish
2 pounds (907 g) ground lamb or ground beef
1 cup (160 g) diced onion
1 cup (130 g) diced carrots
3 cloves garlic, minced or pressed
1 cup (235 ml) reduced-sodium beef broth
1 tablespoon (16 g) tomato paste
1 teaspoon salt, divided, plus more for seasoning
¾ teaspoon freshly ground black pepper, divided, plus more for seasoning

2 tablespoons (16 g) cornstarch
3 tablespoons (45 ml) cold water
½ cup (83 g) frozen corn
½ cup (65 g) frozen peas
2 tablespoons (8 g) fresh parsley leaves, finely chopped
2 pounds (907 g) potatoes, peeled and quartered
½ cup (120 ml) whole milk
¼ cup (55 g) unsalted butter, melted
2 cups (225 g) shredded Cheddar cheese

Preheat the oven to 375°F (190°C, or gas mark 5). Lightly grease a 2-quart (1.9 L) casserole dish or a 9-inch (23 cm) deep-dish pie plate.

Select Browning/Sauté and add 1 tablespoon (15 ml) vegetable oil to the pressure cooking pot. When the oil is hot, add the meat. Cook for about 5 minutes to brown, crumbling it as it cooks. Transfer to a paper towel–lined plate. Drain any excess fat from the pot.

Add the remaining 1 tablespoon (15 ml) vegetable oil, onion, and carrots to the pot. Sauté for about 3 minutes until the onion is translucent. Add the garlic and sauté for 1 minute more. Stir in the beef stock, tomato paste, ½ teaspoon salt, ½ teaspoon pepper, and the browned meat. Lock the lid in place. Select High Pressure and 3 minutes cook time.

When the cook time ends, turn off the pressure cooker. Use a quick pressure release. When the valve drops, carefully remove the lid.

In a small bowl, whisk the cornstarch and cold water until smooth. Add the slurry to the pot. Select Simmer/Sauté and bring the sauce to a boil, stirring constantly until it thickens. Stir in the corn, peas, and parsley. Season with additional salt and pepper to taste. Pour the meat mixture into the prepared baking dish.

Rinse out the pressure cooking pot. Place a steamer basket or a metal trivet in the pot and add 1 cup (235 ml) water. Add the potatoes to the basket. Lock the lid in place. Select High Pressure and 5 minutes cook time.

When the cook time ends, turn off the pressure cooker. Use a quick pressure release. When the valve drops, carefully remove the lid. Drain the potatoes and put them into a large bowl. Mash with a potato masher. Stir in the milk, butter, Cheddar, and the remaining ½ teaspoon salt and ¼ teaspoon pepper.

Spread the mashed potatoes evenly over the meat mixture, right to the edge of the dish. If desired, use a pastry bag with a large star tip to create a decorative topping with the potatoes. Bake for 30 to 35 minutes, until golden-brown. Serve immediately.

Beef Bourguignon

YIELD:
6 SERVINGS

....

TIP: Use a dry red wine, such as a Burgundy, Pinot Noir, or Cabernet Sauvignon.

This classic French stew is one of my favorite meals—chunks of beef paired with smoky bacon and simmered in a burgundy sauce until tender.

6 slices bacon, chopped into ½-inch (1 cm) pieces
3 pounds (1.4 kg) stew beef, cut into 2-inch (5 cm) cubes
1 teaspoon salt, plus more for seasoning
½ teaspoon freshly ground black pepper, plus more for seasoning
2 cloves garlic, finely chopped or pressed
1½ cups (355 ml) red wine
¾ cup (175 ml) reduced-sodium beef broth
1 tablespoon (16 g) tomato paste
½ teaspoon dried thyme

1 bay leaf
1 tablespoon (15 ml) vegetable oil
1 tablespoon (14 g) unsalted butter
1 package (8 ounces, or 227 g) mushrooms, sliced
2 large carrots, sliced diagonally into ½-inch (1 cm) slices
20 frozen pearl onions
¼ cup (28 g) all-purpose flour
¼ cup (60 ml) cold water
Cooked noodles or Creamy Mashed Potatoes (page 248), for serving
2 tablespoons (8 g) chopped fresh parsley leaves

Select Browning/Sauté and add the bacon to the pressure cooking pot. Fry for about 5 minutes until crisp, stirring frequently. Transfer the bacon to a paper towel–lined plate, leaving the bacon fat in the pot.

Season the beef with salt and pepper. Add it to the pot in batches and brown in the bacon fat for about 5 minutes on one side. Transfer the browned beef to a platter. Add the garlic and sauté for 30 seconds, stirring constantly. Add the red wine to deglaze the pot, scraping up any browned bits from the bottom. Let the wine cook until reduced to about 1 cup (240 ml). Stir in the beef broth, tomato paste, thyme, bay leaf, salt, and pepper. Add the browned beef along with any accumulated juices. Lock the lid in place. Select High Pressure and 20 minutes cook time. While the beef cooks, heat a large skillet or sauté pan over medium-high heat until hot. Add the vegetable oil and butter. When the butter melts, add the mushrooms and cook for about 5 minutes until golden. Season with salt and pepper to taste. Set aside.

When the cook time ends, turn off the pressure cooker. Let the pressure release naturally for 10 minutes and finish with a quick pressure release. When the valve drops, carefully remove the lid. Add the carrots and onions to the pot. Lock the lid in place. Select High Pressure and 5 minutes cook time.

When the cook time ends, turn off the pressure cooker. Let the pressure release naturally for 10 minutes and finish with a quick pressure release. When the valve drops, carefully remove the lid.

In a small bowl, whisk the flour and water until smooth. Add about ½ cup (120 ml) hot broth to the flour mixture and stir to combine. Add the slurry to the pot. Select Simmer/Sauté and bring the sauce to a boil, stirring constantly until it thickens. Add the mushrooms and bacon and stir to coat with the sauce. Serve over noodles or Creamy Mashed Potatoes (page 248), if desired, garnished with parsley.

Stuffed Cabbage Rolls

YIELD:
6 SERVINGS

....

TIP: Both the filling and the sauce use 1 cup (160 g) onion. Save some time by chopping 2 cups (320 g) onion when you make the filling and saving half for the sauce.

My sweet friend Carol shared her stuffed cabbage rolls on my blog, *Pressure Cooking Today*, and they are a reader favorite. For this cookbook, Carol and I worked together to streamline the process to make the recipe even easier to make.

FOR CABBAGE ROLLS:

1 large head cabbage, cored
1½ pounds (680 g) lean ground beef
1 cup (160 g) finely chopped onion
¾ cup (139 g) long-grain white rice
3 cloves garlic, finely chopped or pressed
1 large egg, beaten
1 teaspoon salt
½ teaspoon freshly ground black pepper

FOR SAUCE:

2 tablespoons (30 ml) vegetable oil
1 cup (160 g) finely chopped onion
3 cloves garlic, finely chopped or pressed
2 cans (14.5 ounces, or 411 g, each) diced tomatoes with juice
1 cup (235 ml) reduced-sodium beef broth
¼ cup (60 ml) white vinegar
2 tablespoons (32 g) tomato paste
½ teaspoon freshly ground black pepper
½ teaspoon Worcestershire sauce
1 tablespoon (8 g) cornstarch
2 tablespoons (30 ml) cold water

TO MAKE THE CABBAGE ROLLS: Fill the pressure cooking pot halfway with water. Select Browning/Sauté and bring to a boil. Add the cabbage to the boiling water. Cook for 5 minutes, turning, until the outer leaves are softened. Drain. Remove 12 leaves from the outside of the cabbage. Coarsely chop the remaining cabbage.

In a large bowl, use your clean hands or a wooden spoon to mix together the ground beef, onion, rice, garlic, egg, salt, and pepper until well blended. Lay the cabbage leaves on a work surface with the stem end nearest you. Divide the filling among the 12 leaves, placing it at the bottom of each leaf. Fold the sides in and roll the leaf around the filling, burrito style. Fasten the rolls with toothpicks if needed.

TO MAKE THE SAUCE: Select Browning/Sauté and add the vegetable oil to the cooking pot. When the oil is hot, add the onion. Sauté for about 3 minutes, stirring occasionally, until the onion starts to soften. Add the garlic and cook for 1 minute more. Stir in the tomatoes, beef broth, white vinegar, tomato paste, pepper, and Worcestershire sauce. Mix in the chopped cabbage.

Gently put the cabbage rolls directly into the sauce in the cooking pot. Lock the lid in place. Select High Pressure and 20 minutes cook time.

When the cook time ends, turn off the pressure cooker. Let the pressure release naturally for 20 minutes and finish with a quick pressure release. When the valve drops, carefully remove the lid. Use a slotted spoon to transfer the cabbage rolls to a serving platter.

In a small bowl, whisk the cornstarch and cold water until smooth. Add the slurry to the pot. Select Simmer/Sauté and bring the sauce to a boil, stirring constantly until the sauce thickens. Spoon the sauce over the cabbage rolls before serving.

Old-Fashioned Pot Roast with Gravy and Vegetables

YIELD:
6 SERVINGS

TIP: When browning the roast, be sure the pot is hot before you add the roast and wait to turn it until it releases easily from the bottom of the pot.

Growing up, my favorite Sunday dinner was pot roast with gravy. My mom cooked it in our stovetop pressure cooker until it was fork-tender and served it with lots of flavorful gravy, potatoes, and carrots.

3 pounds (1.4 kg) beef chuck roast, about 2½ inches (6 cm) thick
Salt and freshly ground black pepper, for seasoning
1 tablespoon (15 ml) vegetable oil
1 cup (160 g) chopped onion
1 can (14.5 fluid ounces, or 429 ml) reduced-sodium beef broth
1 tablespoon (16 g) tomato paste

2 bay leaves
6 medium-size red potatoes, quartered
3 large carrots, cut into 2-inch (5 cm) pieces
1 tablespoon (94 g) minced fresh parsley leaves
¼ cup (28 g) all-purpose flour
¼ cup (60 ml) water

Pat the roast dry with paper towels. Season both sides of the roast well with salt and pepper. Select Browning/Sauté to preheat the pressure cooking pot. When hot, add the vegetable oil and the roast. Cook for about 5 minutes per side to brown. Transfer to a plate.

Add the onion to the cooking pot. Sauté for about 3 minutes until tender, stirring occasionally to scrape up any browned bits from the bottom of the pot. Stir in the beef broth, tomato paste, and bay leaves. Return the roast and any accumulated juices to the pot. Lock the lid in place. Select High Pressure and 75 minutes cook time.

When the cook time ends, turn off the pressure cooker. Let the pressure release naturally for 15 minutes and finish with a quick pressure release. When the valve drops, carefully remove the lid. Transfer the roast to a cutting board and cover with aluminum foil.

Add potatoes and carrots to the cooking pot. Lock the lid in place. Select High Pressure and 3 minutes cook time.

When the cook time ends, turn off the pressure cooker. Use a quick pressure release. When the valve drops, carefully remove the lid. Check the potatoes for doneness. If needed, select Browning/Sauté and cook until they reach your desired tenderness.

Use a slotted spoon to transfer the potatoes and carrots to a serving bowl and sprinkle with parsley. Cover with foil until ready to serve. Strain the juices and skim off any excess fat. Return the juices to the pot.

In a small bowl, whisk the flour and water until smooth. Add ½ cup (120 ml) hot cooking juices to the flour mixture and stir to combine. Add the slurry to the pot. Select Simmer/Sauté and bring the gravy to a boil, stirring constantly until it thickens. Taste the gravy and season with salt and pepper to taste.

To serve, cut the roast into large pieces and place on a rimmed serving platter. Ladle half the gravy over the roast and pour the rest into a gravy boat to serve with the potatoes.

Round Steak in Mushroom Gravy

YIELD:
6 SERVINGS

TIP: If your round steak is more than 1 inch (2.5 cm) thick, increase the cook time. Add 15 minutes for every additional inch (2.5 cm) of thickness.

Round steak is a fairly inexpensive cut of beef that can be tough unless cooked properly. Braising it in the pressure cooker tenderizes the meat and creates a flavorful gravy all at once.

1½ pounds (680 g) top round steak (1 inch, or 2.5 cm, thick), cut into 6 pieces

Salt and freshly ground black pepper, for seasoning

2 to 4 tablespoons (30 to 60 ml) vegetable oil, divided

1 cup (160 g) chopped onion

1 package (8 ounces, or 227 g) fresh mushrooms, sliced

2 cups (470 ml) reduced-sodium beef broth

½ cup (56 g) all-purpose flour

1 cup (235 ml) water

Cooked egg noodles or Creamy Mashed Potatoes (page 248), for serving

Generously season the steak with salt and pepper. Select Browning/Sauté and add 1 tablespoon (15 ml) vegetable oil to the pressure cooking pot. When the oil is hot, brown the meat in batches for about 5 minutes per side. Do not crowd the pot. Transfer the browned beef to a plate. Add more oil as needed.

Add the onion to the pressure cooking pot. Sauté for about 3 minutes until tender. Add the mushrooms and sauté for 5 minutes more. Add the browned meat and beef broth to the pot. Lock the lid in place. Select High Pressure and 15 minutes cook time.

When the cook time ends, turn off the pressure cooker. Let the pressure release naturally for 10 minutes and finish with a quick pressure release. When the valve drops, carefully remove the lid.

In a small bowl, whisk the flour and water until smooth. Add 1 cup (235 ml) hot juices from the pot and stir until well combined. Add the slurry to the pot. Select Simmer/Sauté and bring the sauce to a boil. Boil for a few minutes, stirring constantly until it thickens. Season with salt and pepper to taste. Serve with egg noodles or Creamy Mashed Potatoes (page 248).

Pepper-Crusted Steak with Parmesan-Garlic Butter

TIP: If the steaks won't fit side by side on the rack, stack 2 crosswise on top of each other.

Nothing beats a great steak on the grill—but if grilling is not an option, here's how to get great flavor in a pressure cooker.

¼ **cup (56 g) unsalted butter, at room temperature**
1 tablespoon (6 g) finely grated Parmesan cheese
¼ **teaspoon garlic salt**
4 (6 ounces, or 170 g, each) top sirloin steaks
   (about 1½ inches, or 3.5 cm, thick)
Salt and freshly ground black pepper, for seasoning
1 tablespoon (15 ml) olive oil

In a small bowl, blend the butter, Parmesan, and garlic salt. Set aside.

Pat the steaks dry and season with salt and a generous amount of pepper. Press the seasonings firmly to adhere to the meat.

Add 1 cup (235 ml) water to the pressure cooking pot and place a trivet in the bottom. Place the steaks on the trivet. Lock the lid in place. Select High Pressure and 1 minute cook time for a steak that's medium to medium-well. (Adjust the cook time if your steaks are thicker or thinner or to achieve your desired doneness.)

When the cook time ends, turn off the pressure cooker. Let the pressure release naturally for 10 minutes. With 5 minutes left in the natural pressure release, preheat a cast iron or heavy-bottomed skillet over medium-high heat. After 10 minutes, use a quick pressure release. When the valve drops, carefully remove the lid.

Add the olive oil to the preheated skillet. Transfer the steaks to the hot skillet. Cook for about 1 minute until a dark crust forms. Flip and cook for 1 minute more. Remove the skillet from the heat and top each steak with 1 tablespoon (14 g) compound butter. Serve immediately.

Melt-in-Your-Mouth Baby Back Ribs

....

TIP: The ribs can be made ahead and reheated on the grill. After pressure cooking, cool to room temperature and refrigerate until ready to grill.

When you cook ribs in the pressure cooker before grilling them, you get the best of both worlds—moist fall-off-the-bone meat from the pressure cooker and caramelized, finger-licking-good coating from the grill.

2 tablespoons (30 g) packed light brown sugar
1 tablespoon (8 g) chili powder
1 tablespoon (18 g) salt
1 teaspoon freshly ground black pepper
1 teaspoon garlic powder
1 teaspoon onion powder
1 rack pork baby back ribs
1 cup (250 g) barbecue sauce

In a small bowl, combine the brown sugar, chili powder, salt, pepper, garlic powder, and onion powder. Set aside.

Pat the ribs dry with paper towels and place them on a work surface. Peel the membrane off the back of the ribs. Cut the rack into sections to fit inside the pressure cooking pot. Liberally season the ribs on both sides with the spice mixture, rubbing it into the ribs.

Add 1 cup (235 ml) water and a rack to the pressure cooking pot. Place the ribs on the rack, so the bones are facing up. Lock the lid in place. Select High Pressure and 18 minutes cook time.

When the cook time ends, turn off the pressure cooker. Let the pressure release naturally for 10 minutes and finish with a quick pressure release. When the valve drops, carefully remove the lid.

Preheat a grill to medium-high heat. Coat one side of the ribs with barbecue sauce. Place them on the grill, sauce-side down, and grill for 3 minutes. Coat the other side with sauce, flip, and grill for 3 minutes more. Slather on additional barbecue sauce and grill each side for 3 minutes more. Alternatively, finish the ribs under the preheated broiler following the same sequence. Serve immediately.

Country-Style Sweet-and-Sour Pork Ribs

YIELD:
6 SERVINGS

....

TIP: Country-style ribs are meatier than other rib cuts and generally more affordable. Bone-in or boneless country-style ribs work well in this recipe.

Country-style pork ribs cook in a Polynesian style sweet-and-sour sauce until fork-tender—this tastes like you cooked it for hours, but this dish requires only a 20-minute cook time in the pressure cooker.

3 pounds (1.4 kg) country-style pork ribs

½ teaspoon salt, plus more for seasoning

Freshly ground black pepper, for seasoning

1 tablespoon (15 ml) vegetable oil

⅓ cup (78 ml) pineapple juice

⅓ cup (78 ml) white vinegar

¼ cup (60 g) packed light brown sugar

2 tablespoons (30 ml) low-sodium soy sauce

1 clove garlic, finely chopped or crushed

1 teaspoon finely grated peeled fresh ginger

½ teaspoon dry mustard

1 tablespoon (8 g) cornstarch

1 tablespoon (15 ml) cold water

Generously season the ribs with salt and pepper. Select Browning/Sauté and add the vegetable oil to the pressure cooking pot. When the oil is hot, brown the ribs in batches for about 3 minutes per side. Don't crowd the pot. Transfer the browned ribs to a platter.

Add the pineapple juice to deglaze the pot, scraping up any browned bits from the bottom. Stir in the white vinegar, brown sugar, soy sauce, garlic, ginger, salt, and dry mustard. Add the ribs and any accumulated juices. Lock the lid in place. Select High Pressure and 20 minutes cook time.

When the cook time ends, turn off the pressure cooker. Let the pressure release naturally for 10 minutes and finish with a quick pressure release. When the valve drops, carefully remove the lid. With tongs, transfer the ribs to a platter and cover with aluminum foil to keep warm. If desired, use a fat separator to separate the fat from the juices. Return the juices to the cooking pot.

In a small bowl, whisk the cornstarch and cold water until smooth. Add the slurry to the pot. Select Simmer/Sauté and bring the sauce to a boil, stirring constantly until it thickens. Turn off the pressure cooker. Add the ribs and stir to coat with the sauce. Put the lid back on the cooker and let the ribs rest for about 10 minutes to absorb some of the sauce, stirring occasionally if the sauce is still bubbling.

Pork Loin Roast

YIELD:
6 TO 8 SERVINGS

....

TIP: While the roast is in the oven, make a gravy with the juices and broth remaining in the cooking pot. In a small bowl, whisk 1 tablespoon (8 g) cornstarch with 2 tablespoons (30 ml) cold water until smooth. Add the slurry to the juices and whisk to combine. Select Simmer/ Sauté and bring the gravy to a boil, stirring constantly until it thickens. Stir in 1 tablespoon (14 g) unsalted butter and season with salt and pepper to taste. Drizzle the gravy over the roast just before serving.

By finishing this roast in the oven, you avoid overcooking it and create that crispy brown exterior that a good pork roast needs.

1 teaspoon lemon pepper
½ teaspoon coarsely ground black pepper
½ teaspoon salt
1 tablespoon (15 ml) vegetable oil
4 pounds (1.8 kg) boneless pork loin roast

Preheat the oven to 450°F (230°C, or gas mark 8).

In a small bowl, mix together the lemon pepper, black pepper, salt, and vegetable oil. Rub this spice mixture all over the pork roast. Put a trivet into the pressure cooking pot and add 1 cup (235 ml) water. Place the pork on the trivet. Lock the lid in place. Select High Pressure and 15 minutes cook time.

When the cook time ends, turn off the pressure cooker. Let the pressure release naturally for 5 minutes. When the valve drops, carefully remove the lid. Transfer the pork to a broiler pan and place it in the oven. Roast for about 10 minutes, or until the pork is crispy and brown on the outside and reaches an internal temperature of 145°F (63°C). Let the pork rest for 10 minutes before serving.

Fork-Tender Pork Chops in Homemade Mushroom Gravy

YIELD:
4 SERVINGS

TIP: The mushroom gravy is thickened with a flour slurry at the end, which is an easy way to get a thicker sauce without a roux. However, flour doesn't dissolve in water as easily as cornstarch, so adding a little of the hot liquid to the flour mixture first helps the flour dissolve and avoids lumps in your gravy.

My Easy Pork Chops in Mushroom Gravy (page 145) get rave reviews. However, if you have a little extra time, try this version with homemade mushroom gravy—it's even more fabulous.

4 bone-in (1 inch, or 2.5 cm, thick) pork chops

Lemon pepper or other favorite spice, for seasoning

2 tablespoons (30 ml) vegetable oil

¼ cup (55 g) unsalted butter

1 package (8 ounces, or 227 g) mushrooms, finely chopped

¼ cup (40 g) finely diced onion

1 clove garlic, minced or pressed

1 cup (235 ml) reduced-sodium chicken broth

1 teaspoon salt

½ teaspoon freshly ground black pepper

¼ cup (28 g) all-purpose flour

¼ cup (60 ml) water

½ cup (120 ml) heavy cream

Pat the pork chops dry with paper towels and liberally season them with lemon pepper. Select Browning/Sauté and add the vegetable oil to the pressure cooking pot. When the oil begins to sizzle, add 2 pork chops and brown for about 3 minutes per side. Transfer the browned chops to a plate and repeat with the remaining 2 pork chops.

Add the butter to the pressure cooking pot to melt. Add the mushrooms and onion. Sauté for about 3 minutes until tender. Add the garlic and sauté for 1 minute more. Stir in the chicken broth, salt, and pepper. Add the pork chops and any accumulated juices. Lock the lid in place. Select High Pressure and 18 minutes cook time.

When the cook time ends, turn off the pressure cooker. Let the pressure release naturally for 10 minutes and finish with a quick pressure release. When the valve drops, carefully remove the lid. Transfer the chops to a large serving bowl.

In a small bowl, whisk the flour and water. Add ¼ cup (60 ml) hot liquid from the cooking pot to the flour mixture and stir to combine. Add the slurry to the pot. Select Simmer/Sauté and simmer, stirring constantly, until the sauce thickens. Stir in the heavy cream. Pour the gravy over the chops to serve.

Heating Ham Slices

YIELD:
8 SERVINGS

TIP: When heating a boneless sliced ham, the top and bottom slices get hot before the middle, so if all the ham isn't warm enough after the natural pressure release, move the middle slices to the top and bottom of the stack and return to the pressure cooker. Cook at High Pressure for a few minutes more.

Heating ham slices in the oven often dries them out, but warming them in the pressure cooker helps avoid that problem. I generally use a bone-in, spiral-sliced ham, but this method heats any precooked sliced ham.

4 pounds (1.8 kg) precooked sliced ham

Pour 1 cup (235 ml) water into the pressure cooking pot and place a rack in the bottom of the pot. Wrap the ham tightly in aluminum foil (if needed, stack or cut the ham so that it fits in the pressure cooker). Put the wrapped ham on a sling and carefully lower it onto the rack. Lock the lid in place. Select High Pressure and 12 minutes cook time.

When the cook time ends, turn off the pressure cooker. Let the pressure release naturally for 10 minutes and finish with a quick pressure release. Remove the ham from the foil, cut the slices away from the bone, and serve immediately.

Red Beans and Rice

A Louisiana favorite, red beans and rice was traditionally made on Mondays using the leftover ham bone from Sunday dinner.

- 1 package (1 pound, or 454 g) dried red kidney beans
- 2 quarts (1.9 L) water
- 1 tablespoon (14 g) unsalted butter
- 6 ounces (170 g) andouille sausage, halved lengthwise and cut crosswise into ¼-inch -thick (0.6 cm) slices
- 1 tablespoon (15 ml) vegetable oil
- 1 large onion, diced
- 2 ribs celery, diced
- 1 green bell pepper, chopped
- 4 cloves garlic, minced
- 3 cups (705 ml) ham stock or reduced-sodium chicken broth
- 2 bay leaves
- 1 teaspoon dried thyme, crushed
- 1 teaspoon salt, plus more as needed
- ½ teaspoon freshly ground black pepper, plus more as needed
- Dash Tabasco sauce, plus more as needed
- Cooked white rice, for serving

In the pressure cooking pot, combine the kidney beans and 2 quarts (1.9 L) water. Lock the lid in place. Select High Pressure and 1 minute cook time.

When the cook time ends, turn off the pressure cooker. Let the pressure release naturally for 1 hour. Drain the beans in a colander, discarding the soaking water.

Select Browning/Sauté and melt the butter in the pressure cooking pot. Add the sausage. Sauté for about 3 minutes until it starts to brown. Use a slotted spoon to transfer the sausage to a plate. Drain any excess fat from the pot.

Add the vegetable oil, onion, celery, and green bell pepper to the pot. Sauté for about 3 minutes, stirring occasionally, until tender. Add the garlic and sauté for 1 minute more. Stir in the ham stock, bay leaves, thyme, salt, pepper, and Tabasco. Stir in the drained beans. Lock the lid in place. Select High Pressure and 5 minutes cook time.

When the cook time ends, turn off the pressure cooker. Let the pressure release naturally for 10 minutes and finish with a quick pressure release. Remove and discard the bay leaves.

Use a potato masher to mash some of the beans to make a creamy broth. Stir in the sausage. Season with salt, pepper, and Tabasco to taste. If needed, select Simmer/Sauté and simmer to thicken the broth. Serve over white rice.

Chicken Marsala

YIELD:

6 SERVINGS

TIP: When I make chicken in the pressure cooker, I prefer chicken thighs. The pressure breaks down the fat and tissue, which leaves the meat much more tender and moist than chicken breasts. However, substitute chicken breasts in this recipe, if you prefer.

Chicken Marsala is a classic dish made with chicken, mushrooms, and Marsala wine. This version includes bacon, which gives the dish a smoky taste that complements the richness of the wine.

4 slices peppered bacon, diced

3 pounds (1.4 kg) boneless skinless chicken thighs, trimmed

Salt and freshly ground black pepper, for seasoning

½ cup (120 ml) sweet Marsala wine

1 cup (235 ml) reduced-sodium chicken broth

1 tablespoon (15 ml) vegetable oil

3 tablespoons (42 g) unsalted butter, divided

1 package (8 ounces, or 227 g) mushrooms, sliced

2 tablespoons (16 g) cornstarch

3 tablespoons (45 ml) cold water

2 tablespoons (8 g) chopped fresh parsley leaves

Select Browning/Sauté and add the bacon to the pressure cooking pot. Fry for about 5 minutes until crisp, stirring frequently. Transfer the bacon to a paper towel–lined plate, leaving the bacon fat in the pot.

Season the chicken with salt and pepper. Add it to the pot in batches and brown for about 3 minutes per side in the bacon fat. Transfer the browned chicken to a platter.

Add the Marsala wine to deglaze the pot, scraping up any browned bits from the bottom. Let the liquid almost completely evaporate to concentrate the flavor. Stir in the chicken broth and return the browned chicken to the pot along with any accumulated juices. Lock the lid in place. Select High Pressure and 10 minutes cook time. When the cook time ends, use a quick pressure release. When the valve drops, carefully remove the lid. Transfer the chicken to a serving dish.

Heat a large skillet or sauté pan over medium-high heat until hot. Add the vegetable oil and 1 tablespoon (14 g) butter. When the butter melts, add the mushrooms and cook for about 5 minutes until golden. Season with salt and pepper.

In a small bowl, whisk the cornstarch and cold water until smooth. Add the slurry to the pot. Select Simmer/Sauté and bring the sauce to a boil, stirring constantly. Stir in the remaining 2 tablespoons (28 g) butter. Add the mushrooms and stir to coat with the sauce. Season with salt and pepper to taste, then combine with the chicken in the serving bowl. Serve topped with crumbled bacon and parsley.

Chicken Cacciatore

YIELD:
4 SERVINGS

TIP: If you have fresh basil, you can substitute 2 teaspoons finely chopped fresh basil for the dried basil.

Cacciatore is Italian for "hunter," so this chicken is prepared hunter style with onions, tomatoes, bell peppers, and herbs.

4 large bone-in skinless chicken breasts (about 2 pounds, or 907 g)
½ teaspoon salt, plus more for seasoning
¼ teaspoon freshly ground black pepper, plus more for seasoning
3 tablespoons (45 ml) vegetable oil, divided
1 green bell pepper, chopped
1 large onion, chopped
2 cloves garlic, minced or pressed
1 can (14.5 ounces, or 411 g) diced tomatoes, undrained
1 jar (4.5 ounces, or 127.5 g) sliced mushrooms, drained
½ teaspoon dried oregano
½ teaspoon dried basil
Freshly grated Parmesan cheese, for serving
Fresh parsley leaves, for serving

Generously season the chicken with salt and pepper. Select Browning/Sauté to preheat the pressure cooking pot. When hot, add 1 tablespoon (15 ml) vegetable oil. Brown the chicken in 2 batches for about 3 minutes per side. Do not crowd the pot. Transfer the browned chicken to a platter.

Add the remaining 2 tablespoons (30 ml) vegetable oil to the pot. Add the green bell pepper, onion, and garlic. Sauté for about 3 minutes, stirring occasionally, until tender. Stir in the tomatoes, mushrooms, oregano, basil, salt, and pepper. Add the chicken and any accumulated juices. Lock the lid in place. Select High Pressure and 6 minutes cook time.

When the cook time ends, turn off the pressure cooker. Let the pressure cooker stand naturally for 5 minutes, then finish with a quick pressure release. When the valve drops, carefully remove the lid. Using tongs, transfer the chicken to a platter and cover with aluminum foil to keep warm. Select Simmer/Sauté and boil the sauce until it thickens. Spoon the sauce over the chicken and sprinkle with Parmesan and parsley to serve.

Coq au Vin

YIELD:
6 SERVINGS

TIP: I prefer cooking the mushrooms separately while the chicken cooks to get perfectly caramelized mushrooms. If you're not as fussy about your mushrooms, sauté them in the cooking pot before you fry the bacon.

A pressure cooker twist on a classic French chicken stew made with chicken thighs, onions, carrots, mushrooms, and topped with bacon.

½ cup (about 4 ounces, or 113 g) diced bacon

3 pounds (1.4 kg) boneless skinless chicken thighs, well trimmed

Salt and freshly ground black pepper, for seasoning

1 medium-size yellow onion, chopped

2 cloves garlic, chopped

1 cup (235 ml) red wine (such as Pinot Noir)

1 cup (235 ml) reduced-sodium chicken broth

1 tablespoon (16 g) tomato paste

2 carrots, sliced

2 sprigs fresh thyme

1 bay leaf

1 tablespoon (15 ml) vegetable oil

1 tablespoon (14 g) unsalted butter

1 package (12 ounces, or 340 g) white mushrooms, quartered

2 tablespoons (16 g) cornstarch

3 tablespoons (45 ml) cold water

2 tablespoons (8 g) chopped fresh parsley leaves (optional)

Cooked noodles, rice, or Creamy Mashed Potatoes (page 248), for serving

Select Browning/Sauté and add the bacon to the pressure cooking pot. Fry for about 5 minutes until crisp, stirring frequently. Transfer the bacon to a paper towel–lined plate, leaving the bacon fat in the pot.

Season the chicken with salt and pepper. Add it to the pot in batches and brown for about 3 minutes on each side. Transfer the browned chicken to a platter, leaving the fat in the pan.

Add the onion. Sauté for about 3 minutes, stirring frequently, until softened and lightly caramelized. Add the garlic and cook for 1 minute more. Stir in the red wine to deglaze the pot, scraping up any browned bits from the bottom. Let the liquid almost completely evaporate to concentrate the flavor. Stir in the chicken broth, tomato paste, carrots, thyme, and bay leaf. Add the browned chicken, along with any accumulated juices. Lock the lid in place. Select High Pressure and 10 minutes cook time.

While the chicken cooks, heat a large skillet or sauté pan over medium-high heat until hot. Add the vegetable oil and butter. When the butter melts, add the mushrooms and cook for about 5 minutes until golden. Season with salt and pepper to taste.

When the cook time ends, turn off the pressure cooker. Use a quick pressure release. When the valve drops, carefully remove the lid. Transfer the chicken to a serving dish.

In a small bowl, whisk the cornstarch and cold water until smooth. Add the slurry to the pot. Select Simmer/Sauté and bring the sauce to a boil, stirring constantly until it thickens. Add the mushrooms and stir to coat with the sauce. If using, add the parsley and season with salt and pepper to taste. Combine the sauce with the chicken in the serving bowl. Top with crumbled bacon and serve over noodles, rice, or Creamy Mashed Potatoes (page 248), if desired.

Lemon Thyme-"Roasted" Chicken

YIELD:
6 SERVINGS

....

TIP: You don't have to brown the chicken once it's finished in the pressure cooker—this step crisps the outside of the chicken and provides a nice brown color. Also, the chicken will be nearly fall-apart tender, so use caution when removing it from the pot.

The beauty of this recipe is you get moist, tender chicken, and the gravy is made right in the pot while the chicken crisps under the broiler.

2 tablespoons (28 g) unsalted butter, at room temperature

2 teaspoons salt, plus more for seasoning

1 teaspoon finely grated lemon zest

¼ teaspoon dried thyme

1 (4 pounds, or 1.8 kg) whole roasting chicken, rinsed well

Freshly ground black pepper, for seasoning

2 tablespoons (16 g) cornstarch

3 tablespoons (45 ml) cold water

In a small bowl, mix together the butter, salt, lemon zest, and thyme. Pat the chicken dry and rub the butter mixture under the skin. Generously season the chicken cavity with salt and pepper.

Put a trivet in the pressure cooking pot. Add ½ cup (120 ml) water. Place the chicken, breast-side up, on the trivet. Lock the lid in place. Select High Pressure and 32 minutes cook time. (If you chose a larger or smaller chicken, the cook time should be 8 minutes per pound, or 454 g.)

When the cook time ends, turn off the pressure cooker. Let the pressure release naturally for 10 minutes and finish with a quick pressure release. When the valve drops, carefully remove the lid.

Preheat the broiler.

Check that the chicken has reached 170°F (76.6°C) for the breasts and 180°F (82°C) for the thighs on an instant-read thermometer. Carefully transfer the chicken to a broiler pan. Broil for about 5 minutes until the skin is crisp and brown.

While the chicken broils, in a small bowl, whisk the cornstarch and cold water until smooth. Add the slurry to the pot. Select Simmer/Sauté and bring the gravy to a boil, stirring constantly until it thickens.

Turkey Breast with Turkey Gravy

YIELD:

8 SERVINGS

TIP: My family doesn't care for the skin; if your family does, place the turkey on a broiling pan after pressure cooking and pop it in a 450°F (230°C or gas mark 8) oven for 5 to 10 minutes to crisp the skin.

Turkey breast cooked in the pressure cooker is super moist and juicy, and cooking a turkey this way saves you lots of flavorful liquid to make a wonderful turkey gravy.

6½ pounds (3 kg) bone-in skin-on turkey breast
Salt and freshly ground black pepper, for seasoning
1 can (14.5 fluid ounces, or 429 ml) reduced-sodium
   turkey broth or chicken broth
1 large onion, quartered
1 rib celery, cut into large pieces
1 sprig fresh thyme
3 tablespoons (24 g) cornstarch
3 tablespoons (45 ml) cold water

Season the turkey breast liberally with salt and pepper. Put a trivet in the bottom of the pressure cooking pot. Add the turkey broth, onion, celery, and thyme. Place the turkey in the pot, breast-side up. Lock the lid in place. Select High Pressure and 30 minutes cook time.

When the cook time ends, turn off the pressure cooker. Let the pressure release naturally for 10 minutes and finish with a quick pressure release. When the valve drops, carefully remove the lid. Use an instant-read thermometer to check the turkey. It should be 165°F (74°C) in the thickest part of the breast. If needed, relock the lid and cook at High Pressure for a few more minutes.

Carefully transfer the turkey to a large plate. Cover with aluminum foil. Strain the broth and skim off the fat. Return it to the pot.

In a small bowl, whisk the cornstarch and cold water until smooth. Add the slurry to the pot. Select Simmer/Sauté and bring the broth to a boil, stirring constantly until it thickens. Season with salt and pepper to taste.

Remove and discard the skin. Slice the turkey and serve immediately with the gravy.

Peppered Boneless Turkey Breast and "Baked" Potatoes

YIELD:
6 SERVINGS

....

TIP: A boneless turkey breast is simply a breast rolled into a roast and wrapped with string to hold it together. The thickness of the breast determines the cook time. If your turkey breast is long and skinny, your cook time will be less. If your turkey breast is more rounded, your cook time may be longer. You can cook a frozen boneless turkey breast with this same method; increase your cook time by about 10 minutes.

Turkey doesn't have to be reserved for Thanksgiving. With this quick recipe, which cooks the "baked" potatoes at the same time as the turkey, you can enjoy turkey year-round.

2 teaspoons freshly ground black pepper
1 teaspoon paprika
1 teaspoon dried thyme
1 teaspoon salt
1 (about 3 pounds, or 1.4 kg) boneless skinless turkey breast
6 (6 ounces, or 170 g, each) russet potatoes, scrubbed

In a small bowl, mix the pepper, paprika, thyme, and salt. Rub the spice mixture over the turkey breast. Put a trivet in the pressure cooking pot. Add 1 cup (235 ml) water and place the turkey on the trivet.

Prick the potatoes with a fork and wrap them individually in aluminum foil. Tuck them into the cooking pot around the turkey breast. Lock the lid in place. Select High Pressure and 30 minutes cook time.

When the cook time ends, turn off the pressure cooker. Let the pressure release naturally for 10 minutes and finish with a quick pressure release. When the valve drops, carefully remove the lid. Remove the potatoes, unwrap them, and place them on a serving plate. Use an instant-read thermometer to check that the center of the turkey has reached 165°F (74°C). If needed, relock the lid and cook at High Pressure for a few minutes more.

Eggplant Lasagna Rolls

YIELD:
4 SERVINGS

TIP: Salting the eggplant before cooking draws out excess moisture so that your sauce and filling aren't too watery.

A cross between eggplant Parmesan and lasagna, these Eggplant Lasagna Rolls are easy to make and easy to serve.

1 large eggplant, ends removed, peeled, and sliced lengthwise into ¼-inch (0.6 cm) slices

½ teaspoon salt, plus more for salting the eggplant

1 cup (250 g) whole-milk ricotta cheese

⅓ cup (33 g) grated Parmesan cheese

1 large egg

2 tablespoons (8 g) chopped fresh parsley leaves

½ teaspoon garlic powder

¼ teaspoon ground black pepper

1 cup (240 ml) marinara sauce (store-bought or homemade), divided

1 tablespoon (15 ml) vegetable oil

1 cup (115 g) shredded mozzarella cheese

Lay the eggplant slices on a clean kitchen towel. Generously salt both sides of each slice and let sit for 30 minutes. Rinse the slices under cold water to remove the excess salt.

Spray a 7 × 3-inch (18 × 7.5 cm) baking dish with nonstick cooking spray. In a large bowl, stir together the ricotta, Parmesan, egg, parsley, garlic powder, salt, and pepper. Spread about ½ cup (120 ml) marinara sauce in the bottom of the prepared pan.

Preheat an outdoor grill, or grill pan, to medium heat. Lightly coat the eggplant slices with the vegetable oil. Grill for about 3 minutes per side until lightly browned and tender then transfer them to a work surface. Place a large dollop of cheese filling on the large end of each slice and wrap the eggplant around it. Place the eggplant rolls in the prepared pan, seam-side down. Top with the remaining ½ cup (120 ml) sauce and the mozzarella. Cover the pan with aluminum foil.

Place a trivet in the pressure cooking pot and add 1 cup (235 ml) water. Use a sling to place the dish on the trivet. Lock the lid in place. Select High Pressure and 8 minutes cook time.

When the cook time ends, turn off the pressure cooker. Let the pressure release naturally for 10 minutes and finish with a quick pressure release. When the valve drops, carefully remove the lid. Remove the dish from the cooking pot and serve.

Brown Rice Fiesta Bake

YIELD:
6 SERVINGS

....

TIP: I like to use leftovers as a burrito filling for lunch the next day.

A hearty meatless meal made with good-for-you brown rice and black beans. The tomatoes and green chilies give it a mildly spicy flavor, and the cheese finishes it with a gooey deliciousness.

1 tablespoon (15 ml) vegetable oil

1 large onion, diced

4 cloves garlic, minced or pressed

2 cans (10 ounces, or 284 g, each) mild diced tomatoes and green chilies

1 cup (235 ml) water

1 cup (190 g) brown rice

1 teaspoon chili powder

½ teaspoon ground cumin

½ teaspoon salt

¼ teaspoon freshly ground black pepper

1 cup (165 g) frozen corn, thawed

1 can (15 ounces, or 425 g) black beans, drained and rinsed

¼ cup (4 g) chopped fresh cilantro leaves

1½ cups (173 g) shredded Cheddar cheese

Sour cream and tortilla chips, for serving

Select Browning/Sauté and add the vegetable oil to the pressure cooking pot. When the oil is hot, add the onion. Sauté for about 3 minutes until the onion softens. Add the garlic and cook for 1 minute more. Stir in the tomatoes and green chilies, water, rice, chili powder, cumin, salt, and pepper. Lock the lid in place. Select High Pressure and 22 minutes cook time.

When the cook time ends, turn off the pressure cooker. Let the pressure release naturally for 10 minutes and finish with a quick pressure release. When the valve drops, carefully remove the lid.

Select Simmer/Sauté and stir in the corn and black beans. Cook for about 3 minutes until heated. Stir in the cilantro.

Preheat the broiler. Spray a 9 × 9-inch (23 × 23 cm) ovenproof dish with nonstick cooking spray. Pour the rice mixture into the prepared dish and top with the Cheddar. Broil until the cheese melts and starts to brown. Serve topped with sour cream and tortilla chips, if desired.

Three-Cheese Lasagna

YIELD:

4 SERVINGS

TIP: The cheese on top comes out of the pressure cooker melted, gooey, and delicious; if you'd like to brown it for presentation, place the pan under the preheated broiler for a few minutes. Watch it carefully since the cheese browns quickly once it starts.

Lasagna doesn't have to be time-consuming. No-boil noodles have this easy pressure cooker dish ready in half the time.

8 ounces (227 g) country-style sausage
1 can (14.5 ounces, or 411 g) diced tomatoes, well drained
1 can (8 fluid ounces, or 235 ml) tomato sauce
1 teaspoon garlic powder
1 teaspoon dried basil
¼ teaspoon red pepper flakes

¼ teaspoon salt
1 cup (250 g) part-skim ricotta cheese
1½ cups (173 g) shredded mozzarella cheese, divided
½ cup (40 g) shredded Parmesan cheese
1 large egg
6 no-boil lasagna noodles

Select Browning/Sauté and when hot, add the sausage. Cook for 5 minutes, stirring often to break up the meat, until the sausage is no longer pink. Drain excess fat from the pot. Stir in the tomatoes, tomato sauce, garlic powder, basil, red pepper flakes, and salt. Transfer to a large bowl and set aside. Wipe out the pressure cooking pot.

In another large bowl, mix together the ricotta cheese, ½ cup (57.5 g) mozzarella, the Parmesan, and egg until blended.

Spray a 7 × 3-inch (18 × 7.5 cm) round cake pan or 1½-quart (1.4 L) baking dish with nonstick cooking spray. Spread a thin layer of meat sauce on the bottom of the prepared pan. Break the noodles into pieces to form a single layer on top of the meat sauce. Spread another thin layer of sauce on the noodles. Spread half the cheese mixture on top of the sauce. Add a second layer of noodles, another thin layer of meat sauce, and the remaining cheese mixture. Top with a third layer of noodles and the remaining meat sauce, and finish with the remaining 1 cup (115 g) mozzarella. Cover the pan with aluminum foil.

Add 1 cup (235 ml) water to the pressure cooking pot and place a trivet in the bottom. Place the pan of lasagna on the trivet. Lock the lid in place. Select High Pressure and 20 minutes cook time.

When the cook time ends, turn off the pressure cooker. Let the pressure release naturally for 10 minutes and finish with a quick pressure release. When the valve drops, carefully remove the lid. Remove the lasagna pan from the cooking pot and let rest for 5 minutes before serving.

Fish en Papillote

YIELD:
4 SERVINGS

TIP: Flounder, tilapia, and haddock are other types of white fish that work well in this recipe. The fish won't brown like it would in the oven—instead, it retains its pretty pale-white color and stays tender and flaky.

Fish "en papillote" sounds fancy, but it's just fish cooked in parchment paper. Cooking it this way lets the fish cook deliciously in its own juices and butter!

4 (6 ounces, or 170 g, each) cod fillets, about 1 inch (2.5 cm) thick
Salt and freshly ground black pepper, for seasoning
¼ red onion, thinly sliced

1 lemon, thinly sliced, seeds removed
¼ cup (56 g) unsalted butter
4 sprigs fresh thyme or fresh dill

Place one fillet in the center of a 12 × 16-inch (30 × 40.5 cm) piece of parchment paper. Season with salt and pepper. Place about one-fourth of the red onion and lemon slices on the fillet. Top with 1 tablespoon (14 g) butter and 1 thyme sprig. Repeat with the remaining fillets.

Fold the parchment paper by bringing the opposite sides of the paper together in the center above the fish. Fold the top of the paper over and continue folding tightly until the paper reaches the fish, crimping to seal. Then roll and crimp the ends closed. Repeat to seal all packets.

Add 1 cup (235 ml) water to the pressure cooking pot and place a trivet in the bottom. Stack the 4 packets of fish on the trivet, with 2 on the rack and 2 stacked crosswise on top of those. Lock the lid in place. Select High Pressure and 8 minutes cook time.

When the cook time ends, turn off the pressure cooker. Let the pressure release naturally for 5 minutes and finish with a quick pressure release. When the valve drops, carefully remove the lid. Carefully remove and open the packets and serve immediately.

Chile Verde

YIELD:
8 SERVINGS

TIP: Boston butt or pork butt are also cuts of pork that come from the shoulder, and both work well in this recipe.

The Red Iguana is the best Mexican restaurant in Salt Lake City. My husband is crazy about their chile verde—a stew with tender cubed pork cooked in a green chile-tomatillo sauce and served with tortillas on the side. With this quick pressure cooker version, I can make it in less time than it takes for us to drive to the restaurant.

1 can (28 ounces, or 796 g) whole tomatillos

4 pounds (1.8 kg) boneless pork shoulder, trimmed and cut into 1-inch (2.5 cm) cubes

1 tablespoon (15 ml) vegetable oil

1 large onion, finely chopped

2 cloves garlic, minced or pressed

1 jar (16 ounces, or 454 g) salsa verde

½ teaspoon ground cumin

½ teaspoon salt, plus more for seasoning

¼ teaspoon freshly ground black pepper, plus more for seasoning

¼ cup (4 g) chopped fresh cilantro leaves

Flour tortillas, for serving

Drain the liquid from the tomatillos into the pressure cooking pot and set aside the tomatillos. Add the pork to the pressure cooking pot and stir to combine. Lock the lid in place. Select High Pressure and 20 minutes cook time.

When the cook time ends, turn off the pressure cooker. Let the pressure release naturally for 10 minutes and finish with a quick pressure release. When the valve drops, carefully remove the lid. Drain the pork into a colander sitting in a large bowl to reserve the cooking liquid. Skim and discard the fat from the top of the cooking liquid, using a fat separator if you have one.

Select Browning/Sauté and add the vegetable oil to the cooking pot. When the oil is hot, add the onion. Sauté for about 3 minutes, stirring occasionally, until tender. Add the garlic and cook for 1 minute more.

In a blender, pulse the tomatillos until smooth. Combine the tomatillo purée with the onion and garlic in the cooking pot. Add the pork, salsa verde, cumin, salt, pepper, and ½ cup (120 ml) reserved cooking liquid. Select Simmer/Sauté and simmer for 5 minutes. Stir in the cilantro and season with salt and pepper to taste. Serve with warmed flour tortillas, if desired.

{ Chapter 7 }

On the Side

The pressure cooker is perfect for making short work of side dishes. A number of readers of my blog, *Pressure Cooking Today*, have found themselves buying a second electric pressure cooker so that they can make the main dish in one and the side dish in the other.

Cheesy Potatoes au Gratin

YIELD:
6 SERVINGS

....

TIP: Panko are Japanese-style bread crumbs that are lighter and crispier than traditional bread crumbs. Substitute regular dried bread crumbs in this recipe or omit the topping all together.

Thinly sliced potatoes surrounded with a rich, creamy cheese sauce and crowned with a crispy panko topping. These scalloped potatoes are a perfect side dish for a holiday dinner—or a simple way to make any weeknight meal special.

2 tablespoons (28 g) unsalted butter

½ cup (80 g) chopped onion

1 cup (235 ml) reduced-sodium chicken broth

½ teaspoon salt

⅛ teaspoon freshly ground black pepper

6 medium-size russet potatoes, peeled and sliced ⅛ -inch (0.3 cm) thick

1 cup (50 g) panko bread crumbs

3 tablespoons (42 g) unsalted butter, melted

½ cup (115 g) sour cream

1 cup (115 g) shredded Monterey Jack cheese

Select Browning/Sauté and melt the butter in the pressure cooking pot. Add the onion. Sauté for about 3 minutes, stirring occasionally, until tender. Add the chicken broth, salt, and pepper. Put the steamer basket in the cooking pot and add the potatoes. Lock the lid in place. Select High Pressure and 5 minutes cook time.

While the potatoes cook, preheat the broiler. Spray a 9 × 13-inch (23 × 33 cm) ovenproof dish with nonstick cooking spray. In a small bowl, stir together the panko and butter. Set aside.

When the cook time ends, turn off the pressure cooker. Use a quick pressure release. When the valve drops, carefully remove the lid. Remove the steamer basket with the potatoes and transfer the potatoes to the prepared dish.

Stir the sour cream and Monterey Jack into the cooking liquid in the pot and pour the mixture over the potatoes. Use 2 forks to gently mix the sauce with the potatoes. Top with the panko topping and broil for 5 to 7 minutes, or until golden-brown.

Old-Fashioned Potato Salad

YIELD:
8 SERVINGS

....

TIP: Skip the steamer basket and cook the potatoes and eggs right in the water in the bottom of the cooking pot—but be aware the potato pieces will be firmer if you use the steamer basket.

This quick potato salad recipe is so easy you'll rediscover home-made potato salad. By cooking the eggs and potatoes together in the pressure cooker, you save time and get perfectly cooked eggs and potatoes every time.

6 medium-size russet potatoes, peeled and cubed
4 large eggs
1 cup (225 g) mayonnaise, plus more as needed
¼ cup (40 g) finely chopped onion
2 tablespoons (8 g) finely chopped fresh parsley leaves
1 tablespoon (15 ml) dill pickle juice
1 tablespoon (11 g) yellow mustard
Salt and freshly ground black pepper, for seasoning

Put the steamer basket in the pressure cooking pot and add 1½ cups (353 ml) water. Add the potatoes and carefully place the eggs on the potatoes. Lock the lid in place. Select High Pressure and 4 minutes cook time.

While the potatoes cook, fill a medium-size bowl with ice water. In a large bowl, stir together the mayonnaise, onion, parsley, pickle juice, and mustard. Set aside.

When the cook time ends, turn off the pressure cooker. Use a quick pressure release. When the valve drops, carefully remove the lid. Remove the steamer basket from the cooking pot. Immediately place the eggs into the ice water to cool. Add the potatoes to the mayonnaise mixture and gently stir to combine.

Peel and dice 3 cooled eggs and stir them into the potato salad. Season with salt and pepper to taste. If needed, add more mayonnaise to achieve your desired consistency. Chill for at least 1 hour before serving. Top with slices of the remaining hard-boiled egg.

Creamy Mashed Potatoes

YIELD:
6 SERVINGS

TIP: For extra-smooth and creamy mashed potatoes, my husband likes to use a ricer. Sometimes we also substitute heavy cream for the milk.

Since I first made mashed potatoes in the pressure cooker, I have never cooked them on the stove again. Steaming the potatoes above the water gives them a better texture—and makes this dish faster and easier, since you don't have to worry about the water boiling over.

6 medium-size russet potatoes (about 2 pounds, or 907 g), peeled and quartered
¼ cup (56 g) unsalted butter, melted
½ to ¾ cup (120 to 175 ml) milk, warmed
Salt and freshly ground black pepper, for seasoning

Add 1 cup (235 ml) water to the pressure cooking pot. Put a steamer basket in the pot and place the potatoes in the basket. Lock the lid in place. Select High Pressure and 5 minutes cook time.

When the cook time ends, turn off the pressure cooker. Use a quick pressure release. When the valve drops, carefully remove the lid. Use a fork to test the potatoes. If needed, relock the lid and cook at High Pressure for a few minutes more. Transfer the potatoes to a large serving bowl. Use a potato masher to mash the potatoes until mostly smooth. Mash in the butter. Gradually stir in the milk. Season with salt and pepper to taste.

Loaded "Baked" Potatoes

YIELD:
6 SERVINGS

TIP: It can be difficult to tell by squeezing a potato if it's done in the center. The size of the potato can make the cook time vary—increase the cook time at High Pressure for larger, thicker potatoes and reduce the cook time for smaller, thinner potatoes.

These potatoes taste just as good as oven-baked potatoes, and they're ready in half the time. I like mine loaded with toppings.

**6 large russet potatoes (about 8 ounces, or 227 g,
    each and 2 inches, or 5 cm, thick), scrubbed**
Olive oil, for coating
Fine sea salt, for seasoning
Toppings of choice, for serving

Pierce the skin of each potato in several places with a fork.

Add 1 cup (235 ml) water to the pressure cooking pot and place a trivet in the bottom. Place the potatoes on the trivet, stacking them crosswise if needed. Lock the lid in place. Select High Pressure and 25 minutes cook time.

When the cook time ends, turn off the pressure cooker. Let the pressure release naturally for 5 minutes and finish with a quick pressure release. When the valve drops, carefully remove the lid. Use an instant-read thermometer to check that the center of the potatoes reaches 205°F (96°C). If needed, re-cover the pot and let them steam for a few minutes longer.

If you like a crispy skin, preheat the oven to 500°F (260°C, or gas mark 10). Carefully remove the potatoes from the cooking pot and lightly coat with olive oil and sea salt. Roast for 5 minutes.

To serve, slice the potatoes lengthwise and load them with butter, sour cream, chives, bacon, shredded cheese, steamed broccoli, or other toppings of your choice.

Twice-Baked Potatoes

YIELD:
6 SERVINGS

....

TIP: Prepare the potatoes earlier in the day and bake them right before serving.

"Baking" the potatoes first in the pressure cooker reduces the cook time from more than an hour in the oven to only 15 minutes in the pressure cooker.

4 large unpeeled russet baking potatoes (8 to 10 ounces, or 227 to 284 g, each), gently scrubbed and halved lengthwise

¼ cup (55 g) unsalted butter, at room temperature

¼ teaspoon salt

⅛ teaspoon freshly ground black pepper

⅓ to ⅔ cup (78 to 156 ml) milk

1 cup (115 g) shredded Cheddar cheese

1 tablespoon (3 g) chopped fresh chives

Add 1 cup (235 ml) water to the pressure cooking pot and place a trivet in the bottom. Place the potatoes on the trivet, stacking them crosswise if needed. Lock the lid in place. Select High Pressure and 15 minutes cook time.

When the cook time ends, turn off the pressure cooker. Use a quick pressure release. When the valve drops, carefully remove the lid. Use a fork to check that a potato's center is tender. If needed, relock the lid and cook at High Pressure for 2 to 3 minutes more.

Preheat the oven to 400°F (200°C, or gas mark 6).

Let the potatoes cool in the cooker until cool enough to handle. Carefully remove them from the trivet and scoop the insides into a large bowl, leaving ¼-inch -thick (0.6 cm) shell. Place 6 shells on a rimmed baking sheet and set aside. (Discard the remaining 2 shells.)

With a potato masher, mash the potatoes until no lumps remain. Mash in the butter and season with salt and pepper. Add the milk a little at a time, mashing after each addition until the potatoes are light and fluffy. Stir in the Cheddar and chives. Fill the shells with the mashed potato mixture. Bake for about 15 minutes, or until the potatoes are hot and the tops are browned.

Garlic and Parsley Red Potatoes

TIP: It's important to cut the potatoes into similar-size pieces so that they cook evenly—otherwise, the smaller pieces will be done before the larger ones.

Red potatoes are thin-skinned potatoes, so there's no need to peel them. Prep time (and cook time) is minimal for this flavorful side dish.

2 tablespoons (30 ml) olive oil
2 cloves garlic, minced or pressed
2 pounds (907 g) small red potatoes, halved, or quartered if large
1 tablespoon (4 g) chopped fresh parsley leaves
Salt and freshly ground black pepper, for serving

Select Browning/Sauté and add the olive oil to the pressure cooking pot. When the oil is hot, add the garlic and sauté for 1 minute. Pour the oil and garlic into a serving bowl.

Add 1 cup (235 ml) water to the pressure cooking pot. Put a steamer basket in the pot and place the potatoes in the basket. Lock the lid in place. Select High Pressure and 6 minutes cook time.

When the cook time ends, turn off the pressure cooker. Use a quick pressure release. When the valve drops, carefully remove the lid. Use a fork to check that a potato's center is tender. If needed, select Simmer/Sauté and cook the potatoes a few minutes more. Remove the steamer basket from the pot. Transfer the potatoes to the serving bowl with the olive oil and garlic. Add the parsley and season with salt and pepper to taste. Toss to combine.

Caramelized Onion Mashed Potatoes

YIELD:
6 SERVINGS

TIP: The cook time for the onions may vary depending on how thinly sliced they are and how much moisture is in the pot. Be patient and keep a close eye on them, adjusting the sauté level up or down as needed.

Golden caramelized onion, mashed potatoes, bacon, butter, sour cream, and cheese—it's a perfect combination!

1 tablespoon (15 ml) vegetable oil

2 large onions, thinly sliced

1 teaspoon salt, divided

6 medium-size russet potatoes (about 2 pounds, or 907 g), peeled and quartered

$1/3$ cup (77 g) sour cream

3 tablespoons (45 ml) milk, plus more as needed

$1/4$ teaspoon freshly ground black pepper

1 tablespoon (14 g) unsalted butter, melted

$1/2$ cup (58 g) shredded Cheddar Jack cheese

2 slices bacon, cooked and crumbled

Select Browning/Sauté and add the vegetable oil to the pressure cooking pot. When the oil is hot, add the onions and $1/2$ teaspoon salt. Sauté for 10 minutes, stirring frequently, or until the moisture evaporates and the onions are completely wilted. Reduce the heat to Simmer/Sauté and cook for 20 minutes, stirring occasionally, or until caramelized. (If the onions begin to stick to the pan, add water, 1 tablespoon [15 ml] at a time.) Cut the onions into 1-inch (2.5 cm) pieces. Transfer to a plate.

Add 1 cup (235 ml) water to the pressure cooking pot. Place a steamer basket in the pot. Add the potatoes to the steamer basket. Lock the lid in place. Select High Pressure and 5 minutes cook time.

When the cook time ends, turn off the pressure cooker. Use a quick pressure release. When the valve drops, carefully remove the lid. Use a fork to test the potatoes for doneness. If needed, select Simmer/Sauté and steam the potatoes for 1 to 2 minutes more. Transfer the potatoes to a large bowl and mash. Add the sour cream, milk, pepper, and the remaining $1/2$ teaspoon salt. Mash until blended. (Add more milk if needed to achieve your desired consistency.) Stir in the caramelized onions. Transfer to a serving bowl. Drizzle with butter. Sprinkle with the Cheddar Jack and cooked bacon.

Parslied Sweet Potatoes

YIELD:
6 SERVINGS

TIP: Typically in the United States you find two varieties of sweet potatoes: red-skinned sweet potatoes with orange flesh (often called yams) and white sweet potatoes. The red-skinned sweet potatoes are softer and sweeter, and the white sweet potatoes are firmer. Use either in this recipe.

Sweet potatoes are one of the most nutritious root vegetables. They are loaded with good-for-you fiber, beta-carotene, vitamin C, and potassium. This side dish is perfect any time of year.

2 pounds (907 g) sweet potatoes, peeled and cut into bite-size pieces
2 tablespoons (28 g) unsalted butter, melted
½ teaspoon garlic powder
½ teaspoon paprika
½ teaspoon salt
⅛ teaspoon freshly ground black pepper
2 tablespoons (8 g) fresh parsley leaves

Add 1 cup (235 ml) water to the pressure cooking pot and place a steamer basket in the pot. Add the sweet potatoes to the basket. Lock the lid in place. Select High Pressure and 3 minutes cook time.

When the cook time ends, turn off the pressure cooker. Use a quick pressure release. When the valve drops, carefully remove the lid. Use a fork to check that a potato's center is tender. If needed, select Simmer/Sauté and cook the potatoes a few minutes more. Transfer the sweet potatoes to a serving dish and drizzle with butter.

In a small bowl, combine the garlic powder, paprika, salt, and pepper. Add the spices and parsley to the sweet potatoes and gently toss to combine.

Dirty Rice

YIELD:
6 SERVINGS

....

TIP: If you haven't eaten chicken livers before, don't be afraid of them in this dish! They blend well with the pork and give dirty rice its color.

You don't have to live in Louisiana to enjoy this Louisiana favorite. This not-too-spicy dirty rice is easy to make at home. My sister, who lives in Louisiana, said it was a huge hit with her family, even her grandsons kept coming back for more.

2 slices bacon, chopped
2 tablespoons (30 ml) vegetable oil
8 ounces (227 g) ground pork
½ cup (about 5 ounces, or 150 g) chicken livers, finely chopped
½ large onion, chopped
2 ribs celery, chopped
1 jalapeño pepper, seeded and finely chopped

1 teaspoon salt
½ teaspoon freshly ground black pepper
½ teaspoon chili powder
1½ cups (278 g) long-grain rice
2 cups (470 ml) reduced-sodium chicken broth
2 scallions, white and green parts, chopped

Select Browning/Sauté and add the bacon to the pressure cooking pot. Fry for about 5 minutes until crisp, stirring frequently. Transfer to a paper towel–lined plate, leaving the bacon fat in the pot.

Add the vegetable oil, pork, and chicken livers. Cook for about 5 minutes until browned. Add the onion, celery, and jalapeño. Sauté for about 3 minutes until tender. Add the salt, pepper, and chili powder. Stir in the rice and chicken broth. Lock the lid in place. Select High Pressure and 4 minutes cook time.

When the cook time ends, turn off the pressure cooker. Let the pressure release naturally for 10 minutes and finish with a quick pressure release. When the valve drops, carefully remove the lid. Fluff the rice with a fork. Stir in the bacon and scallions.

Cilantro-Lime Rice

YIELD:
4 SERVINGS

TIP: My daughter is crazy about this rice. She makes a double batch and freezes it in ½-cup (98 g) portions so that she always has some on hand. When you double this recipe, you do not need to increase the cook time.

The lime and cilantro give this rice a bright, fresh flavor—perfect as a side dish with your favorite Mexican meal or as the base of a burrito bowl.

1 cup (185 g) long-grain white rice
1¼ cups (295 ml) water
2 tablespoons (30 ml) vegetable oil, divided
1 teaspoon salt
3 tablespoons (3 g) chopped fresh cilantro leaves
1 tablespoon (15 ml) fresh lime juice

In the pressure cooking pot, stir together the rice, water, 1 tablespoon (15 ml) vegetable oil, and salt. Lock the lid in place. Select High Pressure and 3 minutes cook time.

When the cook time ends, turn off the pressure cooker. Let the pressure release naturally for 7 minutes and finish with a quick pressure release. When the valve drops, carefully remove the lid. Fluff the rice with a fork.

In a medium-size bowl, combine the cilantro, lime juice, and remaining 1 tablespoon (15 ml) vegetable oil. Add this to the rice and toss until thoroughly mixed.

Ham Fried Rice

TIP: It's important to use cold, day-old rice when making fried rice. Day-old rice has less moisture and absorbs the sauce properly; if you use just-cooked rice, the finished product is likely to be soggy. I often make a double batch of white rice with a meal and use the leftovers in this recipe the next day.

Ham fried rice is made with day-old rice, so be sure to get this started the night before you serve it. The next day, it comes together in a flash!

1 cup (185 g) long-grain white rice, rinsed
1¼ cups (295 ml) water
½ teaspoon salt
4 slices bacon, diced
½ cup (75 g) cubed ham
1 cup (130 g) frozen peas and carrots, thawed
3 large eggs, lightly beaten
2 tablespoons (30 ml) low-sodium soy sauce
2 scallions, white and green parts, chopped

In the pressure cooking pot, stir together the rice, water, and salt. Lock the lid in place. Select High Pressure and 3 minutes cook time.

When the cook time ends, turn off the pressure cooker. Let the pressure release naturally for 10 minutes and finish with a quick pressure release. When the valve drops, carefully remove the lid. Fluff the rice with a fork. Cool to room temperature and refrigerate overnight.

Select Browning/Sauté and add the bacon to the pressure cooking pot. Fry for about 5 minutes until crisp, stirring frequently. Transfer the bacon to a paper towel–lined plate, leaving the bacon fat in the pot. Turn off the pressure cooker. Add the ham and peas and carrots. Cook for 1 minute. Add the eggs and stir to scramble them. When the eggs are set but still soft, stir in the cooked rice, soy sauce, scallions, and bacon. Turn on the pressure cooker again and select Simmer/Sauté. Cook for 10 minutes, stirring occasionally.

Long-Grain White Rice

TIP: This recipe is easily doubled or tripled without increasing the pressure cook time—add 1 tablespoon (15 ml) vegetable oil to prevent foaming. Rinsing the rice before cooking helps remove surface starch, resulting in rice that is less sticky. This recipe also works well with jasmine and other types of white rice.

One of the selling points of an electric pressure cooker is that it's also a rice cooker. Cooking white rice in the pressure cooker doesn't save a lot of time, but it simplifies the process and gives you consistent results—great-tasting, perfectly cooked white rice, every time!

1 cup (185 g) long-grain white rice, rinsed
1¼ cups (295 ml) water
½ teaspoon salt

In the pressure cooking pot, stir together the rice, water, and salt. Lock the lid in place. Select High Pressure and 3 minutes cook time.

When the cook time ends, turn off the pressure cooker. Let the pressure release naturally for 10 minutes and finish with a quick pressure release. When the valve drops, carefully remove the lid. Fluff rice with a fork.

Classic Mexican Rice

YIELD:
6 SERVINGS

TIP: Don't skip the 10-minute natural release after pressure cooking—the rice needs this time to steam and gently finish cooking.

This side dish takes only a few minutes of hands-on time, and it's the complement for any Mexican-inspired meal.

2 tablespoons (30 ml) vegetable oil
½ cup (80 g) finely chopped onion
1 can (14.5 fluid ounces, or 429 ml) reduced-sodium chicken broth
1 can (8 ounces, or 227 g) tomato sauce
1 cup (235 ml) water

1½ teaspoons chili powder
½ teaspoon ground cumin
½ teaspoon garlic powder
½ teaspoon onion powder
Dash cayenne pepper
2 cups (370 g) long-grain rice

Select Browning/Sauté and add the vegetable oil to the cooking pot. When the oil is hot, add the onion. Sauté for about 3 minutes, stirring occasionally, until tender. Stir in the chicken broth, tomato sauce, water, chili powder, cumin, garlic powder, onion powder, and cayenne. Stir in the rice. Lock the lid in place. Select High Pressure and 4 minutes cook time.

When the cook time ends, turn off the pressure cooker. Let the pressure release naturally for 10 minutes and finish with a quick pressure release. When the valve drops, carefully remove the lid. Fluff the rice with a fork and serve immediately.

Brown Rice

YIELD:
**3 CUPS (495 G)
COOKED RICE**

TIP: Toast your brown rice before cooking to add a slightly nutty flavor. Select Browning/Sauté and add 2 tablespoons (28 g) unsalted butter to the pressure cooking pot to melt. Add the rice and toast for about 3 minutes, stirring constantly, until the rice smells nutty. Add the water and salt and cook as directed.

Brown rice is higher in fiber and nutrients than white rice, but I rarely made it since it takes so long to cook on the stovetop. Now I often cook brown rice in the pressure cooker, since it cooks in half the time. You can double or triple this recipe without any change to the cook time.

1 cup (190 g) long- or short-grain brown rice
1½ cups (355 ml) water
¼ teaspoon salt

In the pressure cooking pot, stir together the rice, water, and salt. Lock the lid in place. Select High Pressure and 22 minutes cook time.

When the cook time ends, turn off the pressure cooker. Let the pressure release naturally for 10 minutes and finish with a quick pressure release. When the valve drops, carefully remove the lid. Fluff the rice with a fork.

Buttermilk Corn Bread

YIELD:
6 TO 8 SERVINGS

....

TIP: I keep buttermilk powder on hand. If you prefer fresh buttermilk, substitute 1 cup fresh buttermilk for the ¼ cup buttermilk powder and 1 cup milk.

Buttermilk is the secret to moist, tender corn bread. Corn bread in the pressure cooker doesn't get a golden-brown exterior, but the texture is exactly what you'd expect from oven-baked corn bread.

1 cup (140 g) cornmeal
1 cup (112 g) all-purpose flour
⅓ cup (67 g) sugar
¼ cup (30 g) buttermilk powder
½ teaspoon baking powder

½ teaspoon salt
2 large eggs
1 cup (235 ml) milk
½ cup (1 stick, or 113 g) unsalted
   butter, melted and cooled

Spray a half-size Bundt pan with nonstick cooking spray.

In a large bowl, stir together the cornmeal, flour, sugar, buttermilk powder, baking powder, and salt. Make a well in the center of the dry ingredients and add the eggs, milk, and butter. Whisk the wet ingredients together with a fork. Stir together the wet and dry ingredients, until just blended—the batter will be lumpy. Spoon the batter into the Bundt pan. Cover the pan with aluminum foil.

Pour 1 cup (235 ml) water into the pressure cooking pot and place a trivet in the bottom. Center the Bundt pan on a sling and carefully lower it onto the trivet. Lock the lid in place. Select High Pressure and 20 minutes cook time.

When the cook time ends, turn off the pressure cooker. Let the pressure release naturally for 10 minutes and finish with a quick pressure release. When the valve drops, carefully remove the lid. Carefully transfer the Bundt pan to a wire rack and cool, uncovered, for 5 minutes. After 5 minutes, gently loosen the edges, remove the corn bread from the pan, and cool on a wire rack.

Sun-Dried Tomato and Spinach Rice Pilaf

YIELD:
6 SERVINGS

TIP: Toast the pine nuts in the pressure cooker on Browning/ Sauté for about 2 minutes before starting the recipe. Watch the nuts closely and stir frequently until golden in spots.

This colorful red, white, and green rice pilaf features a bright lemon flavor and crunchy, toasted pine nuts.

1 tablespoon (15 ml) olive oil
1 cup (160 g) finely chopped onion
2 cloves garlic, minced
1½ cups (278 g) long-grain white rice, rinsed
1 can (14.5 fluid ounces, or 429 ml) reduced-sodium chicken broth
½ cup (120 ml) water
1 tablespoon (6 g) lemon zest
¼ teaspoon salt
¼ cup (14 g) sun-dried tomatoes packed in oil, finely chopped
½ cup (15 g) fresh spinach, finely chopped
⅓ cup (45 g) toasted pine nuts

Select Browning/Sauté to preheat the pressure cooking pot. When hot, add the olive oil and onion. Sauté for about 3 minutes, stirring occasionally, until tender. Add the garlic and cook for 1 minute more. Stir in the rice. Cook for about 2 minutes, stirring frequently, until opaque. Stir in the chicken broth, water, lemon zest, and salt. Lock the lid in place. Select High Pressure and 3 minutes cook time.

When the cook time ends, turn off the pressure cooker. Let the pressure release naturally for 10 minutes and finish with a quick pressure release. When the valve drops, carefully remove the lid. Fluff the rice with a fork. Stir in the sun-dried tomatoes, spinach, and pine nuts.

Classic Risotto

YIELD:
6 SERVINGS

TIP: Substitute other freshly grated, finely shredded hard Italian cheeses for the Parmesan. I usually use a 3-cheese blend.

A creamy, classic risotto made with white wine and Parmesan cheese. Risotto is traditionally made on the stovetop and requires lots of stirring while slowly adding broth. When you make it in the pressure cooker, you get that same creamy slow-cooked texture, but without all the work.

¼ **cup (56 g) unsalted butter, divided**
½ **cup (80 g) finely chopped onion**
½ **cup (120 ml) dry white wine, such as Pinot Grigio**
1½ **cups arborio rice**
3½ **cups (825 ml) reduced-sodium chicken broth, divided,**
    plus more as needed
½ **cup (40 g) finely shredded Parmesan cheese,**
    plus more for serving
Salt and freshly ground black pepper, for seasoning

Select Browning/Sauté and add 2 tablespoons (28 g) butter to the pressure cooking pot to melt. Add the onion. Sauté for about 3 minutes until tender. Add the white wine. Cook until the wine is reduced by at least half. Stir in the rice and 3 cups (705 ml) broth. Lock the lid in place. Select High Pressure and 5 minutes cook time.

When the cook time ends, turn off the pressure cooker. Use a quick pressure release. When the valve drops, carefully remove the lid. Select Simmer/Sauté and stir in the remaining ½ cup (120 ml) chicken broth, the Parmesan, and the remaining 2 tablespoons (28 g) butter. Season with salt and pepper to taste. Add more broth, if needed, to achieve your desired consistency. Serve immediately, topped with Parmesan.

Refried Beans

TIP: Lard is the traditional fat used to make refried beans. My local grocery store carries it, but if you can't find it, vegetable oil or bacon fat are good substitutes.

Refried beans are easy to make from scratch, especially in the pressure cooker.

1 pound (454 g) dried pinto beans
2 quarts (1.9 L) water
¼ cup (50 g) lard or vegetable oil (60 ml)
1 cup (160 g) diced onion
2 teaspoons salt, plus more as needed
½ cup (58 g) Monterey Jack cheese

In the pressure cooking pot, combine the beans and 2 quarts (1.9 L) water. Lock the lid in place. Select High Pressure and 1 minute cook time.

When the cook time ends, turn off the pressure cooker. Let the beans soak for 1 hour.

Lock the lid in place. Select High Pressure and 5 minutes cook time.

When the cook time ends, turn off the pressure cooker. Let the pressure release naturally for 10 minutes and finish with a quick pressure release. When the valve drops, carefully remove the lid. Check that the beans are very tender and the skins are starting to split. If needed, relock the lid and cook on High Pressure for a few minutes longer. Drain the beans into a colander sitting in a large bowl to reserve the cooking water.

Select Browning/Sauté and add the lard to the cooking pot to melt. Add the onion. Sauté for about 3 minutes until tender. Stir in the beans, 1 cup (235 ml) reserved cooking water, and salt. Cook for 5 minutes, stirring frequently. Use a potato masher or immersion blender to smash the beans and create a chunky purée. Add more cooking water as needed. Stir in the Monterey Jack. Season with salt to taste.

Smoky Baked Beans

YIELD:
10 TO 12 SERVINGS

TIP: The secret is soaking the beans before cooking. You can soak them in water overnight or you can quick-soak them in your pressure cooker (see page 102). I think they're best if made the day before serving.

These baked beans, coated in a sweet, smoky sauce, are one of my most popular side dishes in the summer.

8 slices (10 ounces, or 284 g) thick-cut bacon, cut into ½-inch (1 cm) pieces
1 large onion, chopped
2½ cups (590 ml) water
½ cup (170 g) molasses
½ cup (120 g) ketchup
¼ cup (60 g) packed light brown sugar

1 teaspoon dry mustard
½ teaspoon salt
¼ teaspoon freshly ground black pepper
1 pound (454 g) dried navy beans, soaked overnight, or quick-soaked, and rinsed

Select Browning/Sauté and add the bacon to the pressure cooking pot. Fry for about 5 minutes until crisp, stirring frequently. Transfer the bacon to a paper towel–lined plate, leaving the bacon fat in the pot. Add the onion. Sauté for about 3 minutes until tender, scraping up any browned bits from the bottom of the pot as the onion cooks. Stir in the water, molasses, ketchup, brown sugar, dry mustard, salt, and pepper. Stir in the soaked beans. Lock the lid in place. Select High Pressure and 35 minutes cook time.

When the cook time ends, turn off the pressure cooker. Let the pressure release naturally for 10 minutes and finish with a quick pressure release. When the valve drops, carefully remove the lid. Discard any beans floating on top and check several beans to be sure they're tender. If not, relock the lid and cook on High Pressure for a few minutes longer.

Stir in the bacon. Select Simmer/Sauté and simmer the beans uncovered, stirring occasionally so that the bottom doesn't burn, until the sauce reaches your desired consistency. Remember, the beans soak up liquid as they cool.

Grown-Up Mac and Cheese

YIELD:
6 TO 8 SERVINGS

TIP: To quickly chop rosemary, slide your fingers down the stem to strip off the leaves. Push the leaves into a pile and cut them in half with a sharp knife.

Mac and cheese isn't just for kids! This sophisticated, grown-up version with bacon and Gruyère cheese is rich and creamy and the perfectly comforting meal.

½ cup (4 ounces, or 113 g) diced bacon
1 quart (946 ml) water
1 package (14 ounces, or 397 g) macaroni
2 teaspoons chopped fresh rosemary leaves
1 teaspoon salt, plus more as needed
2 tablespoons (16 g) cornstarch
2 tablespoons (30 ml) cold water
8 ounces (227 g) grated Gruyère cheese (about 2 cups)
2 cups (470 ml) heavy cream
½ teaspoon freshly ground black pepper

Select Browning/Sauté and add the bacon to the pressure cooking pot. Fry for about 5 minutes until crisp, stirring frequently. Transfer to a paper towel–lined plate, leaving the bacon fat in the pot.

Add the water, macaroni, rosemary, and salt to the cooking pot. Lock the lid in place. Select High Pressure and 3 minutes cook time.

When the cook time ends, turn off the pressure cooker. Use a quick pressure release. When the valve drops, carefully remove the lid.

In a small bowl, whisk the cornstarch and cold water until smooth. Add the slurry to the pot and stir until the sauce thickens. Stir in the Gruyère, a handful at a time, until melted and the sauce is smooth. Stir in the heavy cream.

Season with pepper and more salt to taste.

Corn on the Cob

YIELD:
4 TO 6 SERVINGS

. . . .

TIP: You can fit more corn in the pressure cooking pot if you break the pieces in half.

Steaming corn on the cob in the pressure cooker is fast and easy. The Keep Warm feature on the electric pressure cooker is especially nice when cooking corn—set the corn to cook and it will be hot and ready to serve when the rest of the meal is ready.

4 to 6 ears fresh corn, shucked

Add 1 cup (235 ml) water to the pressure cooking pot. Add a steamer basket or rack to the pot. Place the corn inside the basket or on the rack. Lock the lid in place. Select High Pressure and 3 minutes cook time for freshly picked corn, or 4 to 5 minutes for corn a few days old.

When the cook time ends, turn off the pressure cooker. Use a quick pressure release. When the valve drops, carefully remove the lid. The corn is done if it is tender and pierces easily.

Israeli Couscous Salad

TIP: This colorful salad can be served hot or cold. If serving cold, add the avocado right before serving.

Israeli couscous, also called pearl couscous, is made from semolina—a type of wheat flour—and was developed in Israel in the 1950s when rice was scarce. Basically, it's pasta shaped like little balls.

1 tablespoon (14 g) unsalted butter
1½ cups (263 g) Israeli couscous
2½ cups (590 ml) water
2 tablespoons (30 ml) fresh lemon juice
1 tablespoon (15 ml) olive oil
¼ teaspoon salt
⅛ teaspoon freshly ground black pepper
1 avocado, cut into bite-size pieces
¼ cup (30 g) dried cranberries
4 scallions, white and green parts, sliced
¼ cup (28 g) sliced almonds, toasted
2 tablespoons (8 g) fresh parsley leaves, chopped

Select Browning/Sauté and melt the butter in the pressure cooking pot. Add the couscous and toast for about 3 minutes, stirring constantly, until it smells nutty. Stir in the water. Lock the lid in place. Select High Pressure and 1 minute cook time.

When the cook time ends, turn off the pressure cooker. Let the pressure release naturally for 10 minutes and finish with a quick pressure release. When the valve drops, carefully remove the lid. Fluff the couscous with a fork.

In a serving bowl, whisk the lemon juice, olive oil, salt, and pepper. Add the couscous and stir to combine. Gently fold in the avocado, cranberries, scallions, and almonds. Top with the parsley before serving.

Green Beans with Toasted Almonds

YIELD:
4 SERVINGS

TIP: You can also toast the almonds in the oven. Preheat the oven to 350°F (180°C, or gas mark 4) and place the almonds on an aluminum foil–lined baking sheet in a single layer. Bake for 5 minutes until they just start to brown and smell toasted, stirring occasionally.

This green been recipe has become my go-to vegetable recipe to accompany family dinners—from everyday meals to fancy holiday spreads. My family always asks me to add extra almonds.

2 tablespoons (14 g) slivered almonds
1 pound (454 g) thin green beans, trimmed
1 tablespoon (15 ml) fresh lemon juice
2 teaspoons olive oil
¼ teaspoon garlic powder
½ teaspoon salt
¼ teaspoon freshly ground black pepper
¼ teaspoon dried basil

Select Browning/Sauté and add the almonds to the pressure cooking pot. Cook for about 5 minutes, stirring frequently, until the almonds start to brown and smell toasted. Transfer to a plate to cool.

Put the steamer basket in the pressure cooking pot and add ½ cup (120 ml) water. Put the green beans in the basket. Lock the lid in place. Select High Pressure and 1 minute cook time for crisp-tender beans, or 2 minutes for very tender beans.

In a serving bowl, whisk the lemon juice, olive oil, garlic powder, salt, pepper, and basil. Set aside.

When the cook time ends, turn off the pressure cooker. Use a quick pressure release. When the valve drops, carefully remove the lid. Transfer the beans to the serving bowl and toss to combine. Stir in the almonds.

Strawberry Applesauce

YIELD:
ABOUT I QUART (980 G)

TIP: I prefer to use an immersion blender to blend the applesauce right in the pot. You can also mash it with a potato masher or put it in the blender to purée. My family prefers the apples peeled, but if you don't mind a little extra texture from the peel, leave it on to retain the extra vitamins and fiber.

The strawberries add a pink color to the applesauce. We like eating this applesauce both hot out of the pressure cooker and chilled overnight in the fridge. Serve it as a side dish with sandwiches or pork chops, but I like it best as a simple dessert.

8 Jonathon or Jonagold apples, peeled, cored, and quartered
12 fresh or frozen whole strawberries, hulled
¼ cup (60 ml) water
¼ teaspoon ground cinnamon
Sugar, as needed for sweetening

Place the apples, strawberries, water, and cinnamon in the pressure cooking pot. Lock the lid in place. Select High Pressure and 3 minutes cook time.

When the cook time ends, turn off the pressure cooker. Let the pressure release naturally—do not use a quick release. When the valve drops, carefully remove the lid. Blend the applesauce in the pot until it reaches your desired consistency. If needed, add a little sugar to taste.

{ Chapter 8 }

Desserts

You don't always think of desserts when you think of pressure cooking, but the moist environment of the pressure cooker is perfect for cooking desserts such as rich, creamy cheesecakes, crème brûlée, and one of the most popular recipes on my blog, *Pressure Cooking Today*—old-fashioned rice pudding.

Key Lime Pie

YIELD:
6 TO 8 SERVINGS

TIP: If you can't find key limes, substitute ¼ cup (60 ml) fresh lemon juice and ¼ cup fresh lime juice.

A classic pie with sour cream and lime zest added to give it just a little more zing.

FOR CRUST:
¾ cup (45 g) graham cracker crumbs, about 6 crackers

3 tablespoons (42 g) unsalted butter, melted
1 tablespoon (12 g) sugar

FOR FILLING:
4 large egg yolks
1 can (14 fluid ounces, or 414 ml) sweetened condensed milk
½ cup (120 ml) fresh key lime juice

⅓ cup (75 g) sour cream
2 tablespoons (12 g) grated key lime zest
Whipped cream, for serving

Spray a 7-inch (18 cm) springform pan with nonstick cooking spray. Pour 1 cup (235 ml) water into the pressure cooking pot and place the trivet in the bottom.

TO MAKE THE CRUST: In a small bowl, stir together the graham cracker crumbs, butter, and sugar. Press the crust evenly in the bottom and slightly up the sides of the pan. Freeze for 10 minutes.

TO MAKE THE FILLING: In a large bowl, with a handheld mixer, beat the egg yolks until they are light yellow. Gradually beat in the sweetened condensed milk until thickened. Slowly add the lime juice and beat until smooth. Stir in the sour cream and lime zest. Pour the batter into the springform pan. Cover the pan with aluminum foil. Carefully center the filled pan on a sling and lower it into the pressure cooking pot. Fold the sling down so that it doesn't interfere with closing the lid. Lock the lid in place. Select High Pressure and 15 minutes cook time.

When the cook time ends, turn off the pressure cooker. Let the pressure release naturally for 10 minutes and finish with a quick pressure release. When the valve drops, carefully remove the lid. Transfer the springform pan to a wire rack to cool and remove the aluminum foil. When cooled, cover with plastic wrap and refrigerate for at least 4 hours or overnight. Serve topped with whipped cream.

Just Right Pumpkin Pie

YIELD:
6 TO 8 SERVINGS

TIP: Change up the crust by using gingersnaps instead—really, most crisp, crumbly cookies work well.

A classic pumpkin pie filling in a crumbly Pecan Sandies cookie crust. When a big pumpkin pie is too much, this 7-inch (18 cm) pie is just right.

FOR CRUST:
½ cup (93 g) crushed Pecan Sandies cookies (about 6 cookies)

⅓ cup (33 g) toasted pecans, chopped
2 tablespoons (28 g) unsalted butter, melted

FOR FILLING:
½ cup (120 g) packed light brown sugar
½ teaspoon salt
1½ teaspoons pumpkin pie spice
1 egg, beaten

1½ cups (368 g) pumpkin purée (also called solid pack pumpkin)
½ cup (120 ml) evaporated milk
Whipped cream, for serving

Spray a 7-inch (18 cm) springform pan with nonstick cooking spray. Pour 1 cup (235 ml) water into the pressure cooking pot and place the trivet in the bottom.

TO MAKE THE CRUST: In a small bowl, stir together the cookie crumbs, pecans, and butter. Spread the crust evenly in the bottom and about 1 inch (2.5 cm) up the sides of the pan. Freeze for 10 minutes.

TO MAKE THE FILLING: In a large bowl, combine the brown sugar, salt, and pumpkin pie spice. Whisk in the egg, pumpkin, and evaporated milk. Pour the batter into the springform pan. Cover the top with aluminum foil. Carefully center the filled pan on a sling and lower it into the cooking pot. Fold the sling down so that it doesn't interfere with closing the lid. Lock the lid in place. Select High Pressure and 35 minutes cook time.

When the cook time ends, turn off the pressure cooker. Let the pressure release naturally for 10 minutes and finish with a quick pressure release. When the valve drops, carefully remove the lid. Remove the pie and check that the middle is set. If not, return it to the cooker, relock the lid, and cook on High Pressure for 5 minutes more. Transfer the pie to a wire rack to cool and remove the foil. When cooled, cover with plastic wrap and refrigerate for at least 4 hours or overnight. Serve with whipped cream.

Mini Creamy Lemon Pies

YIELD:

6 TO 8 SERVINGS

·····································

TIP: You could sub-
stitute sour cream
for the Greek yogurt
in this recipe.

These pies are made creamy—and a little tangy—with yogurt, which contrasts nicely with the crumbly graham cracker crust. If you love key lime pie, you'll go crazy for this lemon version.

FOR CRUST:

**1 cup (60 g) graham cracker crumbs,
    about 8 crackers**

1 tablespoon (12 g) sugar
¼ cup (55 g) unsalted butter, melted

FOR FILLING:

4 large egg yolks
**1 can (14 fluid ounces, or 414 ml)
    sweetened condensed milk**
½ cup (120 ml) fresh lemon juice

¼ cup (60 g) plain Greek yogurt
**2 tablespoons (12 g) grated lemon
    zest**
Whipped cream, for serving

Pour 1 cup (235 ml) water into the pressure cooking pot and place the trivet in the pot.

TO MAKE THE CRUST: In a medium-size bowl, mix together the graham cracker crumbs, butter, and sugar until well blended. Divide the crust evenly among 6 (6-ounce, or 170 g) custard cups. Press the crust evenly in the bottom and slightly up the sides. Freeze for 10 minutes.

TO MAKE THE FILLING: In a large bowl, beat the egg yolks until they are pale yellow. Gradually beat in the sweetened condensed milk. Add the lemon juice and beat until smooth. Whisk in the yogurt and lemon zest. Divide among the custard cups. Place 3 cups on the trivet and put a second trivet on top. Place the remaining 3 cups on it. Lock the lid in place. Select High Pressure and 4 minutes cook time.

When the cook time ends, turn off the pressure cooker. Let the pressure release naturally for 10 minutes and finish with a quick pressure release. When the valve drops, carefully remove the lid. Transfer the cups to a wire rack to cool. Use a paper towel to soak up any water that may have accumulated on the tops of the pies. When cool, cover the pies with plastic wrap and refrigerate for at least 2 hours. Serve topped with whipped cream.

Vanilla Lover's Cheesecake

....

TIP: Use 2 (8 ounces, or 227 g, each) packages of cream cheese and save 2 ounces (57 g) for the white chocolate mousse.

Pressure cooker cheesecake is such a treat—rich, smooth, and creamy. This version is a dream.

FOR CRUST:
¾ cup (45 g) graham cracker crumbs, about 6 crackers
2 tablespoons (24 g) sugar

2 tablespoons (28 g) unsalted butter, melted

FOR FILLING:
14 ounces (397 g) cream cheese, at room temperature
½ cup (100 g) sugar
2 tablespoons (30 ml) heavy cream

2 teaspoons vanilla bean paste or extract
2 large eggs, at room temperature

FOR WHITE CHOCOLATE MOUSSE:
½ cup (120 ml) heavy cream
1 tablespoon (8 g) powdered sugar
½ teaspoon vanilla bean paste or extract
2 ounces (57 g) cream cheese, at room temperature

4 ounces (113 g) white chocolate baking squares, melted
¼ cup (25 g) white chocolate shavings

TO MAKE THE CRUST: Spray a 7-inch (18 cm) springform pan with nonstick cooking spray. In a small bowl, stir together the graham cracker crumbs, sugar, and butter. Spread the crust evenly in the bottom and about 1 inch (2.5 cm) up the sides of the prepared pan. Freeze for 10 minutes.

TO MAKE THE FILLING: In a large bowl, with a handheld mixer, mix the cream cheese and sugar at medium speed until smooth. Beat in the heavy cream and vanilla. Mix in the eggs until just blended. Do not overmix. Pour the batter over the crust.

Pour 1 cup (235 ml) water into the pressure cooking pot and place a trivet in the bottom. Center the filled pan on a sling and carefully lower it into the pressure cooking pot. Fold the sling down so that it doesn't interfere with closing the lid. Lock the lid in place. Select High Pressure and 20 minutes cook time.

When the cook time ends, turn off the pressure cooker. Let the pressure release naturally for 10 minutes and finish with a quick pressure release. When the valve drops, carefully remove the lid. Use an instant-read thermometer to check that the cheesecake has reached 150°F (65.5°C) in the center. If not, relock the lid and cook at High Pressure for 5 minutes more with a second 10-minute natural pressure release. Transfer the cheesecake to a wire rack to cool to room temperature. Use a paper towel to absorb any water on the cheesecake.

TO MAKE THE WHITE CHOCOLATE MOUSSE: In a large bowl, with a handheld mixer, beat the heavy cream until soft peaks form. Add the powdered sugar and vanilla and beat until stiff peaks form. In another large bowl, beat the cream cheese until fluffy. Add the white chocolate and beat until smooth. Fold in the whipped cream. Spread the mousse evenly over the cooled cheesecake. Sprinkle the white chocolate shavings on top. Refrigerate for several hours or overnight before serving.

PERFECT PRESSURE COOKER CHEESECAKE TIPS: Making cheesecake in the pressure cooker is super easy, but the key to perfect pressure cooker cheesecake is having the ingredients at room temperature, especially the cream cheese and eggs.

The easiest way to soften the cream cheese is to leave it at room temperature for several hours. If you're in a hurry, put the cream cheese in a zipper bag and place it in warm (not hot) water for about 15 minutes. Add the eggs to the warm water and they'll be at room temperature in about 5 minutes.

Don't press the crust crumbs too high up the sides of the springform pan to avoid getting moisture in your crust.

Use a sling to lift the hot cheesecake. It's a breeze to lift the hot cheesecake out of the pressure cooker.

Use an instant-read thermometer to check that the cheesecake has reached 150°F (65.5°C) in the center. If not, cook the cheesecake at High Pressure for 5 minutes more, using a second 10-minute natural pressure release.

A longer cook time, generally, results in a denser, New York–style cheesecake. Timing can vary based on the pan you're using, whether you've covered your pan with foil, and your ingredients.

Peanut Butter Cup Cheesecake

YIELD:
8 SERVINGS

....

TIP: I use mini peanut butter cups and cut them in half, rather than unwrapping and chopping the bigger peanut butter cups. Use whichever you'd prefer.

This cheesecake is smooth, rich, and creamy—a little slice is all you need to satisfy your peanut butter cup craving.

FOR CRUST:

1 cup Oreo cookie crumbs (about 12 cookies, 5 ounces, or 142 g)

2 tablespoons (28 g) unsalted butter, melted

FOR FILLING:

12 ounces (340 g) cream cheese, at room temperature

½ cup (100 g) sugar

½ cup (130 g) smooth peanut butter

¼ cup (60 ml) heavy cream

1½ teaspoons vanilla extract

1 tablespoon (7 g) all-purpose flour

2 large eggs, at room temperature

1 egg yolk, at room temperature

FOR GANACHE:

6 ounces (170 g) milk chocolate, finely chopped, divided

⅓ cup (78 ml) heavy cream

⅔ cup (about 3½ ounces, or 99 g) coarsely chopped peanut butter cups

Spray a 7-inch (18 cm) springform pan with nonstick cooking spray. Pour 1 cup (235 ml) water into the pressure cooking pot and place a trivet in the bottom.

TO MAKE THE CRUST: In a small bowl, stir together the cookie crumbs and butter. Spread the crust evenly in the bottom and about 1 inch (2.5 cm) up the side of the prepared pan. Freeze for 10 minutes.

TO MAKE THE FILLING: In a large bowl, with a handheld mixer, mix the cream cheese and sugar at medium speed until smooth. Blend in the peanut butter, heavy cream, vanilla, and flour. One at a time, mix in the eggs and egg yolk, mixing until just blended—do not overmix. Pour the batter over the crust. Cover the pan with aluminum foil. Carefully center the filled pan on a sling and lower it into the cooking pot. Fold the sling down so that it doesn't interfere with closing the lid. Lock the lid in place. Select High Pressure and 50 minutes cook time.

When the cook time ends, turn off the pressure cooker. Let the pressure release naturally for 10 minutes and finish with a quick pressure release. When the valve drops, carefully remove the lid.

Use an instant-read thermometer to check that the cheesecake has reached 150°F (65.5°C) in the center. If not, relock the lid and cook the cheesecake at High Pressure for 5 minutes more, using a second 10-minute natural pressure release. Transfer the cheesecake to a wire rack to cool. Remove the aluminum foil. When cooled, cover with plastic wrap and refrigerate for at least 4 hours or overnight.

TO MAKE THE GANACHE: Place 3 ounces (85 g) of the chocolate in a large bowl. In a small saucepan over medium-high heat, bring the heavy cream to a boil. Immediately remove it from the heat and pour it over the chocolate. Stir until the chocolate melts completely. Add the remaining 3 ounces (85 g) chocolate and stir until it melts completely. Cool until the ganache thickens but is still thin enough to drip down the sides of the cheesecake. Spoon the ganache over the cheesecake, spreading it to the edges and letting it drip down the sides. Pile the chopped peanut butter cups on top. Refrigerate until ready to serve.

Strawberry Cheesecake with Oreo Cookie Crust

YIELD:
6 TO 8 SERVINGS

....

TIP: As with all cheesecakes, using room-temperature ingredients produces better results.

If you need an impressive dessert, look no further. This stunning cheesecake features an Oreo crust topped with a rich and creamy cheesecake, crowned with sweet, whole strawberries dripping with fresh strawberry sauce. Looking at it, you'd never guess how easy it is to make.

FOR CRUST:

1 cup Oreo cookie crumbs (about 12 cookies, 5 ounces, or 142 g)
2 tablespoons (28 g) unsalted butter, melted

FOR FILLING:

2 packages (8 ounces, or 227 g, each) cream cheese, at room temperature
¾ cup (150 g) sugar
2 tablespoons (30 g) sour cream
1 tablespoon (7 g) all-purpose flour
1 teaspoon vanilla extract
Pinch salt
2 large eggs, at room temperature

FOR STRAWBERRY GLAZE:

2 pints (580 g) small fresh strawberries, washed and hulled
1 tablespoon (15 ml) water
2 tablespoons (24 g) sugar
1 teaspoon cornstarch

TO MAKE THE CRUST: Spray a 7-inch (18 cm) springform pan with nonstick cooking spray. In a small bowl, stir together the cookie crumbs and butter. Spread the crust evenly in the bottom and 1 inch (2.5 cm) up the sides of the prepared pan. Freeze for 10 minutes.

TO MAKE THE FILLING: In a large bowl, with a handheld mixer, mix the cream cheese and sugar at medium speed until smooth. Mix in the sour cream, flour, vanilla, and salt until just blended. Add the eggs and mix until just blended. Do not overmix. Pour the batter over the crust.

Pour 1 cup (235 ml) water into the pressure cooking pot and place a trivet in the bottom. Carefully center the filled pan on a sling and lower it into the cooking pot. Fold the sling down so that it doesn't interfere with closing the lid. Lock the lid in place. Select High Pressure and 20 minutes cook time.

When the cook time ends, turn off the pressure cooker. Let the pressure release naturally for 10 minutes and finish with a quick pressure release. When the valve drops, carefully remove the lid. Use an instant-read thermometer to check that the cheesecake has reached 150°F (65.5°C) in the center. If not, relock the lid and cook the cheesecake at High Pressure for 5 minutes more, using a second 10-minute natural pressure release. Transfer the cheesecake to a wire rack to cool. When cooled to room temperature, cover the cheesecake with aluminum foil and refrigerate for at least 4 hours or overnight.

WHEN READY TO SERVE. MAKE THE STRAWBERRY GLAZE: Purée 1 pint (290 g) strawberries in a small food processor or with an immersion blender. Remove the seeds by pressing the purée through a fine-mesh strainer into a small saucepan. Add the water.

In a small bowl, mix together the sugar and cornstarch. Stir this into the strawberry purée. Bring the mixture to a boil over medium-high heat, stirring constantly. Continue cooking and stirring for about 2 minutes until slightly thickened. Set aside to cool.

Arrange the remaining 1 pint (290 g) strawberries in a single layer on the cooled cheesecake. Drizzle the cooled glazed evenly over the strawberries. Refrigerate, covered, until serving.

Triple Chocolate Cheesecake

YIELD:

6 TO 8 SERVINGS

....

TIP: I prefer to use 2 (each 4 ounces, or 113 g) Ghirardelli 60 percent Cacao Bittersweet Chocolate Premium Baking Bars and use 2 ounces (57 g) from 1 bar to make the chocolate curls and chop the remaining 6 ounces (170 g) chocolate for the cheesecake batter. Use a potato peeler to make the chocolate curls.

People new to pressure cooking are often most excited to cook cheesecakes in their new pressure cookers. Who can blame them? My *Pressure Cooking Today* blog readers have been asking me to create a recipe for a chocolate cheesecake. I've gone all out on this one, loading it with chocolate for a triple chocolate cheesecake.

FOR CRUST:
1 cup Oreo cookie crumbs
  (about 12 cookies, 5 ounces, or 142 g, crushed)
2 tablespoons (28 g) unsalted butter, melted

FOR FILLING:
6 ounces (170 g) semisweet or bittersweet chocolate,
  finely chopped
2 (8 ounces, or 227 g, each) packages cream cheese,
  at room temperature
½ cup (100 g) sugar
1 tablespoon (7 g) all-purpose flour
1 teaspoon vanilla extract
Pinch salt
2 large eggs, at room temperature

FOR TOPPINGS:
4 ounces (113 g) white chocolate, finely chopped
2 tablespoons (30 ml) heavy cream
Chocolate curls, for garnish

TO MAKE THE CRUST: Spray a 7-inch (18 cm) springform pan with nonstick cooking spray. In a small bowl, stir together the cookie crumbs and butter. Spread the crust evenly in the bottom and 1 inch (2.5 cm) up the sides of the prepared pan. Freeze for 10 minutes.

TO MAKE THE FILLING: In a small glass bowl, microwave the chocolate on 50 percent power for 1 minute. Stir and heat in 30-second intervals until melted and smooth. Cool until lukewarm but still pourable.

In a large bowl, with a handheld mixer, mix the cream cheese and sugar at medium speed until smooth. Add the flour, vanilla, and salt and mix until just blended. Add the eggs and mix until just blended. Do not overmix. Mix in the melted chocolate. Pour the batter over the crust.

Pour 1 cup (235 ml) water into the pressure cooking pot and place a trivet in the bottom. Carefully center the filled pan on a sling and lower it into the cooking pot. Fold the sling down so that it doesn't interfere with closing the lid. Lock the lid in place. Select High Pressure and 20 minutes cook time.

When the cook time ends, turn off the pressure cooker. Let the pressure release naturally for 10 minutes and finish with a quick pressure release. When the valve drops, carefully remove the lid. Use an instant-read thermometer to check that the cheesecake has reached 150°F (65.5°C) in the center. If not, relock the lid and cook at High Pressure for 5 minutes more, using a second 10-minute natural pressure release. Transfer the cheesecake to a wire rack to cool. When cooled to room temperature, cover with foil and refrigerate for at least 4 hours or overnight.

TO MAKE THE TOPPING: In a microwave-safe dish, heat the white chocolate and heavy cream on 50 percent power for 1 minute. Stir and heat again in 30-second increments until melted and smooth. Spread the white chocolate over the cheesecake, allowing it to drip over the sides. Top with chocolate curls. Refrigerate until serving.

Mini Chocolate Chip Cheesecakes

YIELD:
6 SERVINGS

....

TIP: There's no need to remove the filling from the Oreos before crushing them.

Mini cheesecakes are fun and versatile. You can have one now and save the others in the fridge or freezer for another day. Using mini chocolate chips in this recipe ensures you get chocolate in every bite.

FOR CRUST:

¾ cup crushed Oreo cookie crumbs (about 8 cookies, 3.3 ounces, or 94 g, crushed)

2 tablespoons (28 g) unsalted butter, melted

FOR FILLING:

2 packages (8 ounces, or 227 g, each) cream cheese, at room temperature

½ cup (100 g) sugar

2 tablespoons (30 g) sour cream

½ teaspoon vanilla extract

Pinch salt

2 large eggs, at room temperature

½ cup (90 g) semisweet mini chocolate chips

Whipped cream, for serving

TO MAKE THE CRUST: Spray 6 (6-ounce, or 170 g) ovenproof custard cups with nonstick cooking spray. In a small bowl, stir together the cookie crumbs and butter. Divide the crust evenly among the custard cups and press it into the bottom.

TO MAKE THE FILLING: In a large bowl, with a handheld mixer, mix the cream cheese and sugar at medium speed until smooth. Add the sour cream, vanilla, and salt and mix until just blended. Add the eggs and mix until just blended. Do not overmix. Gently fold in the chocolate chips. Divide the batter evenly among the cups.

Pour 1 cup (235 ml) water into the pressure cooking pot and place a trivet in the bottom. Place 3 cups on the trivet. Place a second trivet on top and set the remaining 3 cups on it. Lock the lid in place. Select High Pressure and 4 minutes cook time.

When the cook time ends, turn off the pressure cooker. Let the pressure release naturally for 15 minutes and finish with a quick pressure release. When the valve drops, carefully remove the lid.

Transfer the cheesecakes to a wire rack to cool. Remove any water from the top of the cheesecakes with a paper towel. When cooled, cover with plastic wrap and refrigerate for at least 4 hours or overnight. Serve topped with whipped cream.

Crème Brûlée

YIELD:
6 SERVINGS

TIP: If you don't have a kitchen torch, caramelize the sugar under the broiler. Place the ramekins on a baking sheet. Sprinkle each with 1 tablespoon (12 g) superfine sugar. Broil for about 5 minutes until the sugar is caramelized, rotating the pan frequently so that it caramelizes evenly.

This rich, creamy custard is finished with a brittle caramelized layer on top. It's a classic, elegant dessert that is easy to make at home— and even easier and faster when prepared in the pressure cooker.

6 egg yolks
⅓ cup (67 g) sugar
Pinch salt
2 cups (470 ml) heavy cream
1½ teaspoons vanilla extract
6 tablespoons (72 g) superfine sugar, divided

Add 1½ cups (360 ml) water to the pressure cooking pot and place a trivet in the bottom.

In a large bowl, whisk the egg yolks, sugar, and salt. Add the heavy cream and vanilla and whisk until blended. Strain the mixture into a pitcher or a large bowl with a pour spout. Pour the mixture into 6 (6-ounce or 170 g) ramekins and cover with aluminum foil. Place 3 ramekins on the trivet and place a second trivet on top. Stack the remaining 3 ramekins on it. Lock the lid in place. Select High Pressure and 6 minutes cook time.

When the cook time ends, turn off the pressure cooker. Let the pressure release naturally for 10 minutes and finish with a quick pressure release. When the valve drops, carefully remove the lid. Carefully transfer the ramekins to a wire rack to cool, uncovered. When cool, cover with plastic wrap and refrigerate for at least 2 hours or up to 2 days.

When ready to serve, sprinkle 1 tablespoon (12 g) superfine sugar over the entire surface of each custard. Working one at a time, hold a kitchen torch about 2 inches (5 cm) above the surface of each custard, moving in a circular motion to melt the sugar and form a crisp, caramelized topping. Serve immediately.

Chocolate Pots de Crème

YIELD:
6 SERVINGS

TIP: If you only have one trivet, use rolled-up aluminum foil on the bottom of the pan to raise the cups off the bottom of the cooking pot.

Pots de Crème are thick, rich custards. This dessert is usually baked in the oven in a water bath, so I knew it would be perfect to "bake" in the pressure cooker.

1½ cups (360 ml) heavy cream
½ cup (120 ml) whole milk
5 large egg yolks
¼ (50 g) cup sugar
Pinch salt
8 ounces (227 g) bittersweet chocolate, melted
Whipped cream and grated chocolate, for serving

In a small saucepan over medium heat, combine the heavy cream and milk and bring to a simmer. Remove from the heat.

In a large bowl, whisk the egg yolks, sugar, and salt. Slowly whisk in the hot cream mixture. Whisk in the melted chocolate until blended. Pour the custard into 6 (½-pint, or 235 ml) Mason jars or 6 (6-ounce, or 170 g) custard cups.

Add 1½ cups (360 ml) water to the pressure cooking pot and place a trivet in the bottom. Place 3 jars on the trivet and place a second trivet on top. Stack the remaining 3 jars on it. Lock the lid in place. Select High Pressure and 6 minutes cook time.

When the cook time ends, turn off the pressure cooker. Let the pressure release naturally for 15 minutes and finish with a quick pressure release. When the valve drops, carefully remove the lid. Carefully transfer the jars to a wire rack to cool, uncovered, for about 1 hour. When completely cooled, cover with plastic wrap and refrigerate for at least 4 hours or overnight. Garnish with whipped cream and grated chocolate.

Fudgy Brownies

YIELD:
8 SERVINGS

TIP: Parchment paper is coated with silicone, so it is nonstick. It isn't essential for this recipe, but it does make cleanup a lot easier. You can buy it in rolls at the grocery store, but I prefer precut flat sheets.

Rich, dense, and fudgy brownies to satisfy your chocolate craving. It's easy to make in one bowl.

6 tablespoons (85 g) unsalted butter
1 cup (200 g) sugar
⅓ cup (29 g) unsweetened cocoa powder
2 tablespoons (30 ml) water
1 teaspoon vanilla extract
2 large eggs
1 cup (112 g) all-purpose flour
½ teaspoon baking powder
¼ teaspoon salt
½ cup (87 g) semisweet chocolate chips
Ice cream and powdered sugar, for serving

Spray a 7 × 3-inch (18 × 7.5 cm) round cake pan with nonstick cooking spray. Line the bottom with parchment paper.

In a large microwave-safe bowl, microwave the butter for about 1 minute until melted. Stir in the sugar and microwave for 1 minute more. Whisk in the cocoa powder, water, and vanilla until smooth. Whisk in the eggs. Add the flour, baking powder, and salt. Stir until just smooth. Mix in the chocolate chips.

Spread the batter into the prepared pan. Pour 1 cup (235 ml) water into the pressure cooker and place a trivet in the bottom. Use a sling to carefully lower the pan onto the trivet. Lock the lid in place. Select High Pressure and 20 minutes cook time.

When the cook time ends, turn off the pressure cooker. Let the pressure release naturally for 10 minutes and finish with a quick pressure release. When the valve drops, carefully remove the lid.

Transfer the pan to a wire rack to cool for 10 minutes. Invert the brownies onto a serving plate and carefully peel off the parchment paper. Cool to room temperature and serve topped with ice cream or a sprinkle of powdered sugar, if desired.

Cranberry-Orange Bread Pudding

YIELD:
8 SERVINGS

TIP: Crème anglaise is a silky smooth vanilla custard-sauce. It's easy to make and is one of my favorites because it makes any dessert special.

A decadent bread pudding made with bread and croissants, flavored with orange zest and dried cranberries, and served with a heavenly crème anglaise.

FOR PUDDING:

Butter, for greasing the dish

3 large eggs

½ cup (100 g) sugar

1 teaspoon vanilla extract

Zest of 1 orange

2 cups (470 ml) heavy cream

3 large croissants, torn into bite-size pieces

6 slices white bread, cubed

¼ cup (30 g) dried cranberries

FOR CRÈME ANGLAISE:

¾ cup (175 ml) heavy cream

¼ cup (60 ml) milk

2 egg yolks

⅓ cup (67 g) sugar

1 teaspoon vanilla bean paste or extract

Generously grease a 1½-quart (1.4 L) glass or metal baking dish with butter. (Be sure the dish fits in your pressure cooking pot.)

TO MAKE THE PUDDING: In a large bowl, whisk the eggs, sugar, vanilla, and orange zest. Whisk in the heavy cream. Gently stir in the croissants, bread, and cranberries. Pour into the prepared dish.

Pour 1 cup (235 ml) water into the pressure cooking pot and place a trivet in the bottom. Center the dish on a sling and carefully lower it into the cooking pot. Lock the lid in place. Select High Pressure and 30 minutes cook time.

When the cook time ends, turn off the pressure cooker. Let the pressure release naturally for 10 minutes and finish with a quick pressure release. When the valve drops, carefully remove the lid. Remove the dish from the cooking pot and let cool for at least 15 minutes more before serving.

TO MAKE THE CRÈME ANGLAISE: In a small saucepan over medium heat, whisk the heavy cream and milk. Cook until the mixture just starts to boil. Remove from the heat.

In a medium-size bowl, whisk the egg yolks and sugar. Whisk in half the hot milk

mixture. Add the egg mixture to the saucepan and cook over medium heat, stirring constantly, until the sauce comes to a boil. Reduce the heat to low and simmer for about 2 minutes until the sauce thickens slightly. Remove from the heat and stir in the vanilla. Set aside.

Slice the bread pudding into wedges and drizzle each slice with crème anglaise.

Dangerously Delicious Rice Pudding

YIELD:
8 SERVINGS

TIP: The rice continues to absorb liquid as it chills. Before serving, stir in more milk or cream a little at a time until your desired consistency is achieved.

This is the best, creamiest, old-fashioned rice pudding—it's one of my favorite recipes on my blog, *Pressure Cooking Today*. It's so simple to make in the pressure cooker that readers have told me it's "dangerously delicious."

1 cup (192 g) arborio rice
1½ cups (360 ml) water
¼ teaspoon salt
2 cups (480 ml) whole milk, divided
½ cup (100 g) sugar
2 large eggs
½ teaspoon vanilla extract
¾ cup (110 g) raisins
Whipped cream and cinnamon or nutmeg, for serving

In the pressure cooking pot, combine the rice, water, and salt. Lock the lid in place. Select High Pressure and 3 minutes cook time.

When the cook time ends, turn off the pressure cooker. Let the pressure release naturally for 10 minutes and finish with a quick pressure release. When the valve drops, carefully remove the lid. Stir 1½ cups (360 ml) milk and the sugar into the rice.

In a small bowl, whisk the eggs with the remaining ½ cup (120 ml) milk and the vanilla. Pour through a fine-mesh strainer into the cooking pot. Select Simmer/Sauté and cook, stirring constantly, until the mixture starts to boil. Turn off the pressure cooker, remove the pot, and stir in the raisins. The pudding thickens as it cools. Serve warm or pour into individual serving dishes and chill. Top with whipped cream and sprinkle with cinnamon or nutmeg, if desired.

Coconut, Mango, and Brown Rice Pudding

YIELD:
6 SERVINGS

TIP: Toasted coconut adds a nutty flavor. Toast it quickly on the stovetop in a large skillet over medium-high heat, stirring frequently, until golden-brown.

My *Pressure Cooking Today* blog readers have been asking for a brown rice pudding recipe that's as easy and as delicious as my popular white rice pudding recipe, Dangerously Delicious Rice Pudding (opposite). I tried several different versions and simply adore this tropical twist on brown rice pudding. I think you will, too.

¾ cup (143 g) short-grain brown rice
1½ cups (360 ml) water
¼ teaspoon salt
1 can (14 fluid ounces, or 414 ml) unsweetened coconut milk
½ cup (100 g) sugar
2 large eggs
½ cup (120 ml) milk
½ teaspoon coconut extract
½ teaspoon vanilla extract
1 mango, diced
1 cup shredded coconut, toasted

In the pressure cooking pot, combine the brown rice, water, and salt. Lock the lid in place. Select High Pressure and 25 minutes cook time.

When the cook time ends, turn off pressure cooker. Let the pressure release naturally for 10 minutes and finish with a quick pressure release. When the valve drops, carefully remove the lid. Stir in the coconut milk and sugar.

In a small bowl, whisk the eggs and milk. Pour the mixture through a fine-mesh strainer into the cooking pot. Select Simmer/Sauté and cook, stirring constantly, until the mixture starts to boil and thicken. Turn off the pressure cooker. Stir in the coconut and vanilla extracts. Pour the pudding into a large serving bowl and cool to room temperature. When cool, cover with plastic wrap and refrigerate for 3 hours. Serve topped with mango and shredded coconut.

Cinnamon–Zucchini Bread with Cinnamon Icing

YIELD:
8 SERVINGS

TIP: Removing excess moisture from the zucchini is essential for a good zucchini bread. I like to use a salad spinner or wrap the grated zucchini in a clean kitchen towel to squeeze out excess water.

In late summer, when your garden overflows with zucchini, the last thing you want to do is turn on the oven and heat up the house. Instead, "bake" your zucchini bread in the pressure cooker.

2 cups (224 g) all-purpose flour

2 teaspoons ground cinnamon

1½ teaspoons baking powder

½ teaspoon salt

½ cup (100 g) sugar

½ cup (120 g) packed light brown sugar

⅔ cup (157 ml) vegetable oil

2 large eggs

1 teaspoon vanilla extract

½ cup (115 g) sour cream

1 cup (120 g) grated zucchini

½ cup (50 g) pecans, chopped and toasted, plus more for serving

¾ cup (90 g) powdered sugar

Pinch ground cinnamon

1 tablespoon (15 ml) milk

Spray a half-size (1.4 L) Bundt pan with nonstick cooking spray. In a small bowl, whisk the flour, cinnamon, baking powder, and salt. Set aside.

In a large bowl, whisk the sugar, brown sugar, vegetable oil, eggs, and vanilla until blended. Whisk in the sour cream. Add the dry ingredients and whisk until just blended. Stir in the zucchini and pecans. Spoon the batter evenly into the prepared pan. Cover the pan with a paper towel and cover both the paper towel and the pan with aluminum foil crimped tightly around the edges.

Pour 1 cup (235 ml) water into the pressure cooker and place a trivet in the bottom. Use a sling to carefully lower the Bundt pan onto the trivet. Lock the lid in place. Select High Pressure and 35 minutes cook time.

When the cook time ends, turn off the pressure cooker. Let the pressure release naturally for 10 minutes and finish with a quick pressure release. When the valve drops, carefully remove the lid. Check the bread for doneness. An instant-read thermometer inserted into the middle should be about 210°F (99°C) or a toothpick inserted into the center should come out clean. If the bread is not done, replace the foil, relock the lid, and cook on High Pressure for 5 more minutes. Carefully transfer the Bundt pan to a wire rack to cool, uncovered, for 10 minutes. Remove the bread from the pan and cool completely on a wire rack.

Right before serving, in a small bowl, whisk the powdered sugar, cinnamon, and milk until smooth. Pour the icing over the bread. Decorate with chopped pecans, if desired.

Acknowledgments

Lorna Sass is often referred to as the "queen of pressure cooking," and the first pressure cooker cookbook I bought was hers. When I started using my electric pressure cooker, there weren't many electric pressure cooking recipes available, so I used Lorna's stovetop pressure cooking recipes as a starting point in creating my electric pressure cooker recipes.

Laura Pazzaglia, who blogs at *Hip Pressure Cooking*, is also a great resource for pressure cooker information. Early on, I used Laura's great pressure cooking charts to supplement my pressure cooking manuals and struck up a friendship with her. Although both Lorna and Laura were hard-core stovetop pressure cooking fans, they've come around to the ease and convenience of electric pressure cookers.

I'm a member of many pressure cooking groups on Facebook, which are a great resource for pressure cooking information. Thousands of people come together in these groups to share their recipes and ideas generously and help each other get the most out of our pressure cookers. I've incorporated some of the ideas I learned in these groups in my daily cooking, so they also appear in the recipes in this cookbook.

I also have fabulous readers of my website, *Pressure Cooking Today*, who share their pressure cooking tips and tricks with me. They bounce recipe ideas off me, and we work together to find solutions to problems and create great new recipe ideas. I cherish the community we've built and am grateful for their enthusiasm and support.

My agent and publisher believed in me and saw the need for an electric pressure cooker cookbook. My blog readers have been asking me when I was going to write a pressure cooker cookbook, and I'm thrilled to be able to share my recipes in this beautiful cookbook.

Every recipe in this cookbook was triple-tested by my wonderful recipe testers. They made suggestions for improving the recipes, pointed out missing ingredients in the directions, and helped add tips to each recipe. All recipes are better because of their help.

Finally, I owe a big thank-you to my family. To my three boys, who ate all the meals I cooked—even the versions that weren't quite right—as I worked to perfect these recipes. To my sweet daughter, Jennifer, who shares my love of pressure cooking. Not only did she test nearly all the recipes in the cookbook, she helped me with early drafts; her advice and hard work were invaluable, and the book is significantly better because of her. And to my husband, my biggest fan and my slicer and dicer. He's in the kitchen with me whenever he can be, and he makes it more fun to cook.

About the Author

Barbara lives in a suburb of Salt Lake City, Utah, with her husband of 39 years, who is often in the kitchen with her. He likes to refer to himself as her slicer and dicer. They have four grown children and two adorable grandsons.

She is the creator of two popular recipe blogs: her pressure cooking site, Pressure-CookingToday.com, where she shares fabulous, family-friendly recipes for the electric pressure cooker/Instant Pot; and BarbaraBakes.com, where she shares her passion for baking. *Pressure Cooking Today* and *Barbara Bakes* receive over 1.5 million pageviews each month. Over the past eight years, her distinctive recipes and conversational style have earned her a dedicated readership across the globe.

Index